PEAKY
BLINDERS

Professor Carl Chinn, MBE, PhD, is a social historian, writer, public speaker, and teacher. An off-course bookmaker himself until 1984, he is the son and grandson of illegal bookmakers in Sparkbrook, whilst his mother's family were factory workers in Aston. His writings are deeply affected by his family's working-class background and life in the back-to-backs of Birmingham, and have earned him a national following. He believes passionately that history must be democratised because each and every person has made their mark upon history and has a story to tell. *Peaky Blinders: The Real Story* is his thirty-third book.

PEAKY BLINDERS

THE REAL STORY

The true history of Birmingham's most notorious gangs

CARL CHINN

JOHN BLAKE

Published by John Blake Publishing,
The Plaza,
535 Kings Road,
Chelsea Harbour,
London SW10 0SZ

www.facebook.com/johnblakebooks
twitter.com/jblakebooks

First published in paperback in 2019

Paperback ISBN: 978 1 78946 172 5
Ebook ISBN: 978 1 78946 173 2

British Library Cataloguing-in-Publication Data:

A catalogue record for this book is available from the British Library.

Design by www.envydesign.co.uk

Printed and bound in Great Britain by Clays Ltd, Elcograf S.p.A.

12

John Blake Publishing is an imprint of Bonnier Books UK
www.bonnierbooks.co.uk

The real gangs of Birmingham ruled the lives of backstreet Brummies for generations, and so it is to the hardworking, law-abiding and decent majority of the working class that this book is dedicated.

Unglamorous as their lives may have been, it is they who are worthy of our respect.

CONTENTS

ACKNOWLEDGEMNTS

Born in 1956, like other Brummies of my generation and those gone before, I had heard of the peaky blinders growing up, but I first wrote about them in 1986 in my doctoral thesis on the Ladypool Road neighbourhood of Sparkbrook. It was also in my thesis that I discussed for the first time the importance of Charles Haughton Rafter, the chief constable of Birmingham, who was credited with putting down the peaky blinders. That I was able to do so was thanks to the memories of my great uncle Bill Chinn and great uncle Wal Chinn, born in 1892 and 1897 respectively, who were amongst the first people whom I interviewed as a young oral historian.

Then in 1987, I began researching for my second book, a social history of illegal bookmaking – a subject relevant to my background. My granddad Richard Chinn had started up as an illegal back-street bookmaker in 1922, whilst my dad, Alfred 'Buck' Chinn, was raised in the game and went on to oversee the move into legal betting shops in 1961. I worked part-time in the business from when I was thirteen and later ran the family's betting shops in Sparkbrook between 1978 and 1984, when we sold up. Dad, though, remained involved in bookmaking affairs and became president of the Birmingham branch of the Bookmakers' Protection Association. It was through his contacts that I was able to interview a number of elderly racecourse bookmakers from London. Amongst them was Simeon Solomon, whose bookmaking name was Sydney Lewis and who was the younger brother of the real Alfie Solomon, fictionalised in the series *Peaky Blinders*. He and the others I spoke with were the first to inform me about the racecourse war of 1921 that was fought between the Birmingham Gang and the Sabini Gang.

I am deeply grateful to all those people who shared their stories with me during that time and to all those who have done so since, because this book has been enriched by their memories. Similarly, my appreciation goes to those who have allowed me to include photographs from their personal collections. They are: Brian McDonald, who has also generously imparted his unrivalled knowledge of the London gangs; Juliet Banyard and her brother, Justin Jones, the great-grandchildren of the real Billy Kimber from his first marriage; Lesley and Robert Staight, the great-grandchildren of Birmingham Gang member Edward Tuckey; Tommy Garnham, whose father led a small gang from Islington that worked for Billy Kimber; and Mark Hanson, the great-nephew of the labour-movement activist, Jessie Eden.

ACKNOWLEDGEMENTS

For the inclusion of photographs from their collections, I thank the Library of Birmingham, the Islington Local History Centre and the West Midlands Police Museum, whose Sparkhill police station volunteers have also delved into their archives for me. The existence of that museum owes much to the indefatigable efforts of the late Dave Cross, who introduced me to its priceless collection of prisoners photographs. Other photos are from the Birmingham Lives Archive at the Library of Birmingham, which developed from my own personal collection.

A book of this type and scale could not have been published without the support and expertise of a highly talented team – in fact, two teams. From History West Midlands, I thank: Dr Jenni Butterworth for her thoughtful editing; John and Averil Maskew for the photographic retouching; Peter Bounous for securing the permissions for various photographs. I wish to pay especial tribute to Mike Gibbs, Publishing Director at History West Midlands, for his enthusiasm and commitment to the history of Birmingham and the Black Country and for his belief in my work. The second team is that of Bonnier Books UK and in particular, for their input, enthusiasm and support, I am grateful to: Kelly Ellis, Publishing Director – Adult Non-Fiction, Bonnier Books UK; Ellie Carr, Assistant Editor, Bonnier Books UK; and Liz Marvin, Copy Editor. Thanks to all those from other departments within Bonnier Books UK who have contributed to this book.

Finally, I thank my extended family from Sparkbrook, Aston and Highgate for all the stories that they told me and which inspired to be a social historian, and my Dublin wife,

Kay, for her understanding of my passion for the history of Birmingham and the urban working class, for her insights into growing up in Finglas West, and for her unwavering backing.

INTRODUCTION

In 2013, the BBC2 series *Peaky Blinders* grabbed a riveted audience from its first scene, when Tommy Shelby rides into town like a feared outlaw from the American West. Frightened women scurry out of his way, children peer furtively at him from their hiding places and all that can be heard is the clopping of his thoroughbred horse. With nobody around, the rider stops. But he is not in the Wild West and nor is he a gunslinger: he is a man of power in back-street industrial Birmingham in 1919. Dressed distinctively and stylishly in a three-piece suit and a shirt with a stiff collar but no tie, he is a commanding yet mysterious presence – a feeling heightened by the newsboy-type cap overshadowing his eyes.

After a brief encounter with a deferential Chinese man and woman in traditional dress, Shelby rides off slowly to the theme tune of 'Red Right Hand' by Nick Cave and the Bad Seeds. With its clanging, pounding sound, haunting almost sinister feel and hypnotic bluesy beat, its foreboding lyrics seem as if they have been written specially for Tommy Shelby: 'He's a man, he's a ghost, he's a god, he's a guru'.[1] As he makes his way through a grim urban setting, steam swirls around, smoke disgorges from factory chimneys and the dark atmosphere is punched through with bursts of flame from a foundry. Disabled Great War veterans are begging, other men are drinking and gambling on the tossing of coins into the air and two uniformed police officers touch their helmets respectfully to 'Mr Shelby', who carries on along a street that burrows between brooding factories.[2]

This captivating opening set the standard for a gangster epic that is beautifully shot with a cinematic feel and which is enhanced by stunning set designs, clever direction, classy production, slow-motion fights and compelling performances by famous actors. Above all, the story by Steven Knight, a Brummie himself, is engrossing, telling as it does of a feared and dangerous gang called the Peaky Blinders that rules the Small Heath district of Birmingham in the immediate aftermath of the First World War. This name, infused with fear, is taken from the disposable safety razor blades stitched into the peaks of their caps. In a fight, they are whipped off and slashed across the eyes of their enemies, blinding them.

From their base at the Garrison pub, the Peaky Blinders are making much of their money from illegal bookmaking. They are gathered around the daunting Shelby family led by the second oldest brother, Tommy. Violent and menacing, he is haunted by his harrowing experiences in the First World War and is all the more dangerous because he is not afraid to die. Yet Shelby is no ignorant thug. He is shrewd, resourceful and motivated not only by a thirst to become rich but also by an intense loyalty to his family and a desire to move them away from the back streets and bring them legitimacy. Their path to do so is tortuous, and in a fast-paced drama over several series, the Shelbys' Peaky Blinders fight with other gangsters such as the Londoners Billy Kimber, Darby Sabini and Alfie Solomons; are embroiled both with the IRA and Russian aristocrats; clash with Chief Inspector Campbell, brought in from Northern Ireland to put them down; become factory owners and are challenged by the highly-intelligent trade union leader Jessie Eden; and survive a vengeful mission by a New York mafioso called Luca Changretta.

From the start, *Peaky Blinders* gained a fervent following in the United Kingdom. The rage for all things Peaky grew over the next three series, prompting *Peaky Blinders'* fashion, drinks, bars and tours. Now an international sensation, the series boasts celebrity fans and won numerous awards, including the BAFTA for Best Drama Series in 2015 and 2018. Such accolades have been matched by the praise of many critics, and have led some to declare that *Peaky Blinders* is a 'Brummie *Boardwalk*' because, like the acclaimed American series *Boardwalk Empire*, it is visually stylistic and dramatises historical figures from the 1920s.[3]

This approach has sparked an upsurge in interest in the real characters, events and places drawn from historical obscurity by *Peaky Blinders*. For there was a real Billy Kimber, a real Darby Sabini and a real Alfie Solomon, and there was a real gang war involving them in 1921. There was a real Birmingham Italian family called Changretta. There was a real labour-movement activist named Jessie Eden. There were illegal bookmakers in the poorer neighbourhoods of Birmingham in the 1920s. There was a Birmingham police chief who did hail from Northern Ireland. And there were real peaky blinders in Birmingham. But they thrived before the First World War and not after it, when there was not just one gang, rather there were many. Moreover, these peaky blinders were neither glamorous nor powerful gangsters: they were back-street thugs. Although some of them were also petty criminals, most of them had jobs and none of them belonged to a gang in order to make a living from large-scale gangland activities.

In an era when Birmingham was proclaimed as the 'best governed city in the world', as the American journalist Julian Ralph lauded it in 1890, Birmingham was also notorious for its street gangs and was damned as one of the most violent places in Britain.[4] Behind the façade of a council admired for its municipal socialism and activism, the lives of scores upon scores of thousands of hard-working and respectable citizens in poorer neighbourhoods were blighted by vicious back-street gangs.

These had not suddenly sprung up out of nothing. They had emerged from the late 1850s when the new Birmingham police, under pressure from the middle class, cracked down on the rough sports and gambling of youths in the open in the poorer parts of Birmingham. This police action was resisted by the roughs of the town, who banded together in what were called slogging gangs from 1872. But the sloggers did not just attack the police: they fought each other and also cruelly assaulted anybody who crossed them in any way, whether man or woman, young or old. Similar gangs had arisen in Manchester, Salford, Liverpool and London, and although there were violent men elsewhere, it was only in these cities and Birmingham that street gangs were rampant.

From 1890, the sloggers of the city were also called peaky blinders, a term that would soon be given to brutal bullies whether or not they were in a gang. In Birmingham folklore, their name arose from the story that they had they sewn disposable safety razor blades into the peaks of their flat caps and in a fight, the peak would be slashed across the forehead of an enemy, causing blood to pour into his eyes and temporarily blind him. With a name pervaded with dread, the peaky blinders swiftly gained infamy across Britain as well as in Birmingham, where some families can still identify a peaky blinder ancestor. My family is amongst them as my great grandfather, Edward Derrick, was a peaky blinder and a third-generation criminal. His paternal grandfather was a habitual offender, who was once sentenced to transportation for stealing, whilst his grandmother was also a convicted thief.[5] As for Derrick's father, he was fined for assaulting a police officer after he had struck the wall with a tremendous blow with a poker during a row with his wife.[6]

Derrick's oldest brother, John, was also violent and was a leader in a slogging gang. In February 1891, at the age of 20, John Derrick was charged with assaulting a police constable who had a prisoner in custody in Thomas Street (later

Highgate Road) in Sparkbrook. The incident occurred when he was amongst other roughs and had thrown a brick at the policeman. When Derrick was brought to court, it was stated that he was involved in nearly every row that took place in the district. He was jailed for six weeks with hard labour.[7]

At this time, my great-grandfather, Edward Derrick, was aged eleven and in the Penn Street Industrial School. Boys under fourteen were placed there when they had technically committed crimes, such as begging, or if they were beyond the control of their parents. It was hoped that, in this way, a child in bad circumstances would be saved from his surroundings.[8] That hope was dashed with my great grandfather. Although there is no evidence of him belonging to a slogging gang like his older brother, as with other peaky blinders, he was a thuggish petty thief.

In 1893, he was convicted of vagrancy and, in October 1894, he served seven days in prison for stealing five loaves. Just weeks later, the now sixteen-year-old Derrick was sentenced to four months' hard labour for burglary. Then, in 1897, he was sent down for five months and handed a two-year supervision order for stealing a bicycle. He was not out of prison long before he was convicted of using obscene language and, soon after, in October 1898, he was imprisoned for twelve months for breaking into a counting house. It was stated that he was 5 foot 3½ inches tall, had a blue mark on the back of one forearm and wrist, and a tattoo of a mermaid on the back of the other forearm.

Now a serial offender, in 1899, Derrick assaulted a police constable – constable baiting was especially associated with peaky blinders. A year later, he was arrested for drunkenness, and, in October 1901, under the alias of Fredrick Pitt, he was sent away for three years for bodily harm. Finally, in October 1906, he was sentenced to two months' hard labour for stealing a basket carriage – a basket on three wheels used by hawkers and others to move their goods.[9] Then aged fourteen, my Great Uncle Bill Chinn recollected seeing Derrick and his brother, Fred, with the stolen item and 'pinching a side of bacon from Payne's in Ladypool Road, corner of Colville Road'. He explained, 'I was up there selling [*Birmingham*] *Mails*. I seen Fred Derrick get the long arm, which they was hanging the bacon with outside for show. And he picked one up, they dropped it in this carriage and they went down Colville Road.'[10] Derrick then sold the basket carriage for eight shillings (40p), explaining that he needed that sum as the bailiffs were in his house. He did not use the money for that purpose, though, for he admitted in court that he'd 'blewed it in for the sake of beer'.[11]

A year later, Derrick married my great grandmother, Ada Weldon, at Christ Church, Sparkbrook. He gave himself as a bricklayer, although previously he had said that he was a tailor and later he would call himself a scrap iron dealer and a rag and bone man. Marriage did not change him for the better. When I was researching my doctoral thesis in the early 1980s, I spoke with Lil Nead, née Preston, whose family had lived in the same yard of back-to-back houses in Studley Street, Sparkbrook as the Derricks and their daughter, Maisy, my grandmother. Lil recalled that Derrick was an abusive bully who often smashed up his home when he was drunk and that on occasions his wife and child had to hide from his drunken rages in the communal brewhouse (washhouse) or in the house of Lil's Granny Carey. Known as Old Mother Carey, she was beloved by all the folk of Studley Street and had several strong sons – so Derrick would not pursue his maltreated wife into that house.[12]

There was also a story in the family that my great grandmother went on to divorce him after he had abandoned her. I always doubted this, thinking that it was too expensive for a working-class person to be able to afford the high costs of a divorce. I was wrong. After suffering years of cruelty, she did divorce Derrick in 1922 as 'a poor person' under the rules of the Supreme Court. The divorce documents confirm that from the summer of 1913, he had failed to provide food or clothing for his wife and child. They got by on her wages as a press worker in the brass trade. Then, in April 1915, he had violently assaulted his wife and threatened to kill her at her house at 25 Studley Street.

Six months later, Derrick physically attacked her with his fist and caused her bodily harm. It was emphasised that 'he had frequently given way to drink and had used foul and abusive language' towards her and that he had also often smashed various articles of furniture and broken up two homes. Thankfully, from January 1916, he deserted his wife and daughter and moved to Coventry.[13]

Derrick lived until he was aged eighty-five, dying in 1964, in Nuneaton. As for his wife, Ada, she was later reported as stating that she had left Derrick for a better man.[14] Sadly, she died of stomach cancer in 1925, aged thirty-nine.

INTRODUCTION

I knew of the Derricks growing up but knew little about them until my adulthood. However, they have made a mark upon me. My paternal grandfather Richard Chinn was tall, fairish skinned and blue-eyed. I am short, dark haired, brown-eyed and sallow skinned. So too was my maternal great-grandfather Edward Derrick, my peaky blinder ancestor and a man for whom I have nothing but contempt. As a wife-beater, thief, wastrel and violent ruffian, he was typical of the peaky blinders. Unlike the dramatised peaky blinders, they were not fashionably dressed, they did not have a certain charm, they did not have a certain sense of honour and they were not respected by Birmingham's working class, who were mightily relieved when the reign of the peaky blinders was ended.

Their disappearance by 1914 owed much to the forceful policing initiated by Birmingham's chief constable, Charles Haughton Rafter, who was credited as the man who cleaned up the city's black spots.[15] Yet though the real peaky blinders had been put down, some of them formed the formidable and fierce Birmingham Gang led by the real Billy Kimber. In 1921, they fought a bloody war against an alliance of London gangs led by the real Darby Sabini, and including the real Alfie Solomon, over control of the protection rackets and pickpocketing on the racecourses of southern England. However, no 'battles' in that war were fought in the Midlands or Birmingham, which by now had shed its reputation for violence.

As for the rest of the peaky blinders, some went on to fight for their country in the First World War and returned home changed and more law-abiding men. With the passing of the last of them, the peaky blinders drifted into local folklore. Some older folk used just the mention of their name, like that of the bogeyman, to scare children, whilst others told of the fearsome peaky blinders with disposable razors stitched into their caps. The story went that, in a fight, this weapon was slashed across the foreheads of their enemies, whose eyes were then blinded by blood pouring into them, allowing them to be beaten up.

Slowly, even this tale began fading away, as the children and grandchildren of those who had known the peaky blinders died – fading away, that is, until revitalised for a modern and wider audience by the gripping drama, *Peaky Blinders*. The reality of the gang differs somewhat from that portrayed on our televisions, for the real peaky blinders were unsavoury, unglamorous and unworthy of respect. Yet reprehensible as they were, collectively, they were major figures in late-Victorian and Edwardian Birmingham. Ignored or mentioned merely in passing in studies of the city, in truth the peaky blinders and sloggers affected the lives of scores upon scores of citizens for a generation and more, albeit negatively, and tarnished the reputation of Birmingham. Their actions are as inextricably bound up with the city and its history as those of its leading politicians and great manufacturers. This, then, is the real story of the peaky blinders.

Chapter One

BEFORE THE PEAKY BLINDERS: THE SLOGGING GANGS

A grim and terrifying picture of Birmingham in 1919 was revealed by BBC News on 12 September 2013 when publicising the first episode of *Peaky Blinders*. Under the headline 'Birmingham's Real Peaky Blinders', the city's 'dank, slum streets' were depicted as ruled by gangs made up of hundreds of youths armed with knives, razor blades and hammers. Murders were rife and 'robberies, thefts and riots were a daily occurrence at the hands of young gang members who hold the entire city in a fearful, bloody grip'. The police did their best to control the daily nightmare but were vastly outnumbered. This gang violence had erupted in the 1870s, the article explained, when hundreds of youths fought 'sometimes to the death in mass brawls that lasted for hours' so as to 'own' areas like Small Heath and Cheapside. The most prominent and ruthless of these early gangs were the Sloggers or the Cheapside Slogging Gang, which for 30 years had ruled with protection rackets and violence. Many rival gangs arose, but the most fearful force on the city's streets a century ago was, it was claimed, the Peaky Blinders. As deliberately stylish as they were violent, their chilling nickname was 'derived from the razor blades carefully stitched into the front of their caps which could be used to blind their victims'.[16]

The reality was very different. In 1919, Birmingham was not terrorised by gang warfare. Murder was not rife. There were no riots. And there was no Peaky Blinder Gang. Amongst contemporaries, the best gauge of ruffianism was regarded as the return of assaults on the police. That year, there were 134 convictions for this offence, relating to a police force of 1,341 and a population of around 900,000. This compared to 557 convictions in 1899 for 685 officers in a smaller population of just over 500,000.[17] The fall was remarkable. In fact, so much had violent crime dropped that it did not even warrant a mention in the 1919 annual report of the Chief Constable of Birmingham. He did, though, comment on the increase in street betting, suicides and street vehicular accidents as well as on the marked decline in juvenile crime, especially in serious classes.[18]

Whilst not noted in the report, there was a total of 18 offences of murder and manslaughter over the three years between 1918 and 1920. That averages at six a year. And although the Riot Act was read in Glasgow and Birkenhead in 1919, and there were also riots in the Midlands in Coventry, Bilston and Wolverhampton, among others, there were none in Birmingham.[19] This was despite the turmoil of immediate post-war Britain which was wracked with disorder associated with angry soldiers, widespread strikes, sectarianism in Northern Ireland, and racist attacks in Cardiff, Hull and other ports.[20]

Yet Birmingham did see gang-related battles, riots and murders, but before the First World War, and not after it. In fact, before the war Birmingham had a persistent, longstanding notoriety, so much so that in 1901 the *Birmingham Mail* carried the headline 'Hooliganism Reborn' and bemoaned that the city was:

> . . . rapidly earning the distinction of being one the rowdiest cities in the Kingdom! Admittedly. we had this reputation one time, but since some flattering writer conferred upon us the title of the best governed city in the world we have either improved, or have failed to recognise our faults. Certain it is that the rowdyism of Birmingham nowadays, instead of being chronic, is endemic. It breaks out occasionally in particular neighbourhoods the same way as does smallpox and scarlet fever.[21]

SLOGGING GANGS

Birmingham's bad reputation for violence had arisen from its slogging gangs. Their name came from the word 'slogger' – someone who struck heavy blows. Originally a pugilistic term from the 1820s, its use soon spread outside the ring.[22] And within a generation, the term 'sloggers' would raise up fearful images of Birmingham's back street ruffians, who first came to notice in April 1872.

It was reported that, on Sunday, 7 April, a large body of roughs had gathered in the neighbourhood of Cheapside to the great consternation of the inhabitants. Numbering 400 strong, they termed themselves 'the Slogging Gang'. After creating a great disturbance and smashing several windows, they moved towards the Hill Street area where 'they threw brick bats and stones at the windows of the hucksters (general stores) and confectioners that were open'. The shopkeepers had to put up their shutters to protect their premises, whilst one of them was hit by a brick and had to be taken to hospital. For some time, the rioters terrorised passers-by, whom they stopped and insulted. Finally, they took to their heels when approached by a small body of police. Running back towards Cheapside, the sloggers were dispersed by another detachment of the police.[23]

This outbreak of violence was the culmination of weeks of unrest, during which the police had received 'great complaints' about the large number of boys who had gathered to break windows in and around Cheapside and Barford Street, close to the Bull Ring.[24] These disturbances continued after the first slogging gang outbreak. Three days later, on Wednesday, 10 April, between 70 and 80 youths collected across the town in Northwood Street and Constitution Hill. Armed with sticks and well supplied with large stones, they stoned a police constable and then ran into Cox Street. Two of them were arrested. John Gibbon was an engine driver aged thirteen who lived in Water Street, near to the disturbance. Michael Lowry, a filer aged fourteen, lived not far away on Hospital Street. Both were sentenced to 14 days' imprisonment. Those apprehended from the Sunday riot were also young teenagers.

One of the magistrates before whom they appeared was Alderman Melson, who had himself suffered on the Sunday when some sloggers had met outside his house. He had gone outside and thrashed one of them with an ash stick. His son then followed the gang and grabbed hold of their leader but was set upon and returned home covered in blood and with his lip and ears cut. Melson pronounced that 'this stone throwing nuisance was becoming perfectly intolerable, and the dangerous state of the streets of the town was fast becoming a proverb'. He was determined that when any of these boys were brought before him, whether they had actually been seen to throw stones or not, he should 'deal severely with them'.[25]

Despite these admonitions, stone throwing by gangs was not stopped. On a Friday night in June 1872, about twenty youths on the corner of Great Barr Street and Watery Lane in Bordesley pelted passers-by with stones. As they did so, they shouted, 'We are the slogging band.'[26] As for the stones thrown, there was a plentiful supply of them. The footpaths of many back streets were paved with what were called 'petrified kidneys' – stones that were about as big as a good-sized potato. They were very durable but extremely unpleasant to walk upon and because they came loose they could be lifted up easily.

Stone throwing by gangs was not unique to Birmingham,

given that stones were a readily and freely available weapon. However, from the later 1860s it developed into local but widespread disorder within the city, caused by frightening crowds of young men milling around and attacking property, other gang members, innocent bystanders and the police.[27] In May 1871, a possible explanation for this escalation was put forward at a meeting of the Watch Committee, the body of councillors which oversaw policing. Large numbers of boys were brought before the magistrates each Monday morning for stone throwing and gambling on Sunday. Councillor Lewis believed that one cause of the nuisance was the lack of proper recreation grounds. Because of the Factory Act, 'the lads were not allowed to work after six o'clock, and as there was no place for recreation they turned into the street and commenced stone throwing or playing at bandy' (a game like hockey played with a small ball and, in the case of working-class youngsters, sticks).[28]

There was some justification to this opinion. Birmingham had no recreation grounds at all. Its only public open space was Calthorpe Park in Edgbaston on the south-west outskirts of the city in a middle-class area. This was distant from the densely populated central parts of the town, as was Adderley Park in Saltley to the east, which then lay outside Birmingham's boundaries.

STREET LOYALTY

But the street gangs of early 1870s Birmingham had not suddenly emerged from a void, and there were other reasons for the escalation in violence other than a lack of recreation grounds. These stretched back to the 1840s and included antagonism towards the newly-formed police force and its attempts to control public behaviour, and, in poorer neighbourhoods, the phenomenon of loyalty to the street. The street was the living room and playground of the poor and its people were bound together by kinship networks, communal living and shared experiences. In a nation where so much was denied to the poor, the street belonged to them.

Although it refers to the inter-war years, Jerry White's study of Campbell Bunk, the toughest street in North London, provides an insight into the emotion of 'street belonging' that is suggestive for the nineteenth century. He perceived that in 'The Bunk', the most important collective experience was centred on the street itself, through 'its popular culture, relations between neighbours, its self-identity in the face of a more or less hostile world'. That collective experience was expressed in thought, through shared values, world views, and action.[29]

Poor families inhered to their street: they came from it and it belonged to them, whilst they also belonged to it. The streets in poor quarters became almost living entities, embodying the qualities which the poor themselves lauded: hardness, an ability to fight and a character which was rough and ready and, above all, plain-spoken and down-to-earth. Outsiders amongst the working class did not talk of the residents and the street separately; rather they were one, a unity indivisible and frightening to those who did not belong. Thus, it was not the people of Garrison Lane who were tough, but rather Garrison Lane itself. That loyalty to the street was enhanced by endogamy and matrilocality. In other words, the poor were more likely to marry someone from the same street or nearby, and the wife usually preferred to live close to her mother. These phenomena strengthened kinship networks, to such an extent that in the Bordesley area of Birmingham it was said of the people of St Andrew's Road that 'kick one and they all get a limp'.

For many young men, that sense of belonging to the street stimulated a pride in their own physical prowess and masculinity and through that the toughness of their street. This could and did lead to fights with those from other 'hard' streets, evidence for which emerges in the 1840s from the intriguing memories of Dyke Wilkinson. Born about 1835, he lived from the age of nine at the Dog and Partridge in Kenyon Street, Hockley – a tavern kept by his father. Writing in 1912, he remembered:

> My only playground was the public street. Hundreds of times, I and a gang of lads have played 'pitch back', 'fox and dowdy', 'bear and tender', and other rough games in the middle of the roadway at the junction of Constitution Hill and Livery Street, a spot now crowded with electric tramway cars, cabs and vehicles of all sorts with scores of people – the policeman among them – looking on. These comparatively innocent games were often diversified by street fights; that is one set of lads would make a raid on those of

another locality, often with quite serious results. I suppose there never were such inveterate fighters as the Birmingham lads of those days.[30]

Loyalty to the street among teenaged boys remained a strong feature of poorer working-class life well into the twentieth century. Until he was eight, Donald Phillips lived in a street in the Bull Ring, an area associated with street gangs from the mid-nineteenth century, and he remembered that:

All kids from about six years old to adults (which in the 1920s meant around fourteen) had to belong to the street gang. The warfare between rival streets had to be experienced to be believed. The routine was that one street would gang up, armed with sticks, stones, bottles and any other material ready to hand, and then make a foray into enemy territory. The alarm would go up and every single kid in the home street would rush out, desperately grabbing at any means of retaliation. I've seen props taken from clothes lines, building rubble, cobble stones, anything snatched up for fighting equipment.

The pitched battles that ensued must have frightened many adults and parents. They invariably culminated in much damage to property and person. I still bear some scars from those days including a split eyebrow from a piece of glass. The lump on my forehead from a large stone hurled at short-range is gone – but maybe the results remain! Usually, the skirmish ended when the police arrived on the scene. And, of course, afterwards the kids got it in the neck from the parents although often the fracas led to adult fights if some unfortunate had suffered serious damage and the parents, men and women, went looking for retribution.[31]

My great-uncle, George Wood, was a hard man who would become a sergeant in the 2nd Battalion SAS in the Second World War. Born in 1915, he grew up in Whitehouse Street, Aston – which had been notorious for its slogging gang in the 1880s. He told me that:

> We used to fight as kids with other streets. Avenue Road, Chester Street, Holland Road, Rocky Lane. Oh, we was cock o' the f— north, Whitehouse Street. There was me, Dougie Ayres, Jackie Hunt, Herbert Mortiboy, Bobby Steel and another lot. People used to watch us fight. Fists. Knew you worn't hurting each other. Once you was on your arse you was out the fight. Never seen any kicking. If you was fighting then, you fought with a ring round you, copper'd only muck in if there was somebody getting hurt.[32]

Across the city in Sparkbrook, Fred Franklin had similar recollections: 'The kids used to fight one another with bleeding sticks, props and all sorts. One street against another. We used to have battles.' He came from Chesterton Road but, 'The Studs, Studley Street, they used to come armed with line props, garden forks. They used to meet in combat. Studs, undoubtedly, were the king pins.'[33] My dad, Alfred 'Buck' Chinn, was a child in Studley Street in the 1930s and emphasised that it was 'very, very hard, very hard and you'd always got to be proving yourself'. Dad recalled that as a youngster of seven or eight just before the Second World War:

> A big battle took place, and it looked very big for me as a kid, between Studley Street and Queen Street and I'll always remember the one feller in Queen Street, who was a big lad 'cause I was only a small kid, and they'd got props and brooms and the props of course were these square props and a battle took place and there was dustbin lids. Something had happened where it sparked off and this big battle took place.[34]

It was the only such battle that Dad remembered, although as he got older he was involved in fights on a one-to-one basis with other youngsters: 'But when we fought we fought and that was the finish and we always fought with our fists.' Such fair fighting, which was regarded as the norm by the inter-war years, was a major difference to the fighting with weapons of the sloggers and peaky blinders. So too was the less aggressive attitude of working-class teenagers towards the police. This is manifested by the dramatic drop in the number of assaults on the police between 1915 and 1934, which revealed 'a substantial decline in ruffianism'. In particular, they fell from 240 convictions in 1920 to just 96 in 1934 in a population of one million.[35]

The less belligerent attitude of many young working-class males to the police was encapsulated by Syd Hetherington. Born in 1919, he grew up in poverty in a back-to-back in Holborn Hill, Nechells, and made it plain that:

> There was a curious morality among those communities of the very poor. To cheat authority in the shape of government or a large company was acceptable within limits but robbing or distressing one's peers was beneath contempt. Hence it was an unwritten law among children playing that damage to a neighbour's property had to be made good. A window in a house broken during a game would be replaced immediately, funded by a whip-round among the players, whereas a broken glass in street-lamp would just result in a temporary halt to the game and a quick look around to ensure that no one, especially the local constabulary, had noticed. Our relations with the police were generally as friendly antagonists in that it was their job to stop us playing cricket and football in the streets and our job not to be caught. It was almost a game with justice meted out on the spot by a sharp clip behind the ear. Worse was when the constable decided to take the offender back to his parents for, while the parent would normally berate the policemen for bothering with such trivial offences, immediately he left the offending child would be beaten for bringing the police to the door.[36]

THE PITCH-AND-TOSS NUISANCE

Matters were very different in the mid to late-nineteenth century when the police were regarded by many working class youths as enemies because they were enforcing laws which attacked popular culture and which had been passed on behalf of the middle class. Burgeoning and overcrowded, the urban centres of industrial Britain like Birmingham were often seen as a fearful place for the middling orders. Locally, the population rose from almost 178,000 in 1841 to just over 400,000 in 1881. Throughout most of that period, around 35 per cent were under fifteen, with a majority younger than 30. Many of these people were crammed into a collar of poorer working-class neighbourhoods encircling the town centre and from which the middle class increasingly took flight to salubrious suburbs like Edgbaston. Untrammelled by the rules and order of the old paternalistic society that had been swept away by the surge of industrialisation, urbanisation and class consciousness, much of this young population was boisterous, raucous, less deferential and fond of rough sports and illegal amusements.

The attitudes and worries of the middle class were captured in November 1839 by a writer to the *Birmingham Journal,* a few days before Birmingham's police force was inaugurated. The correspondent strongly objected to 'the constant practice of a set of disorderly boys to congregate in groups on the "Waste Ground" adjoining St. Thomas's Church, (more particularly on the Sabbath Day), to the very great annoyance of every inhabitant in that vicinity'.[37] The annoyances included gambling at pitch-and-toss as well as games like backjumping, racing and tip-cat. This latter was an ancient game played across the world. Basically, the game required a bat (the tip) of about three feet long and a piece of wood (the cat) of about four inches long and tapered at each end. The cat was put on the ground and tipped (struck) at one end to send it upward. In mid-air, the cat was slammed with the tip as far as possible.

As for pitch-and-toss, it was regarded as a problem nationwide. It involved groups of youths and men who threw pennies to a mark. The one whose coin was the closest won the right to toss all the coins into the air, keeping those which landed heads up. If any were left, they were thrown up by the man who had come second closest. This process continued until all the money had been won.

In Birmingham, because of the rapidly growing population, most of the land in the older parts was built upon, whilst the back-to-back houses that predominated in these districts had no gardens. This left only street corners or small plots of waste land for young men to meet. As they worked six days a week, they mostly came together late on a Saturday afternoon or on a Sunday and their favourite pastime was pitch and toss.

Despite the call for the interference of the authorities to stop the gathering of youths by St Thomas's Church, nothing was done. As Geoffrey Floy has indicated in his study on Birmingham's police before the First World War, the force was initiated in 1839 and in its early years its leadership adopted a sensitive attitude towards the enforcement of legislation against street activities.[38] But over the next few years, the police were increasingly encouraged to take an interventionist approach towards 'nuisances', such as boys swimming in the canal and the obstruction of the public way by pigeon flyers, 'black your boot' boys and street traders.[39] This sterner form of policing was accompanied by the stricter enforcement of the law against street gambling. Between 1820 and 1849 there were just six mentions of pitch and toss in the local newspapers – and only one relating to convictions. But from the later 1850s, there was a marked increase in notices on arrests for pitch and toss.

Nationally, there was a growing middle-class concern over activities that were not deemed rational recreation and that attracted large and potentially unruly crowds of working-class youths, particularly on a day meant for worship. In Birmingham, the call for action for action against pitch and toss gatherings was sounded in March 1856, when the influential Reverend G. S. Bull of St Thomas's Church claimed at the annual Church Pastoral Society meeting that no encouragement was given to the police to stop this practice.[40] That situation soon changed and, on 27 September 1857, the *Birmingham Journal* announced a 'Crusade against Street Gambling'.

It was explained that several cases had been brought before the magistrates and that the stipendiary, Mr Kynnersley, had remarked that the game of pitch and toss 'in the public streets, especially on the Sunday, had become prevalent, and was the cause of great public annoyance'. This necessitated making examples of offenders caught transgressing. A man of a very indifferent character was fined 10 shillings. He had been caught with another who was provided with a good character by his employers. [41] Having such a positive reference found some favour with the magistrates and this offender was therefore fined the lesser sum of two shillings. Still he was convicted, and in such a way, otherwise 'respectable' working men could be alienated from the police.

Indeed, it seems that the attempted repression of street gambling was the catalyst for increasing assaults against the police and for the emergence of the street gangs which led to the slogging gangs and peaky blinders. In 1853, only one arrest for causing an obstruction of the thoroughfare through pitch and toss was noted in the Birmingham newspapers. On a Saturday in November, Detective Officer Palmer came upon a crowd of 30 or 40 'thieves', as they were described, playing the game in Thomas Street, a very poor part of the town. After watching them unseen for a minute or two, he went towards them but 'they all scampered off as though there had been a posse of police in pursuit, instead of a solitary detective'. In a smart chase, Palmer managed to capture Joseph Ranford, 'a man nearly six feet high, and strong in proportion'. [42] Yet no attack was made upon the detective.

By contrast, four years later on a Sunday in late April 1857, when Police Constable O'Hara was taking two 'pitch and toss fellows' to the station, an attempt was made to rescue them. James Jennings, a striker from Well Lane, threw a stone at the officer, 'which took violent effect on his head'; Jennings urged his companions to follow his example. Although the prisoner's employer gave him a fair character, he was fined 20 shillings and the costs owing to the serious nature of the assault. If he did not pay, he would face 21 days' imprisonment.[43]

The next year, on 28 April 1858, a headline in the *Birmingham Daily Post* directly connected gambling on the streets with assaults on the police. When two police officers had sought to arrest men playing pitch and toss again in Thomas Street 'volleys of stones, thick as hail, came from the gang of about thirty or forty fellows'. One constable appeared in court with his head bound up as a result of the injuries he had received. Three men were fined, whilst it was observed that the offences of street gambling and throwing stones at the police were almost daily occurrences.[44]

The 'Police Crusade against Pitch and Toss in the Streets' gathered force, and in September 1860 it was pronounced that, for some time past, as many as sixteen lads and youths had been brought before the magistrates in one day charged with the 'evil' that was of 'a very mischievous character in many ways'. [45] Nevertheless, throughout the 1860s, writers to local newspapers continued to complain of the inaction of the police. One such was the Reverend H. H. Horton. In 1861, he was so aggrieved at the most disgraceful acts of Sabbath breaking on the waste ground opposite the end of Dartmouth Street that he called at the Duke Street police station to demand action. Despite assurances that the problem would be remedied, it was not, and the Reverend declared himself to have no faith in the police force, having observed continued pitch and toss games, and confronted individual officers about their lack of action.[46]

It is unsurprising that some, if not many, police officers were loath to take on gangs playing pitch and toss, given the violence they often faced. Floy emphasised that the most turbulent period for street disorder was between 1867 and 1880. During this period, the police, perhaps understandably, were slow in their response to such outbreaks because of the attacks on them when they sought to make arrests.[47] Moreover, in this mid-Victorian battle for the streets, in which the police were entrusted to enforce laws predicated upon middle-class attitudes, they were badly outnumbered. In 1867, the authorised police strength of Birmingham was 400, giving one officer for 813 people. That year there were 465 assaults on constables.[48]

Of course, not all such attacks were connected to pitch and toss gangs. In her important study of law breakers and law enforcers in Birmingham between 1867 and 1877, Barbara Weinberger has shown that in the 1870s 'much of the hostility to the police arose through their attempts to enforce the licensing laws, from their presence around the pubs and from their interference in the drinking habits and drinking places of the working class'.[49] Still, the gathering of crowds of young men playing pitch and toss was intimidating and potentially dangerous as they were prepared to attack the police if attempts were made to stop the gambling.

STREET RUFFIANISM

The increased attention on 'roughs' was associated with the use of a new description for their activities: street ruffianism.

Previously, this was associated with gangs in London and it was apparently first used locally in June 1864, when three young men were charged with causing an obstruction and using obscene language on the corner of Cottage Lane and Nelson Street West in Ladywood.[50] They were Matthew Boyle, aged eighteen and a gas fitter; Alfred Ellis, twenty-six and a shoemaker, and John Sheridan, twenty-two and a caster. The chief officer of the borough's police stated that 'not a day passed but that he received four or five letters complaining of the disgraceful conduct of such ruffians', whilst stipendiary magistrate Kynnersley said that the prisoners belonged to 'a set of fellows who were an intolerable nuisance'. Sheridan and Ellis were each sent to jail for fourteen days with hard labour, but Boyle was discharged as he had been given a good character.[51]

These sentences did not act as a deterrent, and in July 1866 'a gang of roughs' was said to still infest Cottage Lane and Nelson Street, to the danger and annoyance of the peaceable inhabitants.[52] There were similar territorial gangs elsewhere. In March 1868, the attention of the police was called to one which assembled daily on the corner of Loveday Street and Princip Street in the Gun Quarter, where they disturbed the neighbourhood by gambling and using bad language.

In striving to enact the law against such crowds, with the potential to react violently, the police now adopted a different tactic. They sent in larger detachments of men, including those in plain clothes, to certain pitch and toss sites. In one week in 1868, 'about fifty of the street and bye-way pests who amuse and delight themselves to the annoyance of the public in all parts of the town by their pitching and tossing' were brought before the court. They were quickly followed by another fifteen, who were each fined 2s 6d. Aged between twelve and twenty-two, they came from streets across working-class Birmingham, including Bordesley, Hockley, Highgate, the Gun Quarter, Ladywood, Ashted, the town centre and St Bartholomew's (Digbeth).[53]

Pitch and toss locations that drew in gamblers from a wide area were in the town centre. One such was Edmund Street, but as this area was transformed into the civic and business district, these sites were lost. However, spots within working-class neighbourhoods were unaffected and they pulled in a local crowd. It is probable that it was from such gatherings that the street gangs of Birmingham emerged.[54] One such was active in 1870. In April, twenty to thirty youths from Barford Street and Bissell Street were stopped by a policeman because they were shouting and swearing. Armed with sticks and stones, they told him that they were on their way to fight a gang from Sun Street with which they had clashed the previous night. More police officers came to keep the sides apart.[55]

This Barford Street Gang was associated with a pitch and toss site. In 1871, a correspondent complained of 'the disgraceful scenes enacted in Barford Street, more especially on Sundays'. A policeman on the beat was very rarely met with thereabouts, and 'not only are gangs of rough fellows found playing at 'pitch-and-toss' on the Sabbath, but windows are broken and other acts of violence committed by missiles thrown by lawless ruffians, who well know there is no fear of a visit from the gentlemen in blue'.[56]

The gang problem was escalating and it was widespread across working-class Birmingham. In 1870, the roughs who gathered in Islington (by Five Ways) were dubbed 'Mohawks' in a local newspaper, whilst a few miles to the east, a gang in the vicinity of Henrietta Street in the Summer Lane district was damned as a terror to the inhabitants.[57] In September that year, a letter was read out at a meeting of the Birmingham Watch Committee, the group of councillors who supervised the police. The writer complained of the street ruffians who blocked the thoroughfares on the corners of the streets around the Sandpits. They used language so foul that it was unbearable for people to have any comfort in their houses. A surgeon from Exeter Row off Smallbrook Street was also aggrieved at the dangerous stone-throwing by boys on an unfenced piece of ground near to his home, and Alderman Manton observed that on the previous day, sixteen boys had been brought before the magistrates for stone throwing to the annoyance of the inhabitants.[58]

A few months later, on Sunday, 30 April 1871, a gang rioted in the Gun Quarter. Again, the trouble was connected with pitch-and-toss. That evening, police officers Falvey and Palmer were on duty in Weaman Street where they saw a number of roughs gambling. The offenders ran into an entry leading into Slaney Street, and 'stood at the end with bricks in their hands, threatening to throw at the constables if they attempted to touch them'. As the officers rushed at the gang, one of the youths threw a half-brick at PC Palmer.

Fortunately, it missed him. PC Falvey managed to catch hold of Edward Lundy, 'who was very violent and endeavoured to get out of his custody'. Walter Joyce then threw a missile, which struck the officer on the forehead and knocked him down senseless. It was a severe wound, and whilst the constable was 'lying in a state of unconsciousness, Lundy threw several stones at him'. Aged seventeen, Joyce was sentenced to three months' hard labour for violent assault, whilst Lundy was remanded.[59]

The disturbances of the next year brought the term 'slogging gangs' into use. Probably in response to their rise, in 1873, the number of police officers in Birmingham was increased by fifty to a total of 450. Still, this was merely one per 778 residents, and that year there were 473 assaults on constables.[60] On 30 March, there was 'a catalogue of riotous outrages in various parts of Birmingham'. In Rea Street South, a mob attempted to rescue a prisoner from the police and attacked them with stones. Across the town in Great Hampton Street, officers as well as passengers on an omnibus were assailed with mud and stones. The offending youths then climbed onto the roofs of houses and from which they threw slates at the pursuing constables. Nearby in Newtown Row, policemen were injured with stones when a crowd tried to rescue a prisoner and others were stoned in the town centre in Great Queen Street. Trouble was also reported in Aston where a gang of sixty ruffians was 'in the habit of breaking windows and beating passengers in the streets' and on 25 March they had attacked fifteen policemen with stones.[61] These were from the Warwickshire police force as back then Aston lay outside Birmingham. A favoured place for these Aston sloggers to gather and fight others was by the canal bridge in Avenue Road.[62]

On 1 April, the *Birmingham Daily Post* regretted that serious assaults on the police while in the execution of their duty were becoming uncommonly rife in Birmingham. This was especially so on a Sunday, when the pitch and toss gatherings were at their greatest and when 'brutal cowards could give their ruffianism full vent'.[63] Ten days later, the newspaper bemoaned 'eleven weeks of ruffianism in Birmingham' when listing a series of crimes. Damned as a 'melancholy record of the unprecedented ruffianism that has characterised Birmingham for some time past', it included a disgraceful scene in Livery Street, which again took place on a Sunday. The police had sought to disperse some boys assembled in a dilapidated house but were pelted with brickbats (part of a brick). Fourteen of the offenders were taken into custody but 'a large crowd followed them to the station, hooting, and throwing mud and stones'. When the police van came to take the prisoners to the Moor Street public office and lock up, 'a mob of about a hundred of both sexes followed it along Great Hampton Street, Constitution Hill, and Snow Hill pelting it with mud, stones, and other missiles'.[64]

It was now clear that slogging gangs were increasingly associated with certain streets which had a reputation for their tough youths and that, as well as attacking the police and innocent bystanders, these loosely organised gangs were fighting each other. In March 1873, the *Birmingham Daily*

Post noted that a number of youths from the Bradford Street Slogging Band had waylaid a member of the Park Street Gang. After hitting him with a stick, he was knocked down and then kicked.[65] Later that year, a slogging gang in Little Francis Street, Duddeston was confronted by two police officers who stated that the youths were armed with gutta-percha 'neddies' (coshes made of a rubber-like substance) and also sticks with iron at the ends. Another gang of roughs in Great Tindal Street, Ladywood, was described as 'a terror to the neighbourhood'.[66]

Loyalty to the street, police efforts to suppress Sunday gambling and the gathering of young men on corners were key factors in the rise of slogging and they were part of a wider trend identified by Weinberger, a pioneering historian of policing and crime. Her research emphasised that a growing hostility to the police among the working class was most directly expressed by the poorest and most unrepresented. This hostility was rooted in a resistance to new trends in central and local government directives. A passive style of policing, whereby public order was maintained simply by walking the beat, was giving way to a more coercive and punitive approach.

In a drive to enforce urban discipline, increasingly the police were interfering with people with whom they had not previously bothered. As a result, overall working-class tolerance of the police shrank, whilst new police initiatives against behavioural offences such as drunkenness and street gambling provoked resistance. In turn, this led to an upsurge of assaults on constables in towns throughout England in the 1870s. Most particularly, Weinberger argued that the street gangs rejected police claims that they had the right to maintain order in the territories under gang rule.[67]

Yet though changes in policing may have prompted the rise of Birmingham's street gangs, many of the youths and men involved in them were unsavoury characters who blighted the lives of the hardworking and respectable folk amongst whom they lived. According to the *Birmingham Daily Post* on 24 June 1873, despite severe sentences passed by the magistrates, 'ruffianism still prevails to a considerable extent in Birmingham'. In some parts of the town, Sundays were 'monopolised by the roughs who amuse themselves with gambling, throwing brickends at houses, assaulting peaceably disposed foot passengers, and rescuing prisoners from the custody of the police'.

These areas were also given over to mob law on Saturday evenings. Edwin Cook of 40 Potter Street in the Gosta Green neighbourhood was amongst those peaceable citizens viciously assaulted by the sloggers. A gun barrel maker and filer, on the afternoon of Sunday, 8 June, he was taking tea with his family when he heard abusive language outside his house and someone throwing up coins. He went out and saw several roughs playing pitch and toss. Cook asked them to go away but they jeered at him, using bad language. Joseph French was the ringleader and he threatened that 'if you come here I will put you through'. He then pulled out a heavy whip-stock with an iron rod attached to it and with this dangerous weapon, French viciously struck Cook on the forehead as he bravely approached the gang.

Although he had a large wound and his clothes were saturated with blood, Cook took hold of French who handed the whip-stock to another rough, ordering him to 'Lay on the —' (the dash in the newspaper report symbolised a profanity). This he did and then ran off. However, the plucky Cook managed to keep hold of French until a constable arrived, but as he sought to take his prisoner to the station he was rescued by the mob. The following Sunday, Cook saw his assailant in York Street. He told the police, and after a smart chase French was apprehended. As Sergeant Millard was escorting him towards the police station 'a mob came unexpectedly and pelted him with stones'. Taking advantage of the disturbance, French slipped off his jacket and escaped. Finally brought before the magistrates, he was sentenced to two months' imprisonment with hard labour for a very gross assault.[68]

IRISH AND ENGLISH GANGS

The attack on Cook led to increased activity by the police and, in early July 1873, the *Birmingham Daily Post* optimistically hoped that now that the authorities were aroused to 'the gravity of the newly-developed evil of street ruffianism in Birmingham' it would soon become a matter of history.[69] Such a hope was misplaced. In early February 1874, fifteen-year-old John 'Jacky' Joyce stabbed fifteen-year-old John Thomas Kirkham in the neck in what appeared to be a disturbance between the Park Street and Milk Street gangs. The victim died in hospital and, at the Warwick Assizes,

Joyce was found guilty of wilful manslaughter and sentenced to a month's imprisonment and five years in a reformatory.[70]

By now the Milk Street neighbourhood was feared as so 'infested with "roughs" of both sexes that it is dangerous for a policemen to "work a beat" alone, the mob actually hunting and stoning him "off the streets".[71] Nearby, the Barn Street sloggers were also gaining notoriety as was the Allison Street Slogging Gang.[72] That latter street ran parallel with Park Street and it is likely that the gangs from the two streets were one and the same. The 'captain' of this Allison Street Slogging gang was Thomas Joyce, brother of John 'Jacky' Joyce.[73]

Born in Birmingham to Irish parents, the Joyce brothers seem to have moved into the Park Street neighbourhood in the 1870s.[74] Certainly, by the 1881 census, Thomas Joyce was living in Park Lane, the continuation of Park Street. Aged twenty-six, he was a tinsmith.[75] Like his younger brother, Thomas Joyce was violent. On Friday, 23 September 1874, he and Andrew Toy, a tube drawer from Bordesley Street, were involved in a bloody fight with William Smallwood, an eighteen-year-old from River Street. They appeared in court with their heads in hospital bandages. Joyce explained that on returning home from work, he was near to Deritend Bridge when Smallwood and a gang of about twenty came up to him. They wanted to know what he and his friend were looking at. Joyce then accused Smallwood of hitting him and Toy over the head with a strap, attached to which was a buckle, thus inflicting severe injuries. Toy corroborated this evidence, adding that he was also struck with a knife which he took from Smallwood.

Police Constable Butler found no knife upon Toy, whilst Smallwood told the court that he had used his belt only when 'the Allison Street lot tried to stab him'. This version was supported by an independent witness, the son of a local factory owner. He had seen Joyce and Toy wrestling with a youth near the bridge and had heard one of them using very filthy language towards Smallwood, who did not use his buckle until his attackers produced their knives. The magistrates decided that in self-defence, Smallwood had given Joyce and Toy 'a good thrashing – a taste of their own medicine'. He was discharged.[76]

It seems that this fight and the earlier one between the Park Street and Milk Street gangs, when young Kirkham was killed, were heightened by ethnic animosity. Park Street and the adjacent Allison Street were regarded as an Irish area. Just five streets down Digbeth, Milk Street was seen as English. According to Weinberger 'the street gangs of the 1870s came together on the basis of territory and ethnicity, rather than for robbery itself, with each gang staking out and defending its territorial claims against outsiders – whether these were the police or a rival gang'.[77] Philip Gooderson also proposed that 'ethnicity seems to be one of the bases of the early 1870s, at least in the Digbeth area, although it receded as the Irish were assimilated'.[78] Whilst acknowledging that some of the early slogging gangs were associated with ethnicity, it is important not to regard their emergence as an Irish thing. It was not.

By 1871, the Irish-born population of Birmingham had dropped to 9,076 from its peak a decade before. This was just 2.64 per cent of the total of 343,787, although that proportion expanded if the English-born children of migrants were included. Irish people were found in all parts of the town but there were pronounced differences in their concentration. The poorer labouring families from Roscommon and Mayo settled in several streets spread across the older, most insanitary parts of Birmingham. This meant that there was no Irish ghetto as such, although Park Street was widely regarded as the Irish quarter. It was the Irish there who had suffered greatly in the Murphy Riots of 1867, when ethnic conflict convulsed parts of Birmingham, and it was Park Street that had one of the most notorious of the early slogging gangs. Its street gang, therefore, probably came together to protect the Irish from both the police and English roughs.

The Murphy Riots were triggered on 16 June 1867, when the Irish of Park Street gathered to hiss, groan and throw stones at a meeting arranged by William Murphy, a rabblerousing Protestant preacher infamous for his filthy and vile attacks on the Pope, nuns and the Catholic church. A brawl with the police broke out and the next day a massive English mob attacked Park Street. The Irish defended themselves against this band of roughs, described by a more sympathetic observer to the Irish as made up 'principally of pugilists, pick-pockets, garrotters, and that grade in social life termed the "dangerous classes"'. Helped by the police, this misnamed 'party of order' forced out the Irishmen who tried to protect the street and gutted their houses.

Almost every house in Park Street was then broken

into and devastated by the mob. With no protection, Irish women and children huddled in corners, mourning over the wreck of their little homes. They did so 'all in a silence only interrupted by some half frantic wail of lamentation or the bursts of crying from the children'.[79] Eventually, the mayor called out the military from the barracks in Ashted and magistrates read the Riot Act. This legislation authorised local officials to make a proclamation ordering the dispersal of any group of twelve or more people who were unlawfully, riotously, and tumultuously assembled. If they failed to do so within an hour of the proclamation, the authorities could use force to disperse them.

During the Murphy Riots, the Birmingham police had been massively outnumbered but were accused of siding with the English mob and of targeting Irishmen for arrest. In her detailed study of this riot, Patsy Davis revealed that the 450 special constables who were sworn in to support the police became subordinate to the English mob. Furthermore, Birmingham's chief of police, George Glossop, recounted how the Monday riot ended when the 'respectable' portion of the English mob 'formed up in front of the police and stoned the Irish with such force that the police became entire masters of the street'.[80] Having seen their property mangled, the Irish were then made culpable for the riots and punished for them.

Disturbances continued throughout 1867, and in October, an English mob marched on St Alban's, an Anglo-Catholic Church, and tried to attack Irish areas and the Catholic churches of St Chad's, St Peter's and St Michael's. They were defended by the Irish. Tensions remained high over the next few years, and on 28 April 1872, three weeks after the first mention of the slogging gangs, several police constables came upon 'about 400 roughs, divided into two "gangs" Irish and English'. John Morris was arrested for creating a disturbance and throwing stones, which he also incited others to do. Aged thirty-four, he was a bricklayer from Galway living with his parents in Barford Street. Interestingly, this was an overwhelmingly English street.[81]

Gooderson found more evidence of ethnic antagonism in 1874, when Chief Superintendent Glossop showed the Watch Committee a black and green paper flag upon which was a skull and crossbones and a shamrock. It had been found stuck on to the railway viaduct in Allison Street after a fight between rival bands.[82] Still, the localised enmity between English and Irish gangs living close to each other in and around Digbeth faded away as the Irish-born population declined and as intermarriage increased. Moreover, whilst the animosity of the young second generation Irish of Park Street and Allison Street to the police was intensified by the force's complicity in the sack of Park Street during the Murphy Riots, that antipathy was shared by the street gangs in the many areas in which the English poor predominated. It was a hatred that extended towards those who bore witness against sloggers and who were seen as 'coppers' – police informants.[83]

This was made clear in a riot in the summer of 1874, said to involve between 500 and 600 people in the Digbeth area. A few days previously, a local man had come forward as a witness for an attack on the police. The culprit was apprehended and sentenced to six weeks' imprisonment. Then, on the night of 13 July, the witness was sighted locally and chased. Desperately seeking refuge, he ran into a house in Bordesley Street that was stoned. A force of fifteen constables and a sergeant traced the rioters to Allison Street but when they reached Coventry Street 'they were brought to a stand by the stones hurled by the mob and resembling a hail storm'.

The police charged and arrested four ringleaders, aged from twenty to sixty-four. A number of others were charged with riotous conduct, including the fifteen-year-old Julia Giblin, an umbrella maker from New Canal Street. This is a rare case of a young woman in a slogging gang disturbance in the 1870s, although there is a little more evidence of female involvement with sloggers and peaky blinders later in the century. Giblin was of Irish descent as were some of the others arrested – but their number also included those of English heritage. Councillor Arthur Chamberlain, the younger brother of the mayor Joseph Chamberlain, had his factory in the area where the riot had taken place. As a witness of the fracas, he spoke of the frequency of these riots in the district and mention was also made of the Park Street and Milk Street gangs.[84]

THE NAVIGATION STREET RIOT

Assaults on the police continued, as did fighting between street gangs. In March 1875, it was reported that on one

Sunday afternoon, between 100 and 200 youths were throwing stones and brick bats at each other in Hall Street, Ashted, whilst two young men were each fined two shillings and sixpence for throwing stones in Coleshill Street and assaulting a PC Morley.[85] That month, on 7 March 1875, a violent disorder took place in Navigation Street after two detectives arrested William Downes, a man suspected of involvement in a robbery. He was apprehended in the Bull's Head Inn, Wharf Street, which was crowded with his friends. As Downes was marched along Navigation Street, the officers were 'pelted by a party of roughs with stones and mud, and very soon an immense mob assembled'. They were in great danger of being hurt and having their prisoner rescued when Sergeant Fletcher came to their assistance and tried to hold the mob back. He was surrounded and assailed by twenty to thirty ruffians who knocked him down and beat him with bludgeons and stones and jumped upon him.

By now, the detectives had managed to reach the corner of Suffolk Street, where they saw PC Lines coming. One of them exclaimed, 'For God's sake, go to Sergeant Fletcher, they are murdering him!' The gutsy officer immediately ran up the street, drew his staff and rushed to the rescue of Sergeant Fletcher, who had been stabbed in the face and received several scalp wounds. Fletcher succeeded in getting away, however PC Lines was beset by the roughs and, as a witness graphically described it, 'They clung to him like rats, and tried to get him down but failed.' He beat them off, but, 'In the heat of the affray one of the ruffians plunged his knife into his neck, near the left ear, and then Lines fell.' His assailants now kicked and beat him until a cry was raised that more police were coming and they dispersed. PC Lines was taken to Queen's Hospital in Bath Row, where he died on 25 March.

Twelve men were arrested for their part in the Navigation Street Riot. Aged between seventeen and twenty-three, it was stated that all of them were convicted thieves who had given the police a great deal of trouble, whilst several of them had been convicted several times of assaulting the police.[86] One of them, Jeremiah Corkery alias Corcoran, was found guilty of the murder of PC Lines and was hanged. Four other men were convicted of unlawful assault and sentenced to life imprisonment. They were John Creswell, Thomas Whalin, Thomas Leonard and Charles Mee.[87] According to a correspondent to the *Birmingham Weekly News* in 1955, Creswell was released after twenty years, and in the 1890s was living near Broad Street, a respectable working man.[88]

Will Thorne, founder of the Gasworkers' Union, was born in 1857 and grew up in Farm Street, Hockley, and in his life story he wrote that there was 'a very tough gang of roughs who were always looking for trouble' in the Navigation Street locality. It seems that as well as thieving and assaulting the police, they carried out a crude form of protectionism. However, after the murder of PC Lines:

The action of the police resulted in the final clearing up of the neighbourhood. It was a relief, especially for the patrons of the Birmingham Theatre Royal that was adjacent to Navigation Street. This was a favourite place for the gang to operate.

One of their games was to come along when the people were lined up to go into the theatre. I was often in the crowd, and just as the doors were open they would leap-frog over the waiting crowd, run to the gallery and take charge of all the best centre seats. Later they would sell some of these seats, after keeping a number for themselves. Up to the time of the riots neither the police nor the theatre authorities were able to prevent these raids.

Whilst the theatre raids and the murder of a police officer differ greatly in the scale of violence, the testimony of Will Thorne shows the general unrest at the time, revealing an environment that leant itself to the escalation of such violence. This type of social unrest unfortunately was not limited to this area alone. Despite the breaking up of the Navigation Street Gang, elsewhere street gangs carried on blighting the lives of the hard-working and respectable poor as much as they tormented police constables on the beat. So bad was the problem that in May 1875 a deputation from Duddeston Ward met representatives of the borough magistrates to discuss their belief that violent offenders were not punished severely enough. Led by Councillor Derrington, they explained that a great many street rows had taken place in the Duddeston, Nechells and St Bartholomew's wards. Many of these arose from drunkenness, but others seemed like faction fights with 'the opposing forces being drawn up in the neighbourhood, and a general melee ensued'. The *Birmingham Daily Post* thought the deputation misguided, asserting that it had exalted every little street row into an outbreak of ruffianism and that its unfounded claims were refuted by the official criminal statistics.[89]

Such a dismissal would have been scant comfort to Margaret Moran. A steel-toy maker aged twenty-one from the Navigation Street neighbourhood, she was one of a number of witnesses against the rioters who had been persecuted and threatened. In her case, she was also stabbed by Corcoran's sister and was 'afraid of her life'.[90]

By contrast, the magistrates themselves took the complaints of the deputation seriously. Alderman Manton pointed out that not one case in six was reported in the newspapers, whilst the stipendiary magistrate, Kynnersley, said that it was clear that 'great outrages were committed, but those who were brought up had very little to do with the offence and were frequently brought up for refusing to help the police'. It would be a great injustice to punish those people as if they were the perpetrators, whilst the real ringleaders were seldom brought before the magistrates.[91] Still, and perhaps prompted by the deputation and the murder of PC Lines, the Watch Committee increased the police force by 50 men so that double beats could be worked in the most dangerous areas.

It seemed that these actions and the severe sentences passed on the Navigation Street rioters had an effect as, in February 1876, the *Birmingham Daily Post* wrote that, 'We have enjoyed such long immunity in Birmingham from street rows that we were beginning to hope the riotous spirit of the local "residuum" was at length fairly subdued, if not positively extinguished.' Such hopes had been dashed, however, by a recent street fight between roughs and the police and by an organised disturbance.[92]

A year later, it was reported that for several months 'a large number of rough youths had congregated at the corner of Great Charles Street, and indulged in what was vulgarly known as slogging'. They attacked each other with large sticks and pelted each other with stones and brickbats, whilst they watched out for the police and decamped when they were seen.[93]

The ruffianism in Birmingham was now drawing unwelcome attention nationally. In 1877, at the Northampton Assizes, Justice Hawkins commented that 'night after night the streets of Birmingham become the scene of an almost irrepressible violence and brutality'. This was followed by a letter to *The Times*, in which the writer sought an explanation for the discrepancy between the praise bestowed on Birmingham for the perfection of its municipal institutions and the large number of cases of violence in the town. This prompted 'a warm discussion' at a meeting of the Watch Committee. The councillors agreed that recent remarks were a stigma founded upon misrepresentations. Birmingham was being held up to ridicule and scorn not only in every corner of England, but also throughout the whole of the civilized world. Everywhere it would be asked, 'What does *The Times* say?' The answer would be that violent crimes were nightly occurrences in Birmingham. In response, it was resolved that Major Bond, the chief officer of the police, should write to the newspaper with statistics to refute the allegations.[94]

Birmingham's leaders valued highly the recent reputation that they had won, nationally and internationally, for good governance, progressive policies and municipal socialism. Four years before, in 1873, the council had been taken over by young members of the Liberal Party. Under the dominating leadership of Joseph Chamberlain, important reforms were carried out, including the municipalisation of the private gas and water companies. Like Chamberlain, many of the councillors supporting him were Non-Conformists and represented the larger manufacturers. Though they had a connection with the more skilled and regularly employed of the working class, they were sharply separated from the poor in every way: residentially, economically, educationally, and aspirationally as much as by speech, attitudes and beliefs. Consequently, the poor were not embraced by the new civic concept of Birmingham.

As Weinberger has rightly emphasised, the denial of allegations of disorder by the council, together with the lack of decisive action on the part of the magistrates 'points very strongly to an attitude on the part of the authorities that the rowdyism in certain areas of town was of concern to few people other than the local inhabitants'. Weinberger's work focused on the perceived 'criminal class', towards which she concluded that a strategy of exclusion was implemented by the urban elite as it presented 'no real political threat, while it came to serve a diminishing economic function'.[95] These insightful comments could be applied as much to poorer young men in general. Their exclusion from the civic entity was another contributory factor in the expansion of street gangs in 1870s Birmingham, a decade otherwise regarded as a positive period during which Birmingham modernised and went forward.

ASTON SLOGGERS

Street ruffianism was widespread across the working-class districts of Birmingham, and in 1878 there were 478 assaults on the police. Over the next few years that figure dropped noticeably, with only 279 in 1883.[96] This may have been affected by a more cautious approach by constables on the beat towards Sunday gamblers. Certainly, prosecutions against them seem to have fallen and those who were arrested tended to be boys rather than older youths.[97] Such an attitude by the police was intimated by an inhabitant of Aston, who wrote that pitch and toss in the vicinity of Kensington Street was an intolerable nuisance because of a mob of roughs. Yet, whilst a police-officer was stationed to watch for attacks on Salvation Army members in Porchester Street, there was no such oversight of the gamblers.[98]

The infilling of waste land in Birmingham may also have had a temporary effect on the decline in prosecutions for playing pitch and toss. With the loss of bigger spaces, those who threw coins now gathered on Sundays in smaller numbers in side streets in working-class districts.[99] This practice continued into the 1920s, and on a Sunday afternoon when the pubs closed my nan, Lil Perry, and other youngsters would watch the men who came out of the Albion on the corner of Whitehouse Street and Aston Road North 'tossing the pennies till the police came and they would run'.[100]

It may be that the police were acting more warily not only with regard to pitch and toss gatherings but also to the slogging gangs as reports on them diminished in the early 1880s, but any hopes that they had disappeared were mistaken. In June 1882, the Harding Street and Whitehouse Street gangs fought near to Miller Street. The *Birmingham Mail* reported that, 'The affair seems to have cropped up through the existence of a number of roughs who band themselves together and call themselves "slogging gangs". The mission of these seems to be to bring together partisans from certain streets and engage in combats, which have several times resulted in considerable injury being done.' Such was the case in this fight. Thomas Dan was hit by a brick in the head and knocked down and then kicked as he lay on the floor. The onslaught on him was finished with a blow from a piece of iron which broke his skull. Knocked insensible, he received a compound fracture of the skull, a broken arm and a broken thumb.[101]

Later that year, a gang was causing trouble by the corner of New Canal Street with Fazeley Street and the revival of the slogging gangs was announced in the press.[102] The chief of police, Mr Farndale, reassured the Watch Committee that although there been some complaints of the prevalence of what were called slogging gangs, the majority of the stabbing cases occurred in courts of back-to-backs or private houses.[103]

This dismissive observation gives weight to Weinberger's belief that attacks on poorer people were of concern only to those in their neighbourhoods.

The ongoing problem of the sloggers was made plain in 1884 when sloggers were reported as throwing stones at each other in Summer Lane, and two years later the slogging gangs of Aston made the headlines.[104] In July 1886, police constables Dawson and Houghton were taking Alfred Simpson from Whitehouse Street to the police station 'when they were set upon by a gang of roughs, who stoned them, and otherwise behaved in a very violent manner'. The officers were compelled to seek protection in a shop. Simpson then came up to PC Houghton and said that 'he would put it in for him, and immediately afterwards one of the stones which were flying about in all directions struck him on the back of the head', whilst a passer-by was knocked down insensible by one of the stones and had to be conveyed home in a cab.

In court it was said that Simpson was a member of the slogging gang which infested Aston Road, Whitehouse Street and the surrounding neighbourhood. Indeed, 'There was scarcely a day but when the Aston slogging gang met a Birmingham gang and held a pitched battle, the weapons used being stones and brickends.' So serious was the problem that extra police had been put on duty. Simpson, who was from a notorious family, was sent to prison for 21 days with hard labour.[105]

A month later, on Wednesday, 18 August, Superintendent Walker told the Aston police court that on the previous Sunday, 'There was a severe fight between the Aston slogging gang and another gang, and the battle continued up Rocky Lane nearly to Aston Cross.' By five o'clock, nearly 2,000 were involved. They included boys ranging in age from thirteen to sixteen and men of mature age, who were armed with heavy belts, sticks and brick-ends, which they freely used in all directions. So great was the disturbance that the Birmingham police had to send reinforcements to the borough boundary, while the whole of the available force in Aston was required to stop the fighting. Yet, only two men from the large number involved were arrested and charged.[106]

The nearest slogging gangs to Aston were those of Nechells, focused on Charles Arthur Street, and Duddeston, centred on Great Lister Street and Cromwell Street. Gangs also remained in the Digbeth area, such as that in Oxford Street, and, by October 1888, it was feared that ruffianism was increasing in severity both in Birmingham and Aston, whilst there was evidence of a rudimentary organisation to some gangs.[107] Charles Frith, a nineteen-year-old axle filer from Cromwell Street, was named as the 'king' of the Charles Arthur Street gang when he was charged with unlawful wounding, whilst the Aston Slogging Gang was involved in blackmail.[108]

According to newspaper reports in September 1888, apparently the latter had a system of compulsory assurance against fines, whereby gang members made contributions to a common fund. This 'insurance scheme' was checked by the Aston magistrates by sending all convicted members of the gang to prison without allowing them the option of a fine. In response, another ploy was adopted, whereby money was raised for the benefit of any member newly released from jail. In pursuit of this, Simpson and others of the Aston Slogging Gang 'called upon an Aston resident, and asked for a subscription to the fund, and, when they were refused, straightway commenced to beat the man about the head with their buckled belts'. Simpson was arrested and sent to prison for two months.[109]

The infamy of the Aston Sloggers was heightened in February 1889, when five of them were charged with assaulting the police in Birmingham. Named as members of the Whitehouse Street Slogging Gang, they had some grievance against a rough in Digbeth and on a Saturday night went with others to pay off old scores. Two police officers saw William Greening and Frederick Robinson take off their belts and run down Digbeth, where they assaulted an unknown man. As they did so, Greening shouted, 'Whitehouse Street for them! Let them have it!' One of the constables took him into custody, but he struggled so violently that the officer was forced to take his prisoner into a baker's shop close by. From inside, Greening called out, 'Now, lads, lay on; don't give over. We can lick these — ' (in these cases the dash symbolises a profanity). He struck the policeman several times on the head, who was also kicked by Robinson.

Several stones were thrown from the gang members outside. They included John Coley, who shouted, 'Now, Aston boys, we can give it these — .' Seven or eight of the gang took off their belts and struck several policemen. The stipendiary magistrate said the disturbances were a disgrace to a civilised city, and if the law could put them down it should do so. Coley and a Frederick Gibbs were sentenced to two months' imprisonment with hard labour; a Peter Ridding was given six weeks; and Greening and Robinson were each fined 20 shillings and costs, or in default one month's imprisonment with hard labour.[110]

Within Aston, it seemed that the sloggers were unbridled. In February 1889, James Casey and others violently assaulted three constables. He was sentenced to two months imprisonment with hard labour for each of the assaults, but as he was taken away from the dock he informed the magistrates that he would 'make it hot for the "coppers" when he came out'. At that he was ordered back into the dock and sentenced to another month for making the threat. Casey was unperturbed, announcing 'that only makes seven months and a fortnight, and I know you can't give me more than twelve months, so I shall do what I say'.[111]

The ferocity with which the sloggers attacked the police was made clear in July 1889. That month, the Aston Police Court was told that George Guy, a labourer, had attacked PC Payne, who was knocked down by a violent blow. Regaining his feet, Payne was then brutally kicked and beaten by Guy, Joseph English and William Perkins. While struggling on the ground, the constable was robbed of his whistle and armlet and had his helmet taken from him. Fortunately, police constables Lander and Griffiths came to his aid. By now, a vast crowd had collected, and a William Haywood went to help the police. He was a solitary figure. In evidence, he referred not only to Guy's brutality but also to the indifference of the crowd, none of whom assisted the officers who were being 'made footballs of '. Haywood helped the officers take the three prisoners to the police station. One of them was frog marched as he was so violent. Superintendent Walker said that the prisoners were the three biggest blackguards in Aston and that it was impossible to keep good men in the constabulary because of 'the brutality of such roughs, who were prominent members of the slogging gang'.[112]

Only a few other towns had a gang problem like Birmingham and Aston. Liverpool had its corner men, and there were street gangs in London from at least the 1880s, whilst Manchester and Salford had scuttling gangs.[113] The scuttlers have been regarded as Britain's first youth cult, but that designation should be given to jointly to the sloggers. Both sets of youths joined territorial gangs. Both fought each other viciously. And both hurled stones at their enemies and then fought close up with belts. In his deeply researched book on the gangs of Manchester and Salford, Andrew Davies highlighted an article an article on 'Scuttlers and Scuttling' by Alexander Devine. Published in the *Guardian* in 1890, it explained the use of the belt as a weapon:

> The most dangerous part of the belt is the buckle, and this is made of brass, and usually measures about three inches in diameter, though I have seen them both bigger and smaller. They are used by the 'scuttler' fastening one end of the strap into the buckle end, and then, winding his hand round the strap from the wrist, he grasps the leather, leaving about eight or ten

inches of the belt to be used as a weapon, the winding
of it round his arm preventing it from being readily
dragged from him in a fight.

The only thing that differed between the scuttlers and the
sloggers was that the former wore brass-tipped clogs whilst
the latter favoured steel-tipped boots.[114] By the late 1880s,
slogging gangs were causing trouble across Birmingham
as well as in Aston. Newspapers reported frequent stone
throwing, assaults and attacks by named slogging gangs:
Nechells,[115] Floodgate Street,[116] Allison Street, Milk Street
and Charles Henry Street, as well as Blucher Street and
Legge Street.[117] Unsurprisingly, the slogging gangs of Aston
and Birmingham were notorious locally but they had also
gained ill-repute nationally. In 1882, the *Sheffield Daily
Telegraph* noted, sarcastically: 'The latest gift of Birmingham
to the institutions of our country is the "slogging gang". The
name is not a pretty one but it is appropriately descriptive.
Its members are roughs, probably so called because their
manners lack the mildness engendered by a belief in the right
of property and the sanctity of life.'[118] From 1890, the sloggers
and slogging gangs were also known by another name that
would become even more infamous: peaky blinders.

Chapter Two

THE CITY OF PEAKY BLINDERS

FLAT CAPS AND RAZOR BLADES

A planner and a thinker though he is, Tommy Shelby is still a feared fighting man. He makes that clear in series one in a confrontation in the countryside with the Romany Gypsy Lee family. Three of them laugh mockingly at Arthur Shelby. Angered, Tommy moves threateningly towards them, demanding to know if they are laughing at his brother. They step forward to confront Tommy but do not answer him, which fuels his anger. One of the Lees then insults Tommy's mother.

Enraged, Tommy grabs the soft, middle part of his newsboy-type cap with his right hand, from the harder peak of which disposable safety razor blades poke out. In a fight scene enhanced by slow motion, he slashes the peak over the eyes of the offending Lee. Blinded by pain and the blood from the wound inflicted by the razor blades, he falls backwards to the ground, hands to his brow. Arthur swiftly slashes another Lee and, then, with another brother, John, the Shelbys go on to punch, kick and headbutt the Romany Gypsy brothers, who end up battered on the floor.[119]

Speaking in 2013, the creator and writer of the show, Steven Knight, explained that he called it *Peaky Blinders* because at the turn of the twentieth century in Birmingham 'young tearaways used to put these razor-blades in their hats and they were called Peaky Blinders'. After the First World War, 'these young kids that were causing trouble became more organised and this particular gang were known as the Peaky Blinders'.[120] This explanation has filtered into reviews and has come to be accepted as a historical reality. For example, in September 2013, John Crace wrote that the show 'is based on a real-life gang (they got their name from the razor blades they kept in their caps to blind people with) that operated in Birmingham after the First World War, so I have to assume there is some truth in the city's portrayal as a lawless outpost run by gangs of hardened and traumatised veterans who have returned from the trenches armed to the teeth'.[121]

But after 1918, Birmingham was not a lawless outpost run by gangs of hardened and traumatised veterans, and there was there not one gang called the Peaky Blinders. Instead, 'peaky blinders' was a generic term for the city's roughs that had come into popular use from at least 1890 and was originally interchangeable with 'slogging gangs' as a label for any gang member at the time. Moreover, there is no evidence that the real peaky blinder gangs stitched disposable safety razor blades into the peaks of their flat caps to use as weapons. Instead they took their name from their fashion of pulling the peak of their flat cap to one side of their head – thus almost covering or blinding one eye. Yet, in their heyday, these real peaky blinders were as vicious and as violent as their fictional counterparts, but their weapons were buckled belts, stones, knives, coshes and boots – all of which the peaky blinders owned as part of their clothing or else were close to hand and free or cheap to obtain. Although some of the gangs engaged in petty protection, they were only loosely organised and were more concerned with fighting than making money illegally. Most importantly, they were not glamorous. They were brutal and vile.

These peaky blinders were put down before the First World War by strong police action led by Birmingham's chief constable, Charles Haughton Rafter. He was a Northern Irish Protestant, as is Chief Inspector (later Major) Campbell – a character in the first series of the show. However, whereas Campbell is aggressively puritanical, Rafter was respected by Irish Nationalists and his deputy chief constable, Michael McManus, was a Catholic. Supported by the many law-abiding folk in the back streets, by stronger sentencing, and by the growing popularity of association football and the emergence of boxing as a codified sport, Rafter and his men turned Birmingham into a more peaceable city by ridding it of the peaky blinders.

THE MYTH OF THE RAZOR BLADES

In folklore, the infamy of the peaky blinders was heightened by their name, infused as it was gangsterism, violence and fear. The myth that they would sew disposable safety razor blades into the peaks of their flat caps to slash the foreheads of their enemies, causing blood to go into their eyes and blind them, in fact only arose a generation after the peaky blinder and slogging gangs had been put down and was either started in newspapers or else spread through them. The first mention of the use of a cap as a weapon appears to have come in 1929, when the *Warwick and Warwickshire Advertiser* paid tribute to James Ravenhall, the deputy chief constable of the county, on his retirement. He had served as a sergeant in Aston in 1892, where, amongst the peakies, he had shown aptitude in detective work – and he later returned there as a detective inspector. In explaining the term peakies to its readers, the newspaper stated that they:

. . . were also known as peaky-blinders, a name they acquired by reason of their peculiar headdress. They were violent characters and pulled over one eye they wore a peaked cap. The peak often contained a sharp piece of steel metal, which could make a very formidable weapon. Over the other eye there was a carefully trained curl of hair. They went about in rival gangs known 'slogging' gangs, and their principal weapons of attack were heavy belts with enormous buckles attached to them. One gang would come into conflict with another and terrible injuries would often inflicted. Mr. Ravenhall has seen the police station floor, when a 'peaky-blinder' has been arrested, swimming with blood. Enormous bell bottoms to their trousers were another peculiar feature of their dress.[122]

These were the newspaper's words, not those of Ravenhall himself.

The same year, the *Daily Mail* declared that there was a time when Birmingham was known as 'the City of the Dreadful Night', the home of the peaky blinders who had 'the ingenious habit of wearing steel plates in the peaks of their caps with which they playfully butted the eyes of their victims'.[123]

A decade later, in April 1939, in an article entitled 'Belt and Buckle Days. Saga of Birmingham's Peaky Blinders', the *Birmingham Mail* noted that 'the gangster's outfit was crowned with an ordinary cloth cap – ordinary except that it had a reinforced peak. A sudden inclination of the head wearing this weapon could start a fight and very often finish it at the same time.'[124]

In the late 1950s, this story that the peaky blinders wielded their flat caps as weapons gained momentum because of a widely publicised campaign by the noted local controversialist, Norman Tiptaft, against what he perceived was a rise in violent crime in Birmingham. A former lord mayor, he was dubbed a 'vigilante extraordinary'.[125] It was a title that suited him in his involvement with the National Committee of the Anti-Violence League, of which he was a founder and which campaigned for stricter sentences for violent offenders. As such, from 1957 to 1961 he wrote several letters to the press calling for whipping in certain cases of violent crime. In support of this he recalled:

. . . the days at the beginning of this century, of the 'peaky blinders' youths who carried out assaults with razor blades in their peaked caps. They were being fined 10s and 5s by Recorders and magistrates. Then Mr Justice Day came down from Liverpool. He ordered one young thug 20 lashes, sent others to prison for seven, 14 and 20 years. He gave them hell, which was what they thoroughly deserved. Within two years there was not a single peaky blinder left.[126]

So much of what Tiptaft asserted in this hyperbolic piece was incorrect. In the 1880s, Mr Justice Day had ordered the flogging of gang members in Liverpool, but when he was at the Warwick Assizes he did not inflict any such punishment on peaky blinders. This was because flogging could only be sentenced in cases of armed robbery. Moreover, the longest term of imprisonment handed out by Day to a gang member was ten years – and that was exceptional. Finally, Day was no longer in the Midlands by the turn of the century and his actions did not put down the peaky blinders in two years. Tiptaft's claim that the peaky blinders carried out assaults with razor blades in their peaked caps was as wrong as everything else in his statement.

Although he was born in 1883 and grew up during the decades of the slogging gangs and peaky blinders, it is apparent that Tiptaft knew little about them. As a youngster he lived in a house behind his father's ironmongery shop in Spring Hill. He had a prosperous and religious upbringing, sent to a private school in Handsworth, then mostly a middle-class area. His father later became a manufacturing jeweller and Tiptaft entered the business when he left school in 1898, becoming its commercial traveller two years later. As such, he spent a lot of time away from Birmingham. Nowhere in his autobiography does he mention street ruffianism, peaky blinders or slogging gangs.[127]

By the 1960s, the myth of the razor blades had taken hold in the popular imagination, strengthened by the fact that in itself the name peaky blinder suggested a peak that blinded. It was given a boost in 1977 with John Douglas's widely publicised novel, *A Walk Down Summer Lane*. Set in the inter-war years in what was regarded by many as Birmingham's quintessential poorer working-class neighbourhood, it caused a furore as it was seen by many Summer Laners as both playing upon and reinforcing negative stereotypes of the area. Some were angered that it seemed to portray the Lane as a place of squalor, drunken rows, rough people and fighting men. In one section Douglas wrote that:

Groups of men hung around the corners waiting for the pubs to open. They were in their Sunday best; clean shirts with frayed cuffs, some starched; not many had collars and ties but wore a white silk scarf knotted at the throat and, if they had one, a peaky-blinder. The peak of the peaky-blinder was usually slit open and pennies or razor-blades or pieces of slate inserted and stitched up again. The caps, peaky-blinders, were used in fighting to be whipped off the head and swiped across the opponent's eyes, momentarily blinding them or slashing the cheeks. The mark of the 'blinder'. The latest trend was to buy the peaked cap from Zissman's who would ask if you wanted the peak broke to make it come down over the eye at an angle. Smart looking.

Some of the men in the groups were talking about the Saturday night scraps of last night and not a few had scars to show for their part; lumpy faces, black eyes and split lips and ears. Some stood alone on the corners, hands clasped behind their backs, emulating the gangsters showing in the 'pictures' at the 'Globe', Edward G. Robinson type, raising on tip-toe and giving a quick hunch of the shoulders.[128]

In response to the portrayal of Summer Lane by Douglas, Pauline and Bernard Mannion wrote a more straightforward and realistic book about Summer Lane between the wars. They recognised that 'lots of tales have been told about Summer Lane, some true, some fanciful', but stressed that they were genuine Summer Laners 'who want their memories of life in the Lane in the 1920s and 1930s to go on record for all to read about'. The down-to-earth approach of the Mannions emphasised the neighbourliness of the people and their pride in their street – qualities which they shared with many who lived in the poorer working-class neighbourhoods of urban Britain. They accepted that there were fights, especially on a Saturday night, but so too were there fights in many districts of England, whilst there were also gang fights in the side streets: 'perhaps one pub against the other, and the Black Maria vans set off from the [police] station and return loaded up with the offenders'. Yet the Mannions made no mention at all of peaky blinders. That is not surprising as there were none in Birmingham in the 1920s and 1930s.[129]

As for the real peaky blinders of the 1890s and the turn of the twentieth century, there is no evidence to indicate that they sewed disposable safety razor blades into the peaks of their caps. Of all the weapons noted in police, court and newspaper reports of fights involving slogging gangs and attacks by peaky blinders, none mention the use of a disposable razor blade sewn into the peak of a flat cap. Likewise, no such weapon is recalled in the memories of people from the time.

George Morris was born in Thorp Street in 1885 and emphasised that it was in a district that was a hotbed of trouble in the 1890s, when even two police constables 'were not allowed at times without interference'. His father was born on part of the present site of New Street Station in Bread Street and he used to relate stories of the 'Peaky Blinders' and 'the bad old days of gang warfare' in Birmingham, remembering that 'as a boy, I have seen fights with revolvers, knives, bayonets, buckle belts, bottles and half-bricks, and heads bashed in!'[130]

Most pertinently, the type of disposable safety razor blades attributed to the peaky blinders in both Birmingham mythology and the series, were not readily available when the gangs were at their most prolific. In the nineteenth century, men either shaved themselves with a cut-throat (straight) razor or went to a barber, as such razors were costly. Safety razors, which had a guard between the edge of the blade and the skin, were advertised from the 1830s but they were not disposable, which, in the case of examining this myth, is key. The razors would have needed to be disposable in order to have been fitted into the caps – those available at the time would not have been suitable for this purpose. It was not until 1880 that a patent for safety razors with a removable blade was registered in America. This had a handle attached at right angles to a head in which a removable blade was placed. However, the blade was not disposable and like that of a cut-throat razor, its edge had to be stropped and honed. This meant that shaving with a safety razor was expensive.

An advertisement from 1883 gave the price of various safety razors, ranging from one to six shillings. These were prohibitive prices for working-class men, given that an unskilled worker would be lucky to earn fifteen shillings a week – and on top of this, shaving soaps, strops, brushes and blades would have to be bought. By the early twentieth century, the poverty line was given as round about a pound (20 shillings) a week. In 1904, the newest Wilkinson Sword safety razor was selling for eight shillings and sixpence, with a case including six spare blades costing 35 shillings. In total, this was over twice as much as the poverty line.

It was not until the early twentieth century that King C. Gillette succeeded in perfecting a disposable safety razor blade. The first main advertisements for them did not appear in Britain until 1910, just as the peaky blinders and slogging gangs had disappeared. A standard razor set in a velvet-lined leather case, with 12 double-edge blades, cost 21 shillings, whilst a combination set, including Gillette shaving soap and Gillette shaving brush, was on sale for between 25 shillings and £3. Such sums were also out of the reach of working-class men – and as it was, the early peaky blinders did not wear flat caps anyway.

BILLYCOCKS AND FLAT CAPS

Arthur Matthison provided a rare and important first-hand account of peaky blinders. He lived in Summer Lane during their heyday in the 1890s. Born in 1870, when he was about eighteen or nineteen, his father was appointed Registrar for Births and Deaths of St George's District. As such, he had to live the area and took a fairly large house in Summer Lane. Writing in 1937, Matthison remembered that this was:

> . . . one of Birmingham's mean streets with slums abounding all round, and the rendezvous of the Brummagem rough known in that day as a 'peaky blinder'. This product of poverty, squalor, and slum environment was a terror to respectable people forty odd years ago. He took pride in his personal appearance and dressed the part with skill. Bell-bottomed trousers secured by a buckle belt, hob-nailed boots, a jacket of sorts, a gaudy scarf and a billycock hat with a long elongated brim. This hat was worn well over one eye, hence the name 'peaky blinder'. His hair was prison cropped all over his head,

except for a 'quiff' in front which was grown long and plastered down obliquely on his forehead. He usually belonged to a 'slogging' gang, and terrible fights took place between rival gangs. He was also a terror to the police, who went in pairs along Summer Lane every Saturday night, but he never molested any member of my family. Perhaps as we lived on his doorstep, we were treated as members of the gang by courtesy or adoption. I had to go home at all hours of the twenty-four, according to what hours I was working at the Telegraph Office, and the local bullies would always give me curt nods of comradeship. One night, I had been acting in an amateur performance and came home in the dress I had been wearing, a cavalry uniform, about twelve midnight. I passed a brace of beauties lounging at the entrance to a notorious court. One of them said, 'Let's knock the sodger's blinkin' spurs off,' when the other, taking a good look at me, said, 'Strewth, it ain't a sodger; it's only the registrar's barstard.' My presumed illegitimacy no doubt saved me from violent assault and battery on that occasion, but I felt quite proud at having been recognized as a man and a brother in crime.[131]

The clothes described by Matthison are substantiated by contemporary descriptions. In 1890, a rogue called Arthur Cotton was named as a member of the Charles Henry Street 'bell-bottom' gang. Bell-bottomed trousers were announced as the regulation trousers of the slogger, and a year later the gangs were called the 'bell-bottom crew'.[132] The bell part of the trousers was often adorned with a line of pearl buttons.[133] As for the billycock noted as the headgear of the peaky blinders in the early 1890s, it was a type of bowler hat. It was widely regarded as a characteristic of the working man, as made plain in the *Birmingham Daily Post* on 19 May 1891. An older man found dead in the canal at Saltley 'evidently belonged to the working-classes' as he wore a dark blue serge suit, cord trousers, lace-up boots and billycock hat.[134]

Matthison's account highlighting that the peaky blinders originally took their name from the wearing of billycocks with an elongated rim worn well over one eye is an important one and is supported by the memories of others who also had first-hand knowledge. In 1936, an F. Atkins wrote to the *Birmingham Weekly Post*, stating that the clothes of the peaky blinders consisted of trousers that measured 22 inches round the bottom and 15 inches round the knee, although some preferred moleskins or cords. They also sported a silk 'daff' as it was called, twisted twice round their necks and tied at the ends. It was then called a 'choker'. As for the hat, it was a bowler with the brim made to fit the sides, whilst the front of the brim came to a point almost like the spout of a jug. This was achieved by wetting the brim, warming it by the fire and then making it the shape required.

As Matthison also observed, the brim was worn on the side of the head to show the hair on the other side done in a 'quiff'.[135] Norma L. Beattie's father was born in Langley Road, Small Heath, in 1879. She confirms that the peaky blinders were 'definitely not in the 1920s'. They were around when her father was a young man and 'the hats they wore were bowler hats and the front was pulled down into a peak and pulled well over their eyes – hence 'peaky blinders'.[136]

The Birmingham police was the first force in the country to record the images of people in custody and the West Midlands Police Museum has a historically significant collection of prisoners' photos, including a large number from 1892 to 1895.[137] Of those wearing hats, 64 have bowlers/billycocks, 59 flat caps of some sort and four another type of hat. By contrast, in photos of prisoners from 1903–7, 479 have flats caps of some kind and 73 bowlers/billycocks, with only a handful wearing another type of hat. This marked shift in fashion was reflected in the headgear of the peaky blinders.

Born in 1892, V. W. Garrett grew up poor in the Bath Row neighbourhood. In his life story published in 1939, he observed that in his younger days, rival gangs of roughs were composed of peaky blinders 'who wore long-peaked caps and wide, bell-bottomed trousers which tapered towards the knees. A line of vivid brass buttons down the front gave added distinction.' As for weapons, they used belts and knuckle dusters.[138]

Fred Sutton was born in 1898 and grew up in Aston and he was another person who knew peaky blinders first hand. He too mentions their hats, explaining: 'They was only peaky blinders because they used to wear a cap which they used to bend it over the eyes well. You know the peak, well they used to bend the peak over their eyes and you could hardly see their eyes and if they was talking to you you'd have to go like that to see 'em, y'know what I mean. The peak was bent right down, that's what it was like.'[139] Before the First World War, this peaky-blinder style of pulling the peak of their cap well over the face was commented upon in various newspapers.

The change in preference for the flat cap over the billycock was accompanied by a shift in hair fashion, for by the late 1890s, peaky blinders favoured short cropped hair with a donkey fringe.[140] According to a contemporary writer in the *Birmingham Mail*, this tuft 'gave an evil appearance to the face of the wearer'.[141] In the summer of 1906, as the peaky blinders were coming towards their end, a new style in 'peaky' hairdressing was noticed in Birmingham's Victoria Law Courts. Usually, 'the local hooligan has his poll cropped short with the exception of a fringe, which he plasters carefully over whatever expanse of forehead he may possess. This particular mode has apparently gone out of fashion, and the centre parting has taken its place.' In conjunction with the cropped head, the effect was regarded as rather curious.[142]

Geoffrey Pearson, a pioneer of research into hooliganism and gangs, noted that the hooligans of London also adopted 'a uniform dress code of peaked caps, neck scarves, bell-bottom "narrow-go-wide" trousers cut tight at the knee, heavy leather belts with designs worked in metal studs, and a hairstyle which was cropped close to the scalp with a 'donkey fringe' hanging over the forehead'.[143] The scuttlers of Manchester and Salford favoured a similar fashion. They wore bell-bottomed trousers and flashy silk scarves round their necks, whilst their hair was cut short back and sides. However, they had long fringes, 'which were worn and plastered down on the forehead over the left eye. Pigeon-board peaked caps were also worn tilted to the left, and angled to display the fringe.'[144]

Yet, in Birmingham at least, there were some differences in clothing depending on the income of the peaky blinder, as commented upon by a writer in the *Central Literary Magazine* of 1899, signed as J.R.C. The writer explained that a peaky blinder generally went about in a gang of 20 or more and that his clothing varied:

> . . . from well-dressed respectability, in velvet jacket, brightly coloured scarf, huge metal ring, and the crowning cigarette, to the less favoured corduroys – a ragged, unkempt, untidy and uncouth array of togs, pinned or even nailed together – *en masse* they make a somewhat imposing army, a terror to the small shopkeeper, an ever irritating bait on the policeman's otherwise monotonous beat, a continual menace to his peace and pleasure, not to mention safety, or often life.

This writer regarded peaky blinders as young men separated by a gulf from those of true citizenship. Born of careless or indifferent parents, from an early age the streets were his only playground. This is where he found 'his chums amongst similarly ill-favoured lads, feeling no one cares for him, and that he in turn need care for none, the Peaky full soon learns to know, and to measure, the full force of his enemies, who comprise such, to his mind, useless beings as school attendance officers, employers of labour, landlords of house property, "coppers" and "beaks"'. His daily life was one of continual scuffle after meals, mischief or sport, 'from street football to pitch and toss in the seclusion of the court or alley'.[145]

Yet, alienated as they may have been from wider society, peaky blinders and sloggers were not outside their own communities. They lived within working-class neighbourhoods and most worked in a wide variety of occupations. The court cases discussed and to be discussed reveal that many were labourers, but others were in the brass trade and one was a gold beater – whilst some were described by the police as hard-working lads.

Although many in authority looked down upon peaky blinders and sloggers as hailing from an isolated group on the margins of civic life, closer examination reveals a different picture. In occupational terms, they were frequently drawn not from the 'residuum', the criminal class and unemployable, but from the ranks of industrial workers who formed the majority of Birmingham's young male workforce. This was highlighted by 'Bred and Born Brum' in a letter to the *Birmingham Weekly Post*, in 1936, who insisted that the peaky blinder was 'just an ordinary working man ... He could always be found at work during the day in some brass foundry, doing his bit at the lathe or vice or perhaps as a polisher or in the casting shop.'[146]

Heather Shore's in-depth research on London's street fighting gangs and hooligans supports this opinion. She placed the boys and youths involved in street violence within their working-class communities, which were not simply slums. For the most part, these youths 'lived in mixed class communities in which they also worked, drank and socialised'. The rhetoric of the Victorian press may have labelled hooligans as members of the criminal class but 'in reality membership of and identity with streets gangs was probably more disorganised, more flexible and more fleeting than contemporaries believed'. Most of the youths whom she studied in London did work, but mostly in low-level and low-skilled occupations, as seems to be the case in Birmingham, and it may be that gangs offered them a place of refuge. Feeling socially marginalised, the badge of identity from belonging to a street gang linked to the small area in which they lived had meaning.[147]

THE GIRL WITH THE PEAKY BLINDERS

In a 1901 newspaper piece, peaky blinders were referred to as ''Arry' and the young women associated with them as ''Arriet'. These generic terms were used insultingly and could be equated to the derogatory use of 'Kevin' and 'Sharon' in modern society. Generally, though, the young women involved with peaky blinders were little mentioned by the newspapers, other than in an occasional reference to those who had been assaulted. In 1901, for example, readers of the *Birmingham Daily Gazette* were disturbed by the case of a peaky called Dennis Kennedy from Lower Loveday Street who was sent to prison for two months for assaulting Isabel Madden with a file, causing several cuts. He had recently served three months for attacking her sister. In court, Madden stated that Kennedy had called her child a bastard but denied that she was keeping company with him. However, she explained that, 'He was always thick with the young man I walk out with. He always treated me well.' She admitted that she may have scratched Kennedy with her hair pin, and he had a thin red line on his face, but although he had struck her first she forgave him.[148]

The reporter stated that the case threw some not very pleasant sidelights on low life in the city, but like so much evidence about the working class and especially the poor, it was filtered through a middle-class perspective. With this in mind, it is important to take note of the research and findings of the historian Alan Mayne on sensational representations of 'slums' in late Victorian newspapers. Overall, middle-class observers denigrated poorer neighbourhoods as dark, gloomy and iniquitous places pervaded not only with poverty but also with violence, vice, criminality and drunkenness. Men were thugs and women were either good or bad – home makers or slovenly – and often victims of brutal boyfriends and husbands.[149]

Davies discussed these gender issues in his penetrating article on youth, violence, and courtship in late-Victorian Birmingham. It focused on the case of James Harper, an eighteen-year-old metal polisher. In December 1898, he was found guilty of the manslaughter of Emily Pimm, his former 'sweetheart', whom he had kicked about the head and body whilst she was prostrate.

Commentaries on Harper in the Birmingham press dwelled on his alleged status as a gang member, or 'peaky blinder', whilst he and Pimm were identified as slum-dwellers in one of the city's supposedly most notorious districts, Summer Lane. Yet the evidence against Harper made it clear that both he and his family were, to some extent at least, respectable, and he did not dress like a peaky blinder. Nevertheless, in the local press and in the judicial system, the case was easily resolved: Harper was damned as a violent gang member who had anticipated the 'slum' husband's privilege of beating his wife. As a slum-dweller and thus a socially marginal figure, he was seen as unable to restrain his savage impulses and his behaviour was a stain on civilisation. The actions of Harper were in no doubt violent and morally corrupt, but to blame this purely on his social circumstances is both incorrect and unjust upon those who shared his situation in life. The reality behind the violence is elaborated upon by Davies, whose analysis casts doubt on portraying Harper's violence as restricted only to 'slum' dwellers. Whilst violence within courtship and marriage was far from universal it was still customary – and extended across the social classes.[150]

During the outcry over Harper's behaviour, the *Birmingham Mail* sent a reporter to Summer Lane to find out the views of local young people. One of those interviewed was a peaky's 'moll'. Through her, readers were given an 'insight' into 'the methods of love-making which obtain to-day among the bell-bottomed fraternity'. Many of the newspaper's readers would have no doubt have been quite titillated by the description of this 'exotic' figure from what they would have regarded as an 'underclass'. The peaky's moll was easily identifiable through her dress and hairstyle, which mirrored those of the peaky himself. She had a lavish display of pearl buttons, a fringe obscuring the whole of her forehead which descended nearly to her eyes, a gaudy-coloured silk neckerchief covering her throat, and her head was hidden beneath a wide elaborate hat decorated with feathers and poppies.

According to the writer of the piece, the peaky blinder's moll gloried in the scars on her lover's closely cropped head, regarding each one as evidence of his manliness.[151] This point was reiterated by another journalist six years later when it was revealed that a peaky blinder favoured close-cropped hair so that the scars caused by the buckle-belt and the policeman's truncheon could be distinguished. He regarded these scars in much the same light a soldier looked upon medals as honourable evidence of deeds done. But not only did he appreciate these marks, for 'his Moll – as he calls his lady-love – looks upon them with ostentatious pride. The more numerous the scars which adorn the closely cropped pate of the "peaky" the more numerous are the girl lovers who favour the "blinder".'[152] It is important to be aware that the representations of peaky blinders and the young women associated with them are viewed through the prism of middle-class journalists and are infused with class prejudice. As Benny Green has acutely observed, the urban masses as a whole never appeared as themselves 'but only as something which might be turned into something else'.[153] This was all the more so for groups on the margins of the working class, such as the peaky blinders – none of whom spoke for themselves.

In contrast to these middle-class accounts, a rare and valuable source from a poorer working-class perspective about peaky blinders and their girlfriends is provided by Cecilia Costello, née Kelly. Born in 1884, she grew up in back-to-back housing in various streets around the Bull Ring, but her parents were from the west of Ireland and her father, Edward, taught her the traditional songs that he had learned before he had emigrated. Cecilia herself was discovered by folk-music scholars in 1951, and, in 1967, Charles Parker and Pam Bishop collected a large number of reminiscences and songs from her. One she recounted was that, in her day, in the 1890s, the trousers of the young men:

. . . used to flap like a woman's skirt, them was bell-bottom trousers. They always had a cap to match, and they used to have a black silk scarf with a flower on. If they was Irish it'd be the green shamrock; if they was English it'd be the dells [daffodils?], all cut out, knitted onto the scarf. And they never had them tied like they would today, they got them all loose and swinging out; the cap at one side, the bell bottom trousers. If we seen an ordinary man come down like you, we wouldn't dream of looking at you – 'Ain't he common?' and the woman as well. Ladylike with gloves on up to there, and her hat properly on. Whereas the girl with the Peaky Blinders, she'd have a great big hat on, and she'd have the bloke coming down the road with her.

So they'd be singing:

My bloke's a Peaky, none the worse for that

He's got bell bottom trousers

and a Peaker Blinder's hat

Rings on his fingers and

round his neck a daff

So all you nosey parkers can take it out of that![154]

In Manchester and Salford, Davies has found evidence of female scuttlers and there are hints that some young women in Birmingham were also involved actively in the peaky blinder gangs.[155] In his contemporary article, J.R.C. noted that peaky blinders were not solely men, and that 'their sisters too often go on the equally forbidding rampage, and are too often but aiders and abettors of their male companions of the street'.[156] Some support for this statement is found in a report from May 1897, which commented that two gangs had been giving the police some anxiety in the Bath Row area. Two police constables responding to a fight in Owen Street encountered a gang of youths, the majority armed with sticks, and among them were about twenty girls.[157]

THE REAL PEAKY BLINDERS

By the late 1890s, Birmingham had asserted its claims to be considered the best governed city in the world because of its effective and efficient Council, most especially associated with the municipal ownership of the provision of gas, water and other services. As the *Sheffield Evening Telegraph* acknowledged, 'In point of many exhibitions of public spirit, the capital of the Midlands certainly leads way.' Yet it was a humiliation for the city that brutality there was as cheap as it was prevalent. A very serious state of affairs prevailed in which outrages were committed by street corner loafers, 'of whom in point of numbers Birmingham appears to possess an unenviable lead'. The Yorkshire newspaper emphasised that these loafers were the most despicable characters on earth and the city's magistrates needed to award the maximum term of imprisonment in every case of violence carried out by a peaky blinder whose offence was proved before them.[158] Indeed, the reign of these ruffians was so bad that Birmingham was frequently looked down upon as 'the city of the Peaky Blinders'.[159]

This new term for members of the city's slogging gangs was first noted in the press in the spring of 1890, suggesting that it was already in common use because of the sloggers wearing their billycocks pulled well over one eye. On Saturday, 22 March, between teatime and eleven o'clock, a young man called George Eastwood went into the Rainbow public house on the corner of High Street Bordesley and Adderley Street. As a total abstainer from alcohol he ordered a bottle of ginger beer. Shortly afterwards, several men known as the 'peaky blinder gang' came in to the pub. A brass caster, twenty-year-old Eastwood was from nearby Arthur Street in Small Heath and knew the gang by sight as they lived in the same neighbourhood. The men, who had an evil reputation, 'immediately commenced making offensive remarks about his being a teetotaller and drinking ginger beer. He merely appealed to the landlord to whether or not he was liberty to call for what he liked, when one of the party tripped him up from behind.'

Fortunately things calmed down and the three men left, but when Eastwood set off home, he was followed:

On reaching a lonely part of Adderley Street, where two bridges cross, the road the captain of the gang, a man named Thomas Mucklow of Adderley Street, shouted, 'Now, boys, give it him hot!' They then commenced striking him with their fists, and Eastwood tried to defend himself. Eventually, he was overpowered by a terrible blow from a buckled belt, dealt, he alleges, by a man named Groom. He fell and whilst on the ground was kicked about the road, and was struck several time about the head with buckled belts. At last, Eastwood gained his feet, and, chased by the mob, ran as far as the back entrance to Allcock Street Board School, and by scaling the wall, crossing the playground, and then climbing another wall, got into Allcock Street, where he took refuge in the house of Mr Turner. Eastwood was then in a very exhausted condition, and bleeding profusely from the injuries he had sustained. Owing to the attitude of the gang outside Mr Turner's house, who shouted, 'We'll kill him if we cop him!' it was nearly twelve o'clock before it was possible to remove the injured man to the Queen's Hospital.

The unfortunate George Eastwood had suffered severe wounds to the head and contusions all over his body and both legs. On the right side of his forehead there was a wound an inch long and the frontal bone was badly fractured and splintered, whilst 'the brain substance had also been wounded'. He had another serious scalp wound, three quarters of an inch long with the bone bared.

Because of his head injuries, Eastwood was trepanned. Using an instrument resembling a carpenter's brace and bit, medical staff removed a circular section of bone from his skull. Unsurprisingly, he lay in a somewhat critical condition and remained in hospital for 24 days. After the assault was reported to the police, a search was made for the perpetrators and the hunt was kept up all Saturday night and Sunday. But fearing the consequences of their action, they had fled. A warrant for their arrest was issued.[160]

Just over two weeks later, an inhabitant of Birmingham wrote to the London newspaper the *St James's Gazette*, affirming:

> That there exist in Birmingham and the neighbouring manor of Aston what are known as 'Slogging Gangs', who delight in waylaying unsuspecting people in lonely roads and pouncing upon them unawares and brutally ill-treating them. A recent instance is one in which these ruffians knocked a man down and were kicking him when a poor woman came up and begged them to desist. They replied by knocking her down. In another case, which occurred last Saturday week,

a young man named Eastwood was murderously assaulted by a number of members of a gang known as the Small Heath 'Peaky Blinders'. The police appear, from this gentleman's testimony, to come in for an exceptionally large share of such outrages.[161]

This letter gained wide coverage in newspapers from Aberdeen to Chichester, mostly under the heading of the 'Slogging Gangs'.[162] However, although the gang was noted as the Small Heath Peaky Blinders, as Gooderson has made plain, Adderley Street is actually in Bordesley.[163] Like all of the central districts of Birmingham, it merged almost imperceptibly with adjoining areas such as Deritend, Camp Hill, St Bartholomew's, and, indeed Small Heath. This latter straddled the main Coventry Road, which began close to Adderley Street, and although there was much back-to-back housing in the streets on the city side of Small Heath, further along were larger houses in roads associated with the middle class.

The only one of the Adderley Street Gang captured was Thomas Mucklow, a twenty-four-year-old labourer from Adderley Street itself. In May, he was charged with violently assaulting Eastwood and, in the *Birmingham Mail*, it was stated that when the victim had ordered his ginger beer, Mucklow had said, 'What do you drink that tack for?' Eastwood replied, 'Mind your own business,' and then was challenged to fight by Mucklow. Understandably, Eastwood declined. The gang then left a little before eleven but waited outside for when Eastwood started his way home. He admitted that it was not Mucklow's blow that had caused his injuries, but that inflicted by one of the other two men – although a lad named Roberts had heard the prisoner incite his companions to give it to Eastwood. Based on the evidence, the magistrates committed Mucklow to the Sessions for trial. He was allowed bail on his own surety of £50 and one other for the same sum. This was a very large amount for an unskilled working-class man to raise given that he would be lucky to earn 17 shillings and sixpence a week.[164]

In June, Mucklow was found guilty of maliciously inflicting grievous bodily harm. Interestingly, Detective Inspector Drinkwater said that he was not street ruffian but a hard-working man. This highlights an important point: many peaky blinders were not simply wastrels or men who relied solely on petty criminality to earn a living, but youths and men who held down respectable jobs but whose life outside of work seemed intrinsically linked with fighting. Unfortunately for Mucklow, despite not being the leader in the row, the police had been unable to get sufficient evidence to warrant the arrest of the man who had used the belt on the unfortunate Eastwood. In sentencing Mucklow, the assistant barrister stated that the case 'was a very bad one, but that he would take into consideration the good character the prisoner had borne and as a result he would be imprisoned for nine months with hard labour'.[165]

This would have been a gruelling experience for Mucklow. Prisons adhered to the 'Silent System', designed to break the will of convicts through total silence and long, pointless

Above: The real Jessie Eden in later life at a family party. Left to right are her sisters Nell and May; Jessie Shrimpton, their mother; Walter McCulloch, Jessie's second husband; and Jessie herself. Although not a major figure in Birmingham's labour movement in the mid-1920s, she became so a few years later and was instrumental in encouraging many women workers to join trade unions.

© Mark Hanson

Below left: My great-grandfather, Edward Derrick, in 1895 aged seventeen, when he was discharged from house breaking. *© West Midlands Police Museum*

Below right: Edward Derrick, this time in 1906 when he was arrested for stealing a basket carriage. On this occasion, his height was given as 5 foot 4½ inches.

© West Midlands Police Museum

Above: Numbers 33–35 Cheapside. It was in this locality that the first slogging gang to be officially mentioned gathered in 1872. ©*Library of Birmingham MS 2724*

Below: A court in Thomas Street, where two police officers were assailed with a volley of stones by men playing pitch-and-toss in 1858. This was one of the poorest parts of Birmingham. © *Library of Birmingham, LS 2/1-134*

Above: The Rainbow on the corner of High Street Bordesley and Adderley Street in the 1950s. A few yards from here, the first assault for which peaky blinders were blamed took place in March 1890. © *BirminghamLives Archive*

Below: Henry Lightfoot photographed by Birmingham City Police in January 1904, when he was arrested for stealing pork. He was the first individual to be called a peaky blinder in 1895. © *West Midlands Police Museum*

Left: Charles Battle, aged fourteen, photographed by the Birmingham City Police in October 1892. On the right, he is wearing the billycock and silk 'daff' of the original peaky blinders. © *West Midlands Police Museum*

Right: George George is wearing the outsized flat cap with a wide peak and neck scarf of the later peaky blinders. However, he is also sporting a 'quiff' of hair plastered down obliquely on the forehead in the style of the original peaky blinders.

© *West Midlands Police Museum*

Left: Young women and children outside 102, 103 and 105 Bagot Street, which had a longstanding slogging gang. Notice the two young women in the doorway, the one on the right with her arms folded has the long fringe associated with female peaky blinders.

© *Library of Birmingham, MS 2724*

Left: Charles Haughton Rafter in the uniform of an officer of the Royal Irish Constabulary, before he was appointed the Chief Constable of Birmingham.

©*West Midlands Police Museum*

Below: A cutting from the *Birmingham Daily Gazette* from 28 August 1935 showing the dense crowds gathered outside St Martin's in the Bull Ring for the memorial service for Sir Charles Haughton Rafter. ©*Library of Birmingham*

Birmingham Mourns Police Chief: Crowds at Funeral of Sir Charles Rafte

Above: Ladywood United FC, 1913–14, one of the many local football teams emerging by this date. Such teams were a key factor in the demise of the peaky blinders, alongside the popularity of boxing and the cinema, and the work of boys' clubs.

© *BirminghamLives Archive*

Below: Sergeant William Doughty, standing in the middle of the front row, was a physical-training instructor with the Birmingham Police at Digbeth police station, where the Police Training School was based from 1913. Boxing and wrestling were taught for self-defence, and skills in both were needed against the peaky blinders.

© *BirminghamLives Archive*

Deputy Chief Constable Michael McManus, a labourer from Newfield,
Co. Mayo in the west of Ireland, who began his police career in Birmingham
as a constable. He retired in 1918 after forty-five years' service and died ten
years later. He was a key figure in the strategy of forceful policing against the
peaky blinders. © *BirminghamLives Archive*

Right My granddad, Alf Chinn (right), in the early 1950s, outside the Gate pub in Sparkbrook, where he paid out winning punters. He is with one of his runners, Teddy Gustrey, who took bets at the Great Western Railway Loco depot at Tyseley.

© Carl Chinn Personal Collection

Below: The outside of my grandad's illegal betting shop in Sparkbrook just before legalisation. Like so many similar premises it advertised a phone number to give the illusion that it only took credit bets by telephone, which was legal. From May 1961, this became a legal betting shop and was later owned by my Uncle Wal.

© Carl Chinn Personal Collection

Right: Alfie Bottrell, known as Bottle, taking bets as Joe White The Silver King on an English racecourse about 1924.

© Carl Chinn Bookmaking Archive, Cadbury Research Library, University of Birmingham

and exhausting hard labour, like walking the treadmill. This was a giant wheel with slats. Prisoners held on to a bar and walked up the wheel for ten minutes followed by a five minute break. This went on for an eight-hour shift and was the equivalent of climbing over 8,000 feet. Another task was for the prisoner to turn the crank in his cell a specific number of times to earn his food. This crank turned paddles in a box of sand.

After his release from an imprisonment of hard labour, hard fare and hard board, Mucklow was recorded in the 1891 census as a jobbing carter living with his wife, Elizabeth, at 160 Adderley Street in the home of his parents-in-law: George Groom was a haulier and his wife, Mary, was a pearl button worker. Five others also lived in the house. They included the Grooms' son, George, who was aged twenty and a general carter.[166] Of course, it was a man called Groom who had been identified by Eastwood as the one who had overpowered him with a terrible blow from a buckled belt. He escaped justice.

THE CRUSADE AGAINST RUFFIANISM

During the fortnight after the brutal assault on George Eastwood, seven extra policemen were put on in the Milk Street quarter because of the feud between the Milk Street and Barr Street slogging gangs. This was very much a localised battle for supremacy as the two streets were a few hundred yards away from each other. On 5 April 1890, five youths from the two gangs were charged with slogging. Each was fined 20 shillings and costs or, if they failed to pay, one month's imprisonment with hard labour. In another gang fight, one man had fired a pistol and another rough was swinging around a pick axe. In attempting to make an arrest, PC Bertie was struck by half a brick thrown by John Bloxwich – another ruffian with previous convictions for assault – who he was sent to jail for three months' hard labour.

Bloxwich's brother, Benjamin, alias Block, of 21 Court, 4 House, Milk Street was as violent. He was charged with assaulting Frank Nolan of Great Barr Street on 7 April. Nolan belonged to the Barr Street Gang and as he was passing along Coventry Street that evening he was knocked down by Bloxwich. He was with a number of roughs and he then put his foot on Nolan's chest and beat his head severely with the buckle-end of a belt. PC Meeson arrived and heard Bloxwich say that he would knock his victim's brains out. As Bloxwich showed fight, the officer had to draw his staff and knock him down to make the arrest.

In court, Arthur Chamberlain said, 'It was evident that the prisoner belonged to a dangerous gang, who carried on fighting in the street and that the magistrates were determined to put a stop to that sort of thing, and to the use of buckles; and the prisoner would have to go to gaol for two months, with hard labour.' As for Nolan, he had been taken to the Queen's Hospital in an unconscious condition. He had sustained eleven scalp wounds, four of which exposed the bone.[167]

In reporting these fights, the *Birmingham Daily Post* headlined the 'Crusade against Ruffianism'. But it was a campaign that was failing. On Wednesday, 9 April 1890, the Highgate Street Slogging Gang, 'a notorious gang of blackguards', caused a violent disturbance nearby in Longmore Street, Balsall Heath – then in Worcestershire. Some of them had a kind of loaded India rubber staff. Others had pieces of lead attached to catgut strings, which were used for throwing at people, or were wielding belts with heavy and formidable buckles. PC Dysons sought to quell the disorder and arrested one of the most turbulent men, Henry Butterworth, a brass caster and the leader of the gang. He was handcuffed and became very violent, whilst his companions assaulted the officer unmercifully. They kicked him on the side, struck his head and cut his knee badly, whilst his left hand was bitten severely by Butterworth.

A young man tried to help the officer, but he was also attacked and ran away. A large crowd had gathered but 'not another person dared to lift a hand to rescue the policeman for fear of attack, whilst the officer was so hemmed in that it was very difficult for him to ward off the blows aimed him'. One of those who watched the attack 'wanted to give assistance to the officer, but had I done so the result would have been a broken head or a kick in the face or ribs'. The witness explained that the vagabonds trying to rescue their 'pal' were something frightful to see. They were looking about the street for bricks and stones and one said, 'Come on this way; here are some lumps of coal to throw at the policeman.' Straps with buckles at the end were also produced from their pockets.

At last, PC Dysons managed to drag his prisoner into the butcher's shop of Mr Swadkins, but the roughs pulled him out again. Once more, the constable managed to get back into the shop and, 'Mr Swadkins, with spirit in striking contrast to that of the crowd which had passively looked on, stood in the doorway with his cleaver and kept the roughs back.' Two Birmingham police officers then came to Dysons' assistance. Butterworth was given six months' hard labour.[168]

The same week as this disorder, a slogging gang from Birmingham was reported as assaulting a man in Perry Barr, whilst the Sparkbrook Slogging Gang was so terrorising the neighbourhood by waylaying pedestrians, especially women and children, that the police force there had been increased.[169]

With its working-class readership more likely to suffer the depredations of slogging gangs than the middle-class who bought the *Birmingham Daily Post*, the *Birmingham Mail* was deeply worried about this 'mob law in Birmingham', pronouncing on 11 April that rowdyism, another term for violent behaviour, was on the increase. There were slogging gangs in many quarters of the city. Some were harmless enough as they confined themselves to using obscene language in the street, 'but the more notorious of the gangs are composed of youths who individually may be, the police assert, the greatest cowards, but who collectively are the most desperate of ruffians'. These combinations of roughs banded together without any definite intentions: 'Their only object is to form a mutual protection league. It is looked upon the correct thing for each district to have its slogging gang, consisting of youths, ranging in age from 17 to 21 years. Those youths infest the street corners, if the police are on the alert they move into low coffee houses, where they decide upon their movements.'

Amongst the most infamous was the Digbeth Gang, which had recently been involved in a vicious attack on the manager of the Canterbury Music Hall, which had led to his death. Another was the Whitehouse Street gang, 'notorious for its assaults on inoffensive persons, who happen to be found late at night on the waste ground at Aston'. Then there were the Suffolk Street and Summer Lane bands, which were 'famed for their lawlessness and savagery'. Short terms of imprisonment had little effect on these ruffians, with the Park Street gang boasting that one of its most prominent members was a youth who had spent nearly 11 months out of the last 12 in jail.

The *Birmingham Mail* report of 11 April went on to explain that a new favoured weapon of the slogging gangs was the cosh:

A short, heavy stick, well loaded at the end, which can be concealed up the sleeve, but they also have a partiality for pieces of pokers and strong handkerchiefs with stones tied at the end. There is also weapon, which in practised hands can be used in a quarrel with considerable effect. It is piece of gutta percha, sometimes cat gut is used, with stones attached to the end of it. Then, of course, there is the useful brick-end, the buckled belt, and the big clasp knife. The rough who is to use the knife in a row is told off by the leader as the 'chivier'. That means he is to stab the victim in the back, not fatally if he can help it, when all the other methods of assaulting him have been tried and found ineffective.

Each gang had a leader and as well as free fights with other gangs they would sometimes attack the public house favoured by an enemy gang, wrecking it and attacking all the customers who were there. Such actions emphasised the territoriality of the gangs.

Despite all this evidence that violence was increasing, including reports from his own officers, at a meeting of the Watch Committee on 22 April 1890, the chief constable, Joseph Farndale, asserted that, 'he had 'no evidence of slogging gangs in the city for very long time, and the superintendents reported that for years they had been decreasing in numbers and power'. However, Farndale's claim was ridiculed in the *Birmingham Mail*, on 23 April, which quoted the concerns on the prevalence of street ruffianism by the Recorder of Birmingham, Mr Dugdale.[170] Importantly, evidence for challenging the chief constable's belief is provided in several exemplary sentences passed shortly before he sought to pass off the problem of slogging.

At the Worcester Quarter Sessions earlier in April, John Harper of the Sparkbrook Slogging Gang was imprisoned for eighteen months for a savage assault on PC Bayliss. In so doing, the deputy chairman remarked that the court had passed a severe sentence as a deterrent.[171] There was a large number of convictions against Harper as there was against his brother, Thomas, who had kicked PC Bayliss. For this he was sentenced to six months' hard labour. The brothers were 'a terror to the neighbourhood in which they lived. They were frequently assaulting people, especially on Saturday nights and complaints were often made to the police.'[172]

A longer term of imprisonment had been given by the Recorder of Birmingham, on 16 April, to Thomas Henry Everall, a labourer aged eighteen. In November of the previous year, he and Albert Chaplin, aged twenty, and another labourer, had attacked George Onions, against whom they held a grudge for having kicked a dog belonging to a member of their gang. Upon meeting Onions in Summer Lane, they had knocked him down and kicked and struck him with an iron chain. Onions was in the hospital for eleven weeks, having sustained severe injuries. In sentencing the two men, the Recorder said, 'The case was one of those which were becoming more prevalent now in the city than they had been for a long time past. If this sort of thing were not checked it would end in murder being committed.' It was quite intolerable, he added, that 'gangs of young men should go about the streets and make it impossible for peaceable persons to walk about at night without being assaulted and knocked about'. As the leader of the gang which he had brought together to make the attack, Everall was imprisoned for five years with Chaplin sentenced to 15 months with hard labour.[173]

The *Birmingham Mail* stressed:

The sentences are well calculated to strike terror into the leaders of ruffianism which has been rearing its head in Birmingham for the last few months. We shall expect them to have a pacifying effect on the disturbed neighbourhoods; and no one will be disposed to quarrel with their severity. The Recorder sees, everyone else must see, that unless the outbreak is stamped out at once, it will end as the Navigation Street riot ended, in the hanging of someone and with such prospect in view, false sentiment in favour of mercy is mischievous in extreme.[174]

Allowing for alarmist reporting, it was evident that, by the end of the 1880s, many poorer parts of Birmingham were indeed plagued by street gangs – and it was difficult to leave such a gang, as William Davis of Hospital Street found out. On 18 June 1890, he was met by James Cain, a brass worker of Belmont Row, and William Copley from Moland Street. Davis later explained in court that Cain had wanted him to slog the Bagot Street gang but he had not done so as he had had enough of it. This lack of loyalty led Cain to strike Davis on the side of the head and Copley to hit him on the back with a buckled belt, inflicting wounds which bled profusely. Cain, a well-known member of the Cross Street slogging gang, was sentenced to 21 days' imprisonment, and Copley to 14 days.[175]

DANGEROUS PEAKY BLINDERS

It seems that the activities of the sloggers were curtailed for a short time by the stiff sentences passed in 1890, and over the next few years there were fewer mentions of the gangs in the local newspapers. Yet, despite this apparent lull, the slogging gangs had not been put down. In July 1891, Inspector McManus said they were a public nuisance and that he had been forced to send a dozen plain clothes officer to Moorsom Street to stop the encounters between them.

Slogging also continued in Sparkbrook, despite the long sentence on John Harper, and the nearby Charles Henry Street in Highgate had a notorious slogging gang.[176] Like other gangs before and since, it was difficult to leave – serving time or trying to come clean did not ensure the ability to cut ties with former criminal associates. In March 1891, nineteen-year-old George Rutter assaulted a companion because he refused to join the gang on a riotous expedition.[177] The next month, William Rabbit attacked a former member of the gang who was believed to have sent one of them to prison; and two teenagers who were walking along Charles Henry Street were attacked with bricks and buckled belts. Both were treated in hospital for head wounds, whilst one of them was also stabbed.[178]

Then in the autumn of 1891, Arthur Croton was named as one of what was described as the Charles Henry Street 'bell-bottom' gang, when he was found guilty of an assault on Emma Blade, an old woman who kept a refreshment room in the street. Croton had argued with her over his change from a purchase and tried to stab her with a breadknife, which was lying the counter. He dropped the knife and then picked up the advertisement board and struck the shopkeeper with it. Although the magistrates thought this was very bad case, Croton was only fined 40 shillings, with a month's hard labour if he failed to pay.[179] Such a weak sentence gives added justification to Weinberger's assertion that the magistrates did not seem to care about rowdyism in the poorer parts of Birmingham when it affected only local people.

Slogging gangs in Summer Lane and on the Aston Road were also identified in 1892.[180] The latter was probably another manifestation of the long-established Aston Sloggers and Whitehouse Street Slogging Gang. Within Birmingham itself, on 2 August, it was stated that over the previous fortnight a stone-throwing combat had taken place each night between the Cliveland Street and Weaman Street slogging gangs, and, in October 1893, John Cambridge, a labourer aged twenty-two from Rupert Street was named as the chief of a slogging gang that infested Nechells.[181]

Notwithstanding these reports, in June 1894 local commentators believed that the 'epidemic of ruffianism' had settled in the city.[182] This did not last, however, as in late 1895, the slogging gangs and peaky blinders once again attracted unfavourable attention. Although the latter term had been first mentioned in 1890, it does not appear to have been used again in the Birmingham newspapers for the next five years. When it was, it is apparent that it was as another name for sloggers and slogging gangs. On 27 June 1895, under the heading 'Birmingham Slogging Gangs', the *Manchester Evening News* noted that the Birmingham Recorder had passed sentences of six months' imprisonment on two men for maltreating a third with a loaded life preserver, a metal cosh, and fire irons. They were members of rival gangs of 'Peaky Blinders', 'who stand on street corners to assault passers-by, or get into free fights with other gangs. The Recorder said the nuisance would not be stopped till magistrates sent the offenders to gaol.'[183]

This event was followed in October 1895 by a disturbance in Bromsgrove Street. Police constables Bennett and Telfer were called to the Stag and Pheasant pub, at the corner of Pershore Street, to turn out a gang of between 20 and 30 peaky blinders who had caused trouble. In attempting to take out Charles Warner, a twenty-year-old goldbeater of Edgbaston Street, they were assaulted by him and 'the gang commenced to kick and beat them'. James Cuson, a twenty-eight-year-old labourer from Cheapside, kicked Constable Bennett in the stomach so that he had to release Warner, whilst Cuson also got away. Constable Telfer followed Turner and recaptured him in an entry in Inge Street, where 'another desperate encounter ensued, and Telfer was in danger of being badly handled when Bennett came up'. Seventeen-year old Thomas Groves, a brass caster from Hurst Street, went to help Warner, and buckled belts were used on the officers' heads. Cuson was known and arrested on a warrant. He had 18 previous convictions and was sent to prison for six weeks. Warner, who was described as having a very bad character, received six months, whilst Groves, whose name also appeared very frequently in the police books, was handed three months' hard labour. All three men lived in the vicinity of the pub and were obviously part of a local gang.[184]

A month later, it was reported that a slogging gang was operating in the neighbourhood of Northwood Street and Kenyon Street, Hockley. A police officer also explained that in Aston there was a feud between the Park Lane Gang and the Lichfield Road Gang. Interestingly, he stated that the latter was made up of hard-working lads, thereby contrasting them with those who were loafers and who got by as petty thieves or through the work of their wives or girlfriends. Three of this Lichfield Road Gang were charged with feloniously wounding William Latham with intent to do him grievous bodily harm. They were Samuel Preece, Albert Medlicott and Samuel Greer. On 24 August, they hit Latham with the buckle end of a belt and stabbed him in the chest. When the Latham fell, he was kicked on the ground. Taken unconscious to the hospital, he was there for six weeks, during which it was feared that he would die of his injuries.

The attackers were tried at the Warwick Assizes in December 1895 and the judge, Mr Justice Day, avowed that he would 'break up the Lichfield Road arrangement'.[185] Nicknamed as 'Judgement Day', he had become famed for punishing gang members in Liverpool by flogging with the cat o' nine tails.[186] In sentencing the three men he called them 'a gang of ruffians who infested the suburbs of Birmingham', urged the police to take more action and expressed his determination to stamp out the problem. Greer was given ten years' penal servitude and Medlicott and Preece were each handed two years' hard labour.[187]

That same month, the first man to be specifically called a peaky blinder was brought to court. Henry Lightfoot was twenty-two and, unusually, of no fixed abode. Having a grievance against some men drinking in a beer house, he had dashed inside and assaulted several people with a stick. In throwing Lightfoot out, the landlord and his wife were bitten on the hand. The 'ruffian' then marched up Hurst Street into Bromsgrove Street, striking at everyone he met until he came upon Detective Tingle. 'You're a jack!' Lightfoot shouted. 'Hop off!' Lifting the stick over his head, he 'discharged a blow which beat down Tingle's guard and struck his head'. The detective hit Lightfoot in the face and knocked him over, but an associate of Lightfoot came to his rescue and knocked over the policeman, allowing Lightfoot to hit him again with the stick. Lightfoot was finally arrested. In court, Sergeant Richards said that he had been sent to jail many times for assaults on the police, and was dealt with severely at the assizes for an assault in Hay Mills. The magistrates said that he was evidently a 'peaky-blinder' of a dangerous type and he would be sent to jail for six months.[188]

Lightfoot was not the first one in his family to be in trouble with the law. In January 1877, his older brother, Samuel, had been fined one shilling and costs at the Balsall Heath Police Court. His offence was for 'the dangerous practice of playing bandy [a hockey-like game] in the public streets'. The magistrates imposing the fine included men from wealthy manufacturing families. Their fine on the then eleven-year-old Samuel Lightfoot emphasised the middle-class attack on working-class rough sports and on the use of the street as a recreation ground.[189]

Six years later, Samuel Lightfoot was involved in 'a general melee' in Balsall Heath Road. He had been arrested by PC Rudnick for refusing to leave the Sherbourne Hotel Concert Hall, where he had been 'misbehaving'. It was reported that since 1878, 'disgraceful scenes and riots' by the gangs of low, foul-mouthed blackguards had taken place outside this place on Saturday nights.[190] On this occasion, Lightfoot 'incited a mob, which gathered round him, to release him, which they did'. Taken into custody again, he 'acted like madman, kicking and assaulting the police'. The mob now numbered about 200 and once more released Lightfoot got clean away. He was fined 40 shillings and costs.[191]

As for Henry Lightfoot, his first offence was in 1886 for stealing a duck. He was thirteen and jailed for seven days. Two years later, he was described as a 'hardened criminal' when he was sentenced to nine month's imprisonment with hard labour for stealing eight brass door knobs.[192] Previously, he had stolen fruit, a jacket and pigeons and he would go on to be imprisoned numerous times for other minor thefts as well as for gambling, drunkenness, burglary, wilful damage and obscene language. However, as well as being a petty thief, Lightfoot was also a violent man. In December 1892, he was given nine months in prison for malicious wounding; he served another six months in 1894 for assaulting a constable, and he was convicted of six other assaults. His last apparent offence in 1907 was for the theft of 12 scrubbing brushes.[193]

Seven years later, on 14 September 1914, shortly after the outbreak of the First World, Lightfoot joined the Royal Warwickshire Regiment. This man who had spent most of his life breaking the laws of his country decided to fight for his country, as is emphasised by the fact that he gave his age as thirty-four when in fact he was forty-one. Yet old habits die hard and, in November that year he was sentenced to

14 days' detention for insolence and threatening a non-commissioned officer. Within days of finishing his detention, Lightfoot was discharged from the Army as unlikely to make an efficient soldier.[194]

He was then living in Rowington Terrace, Berkley Road, Hay Mills, as he was in January 1915 when he joined up again, this time with the 2/5th Reserve Battalion of the Royal Warwickshire Regiment, a Territorial Army unit. Lightfoot, though, was still a troublesome soldier. In August 1915, he used insubordinate language to a superior officer and 'offered him violence', for which he was detained for 28 days. The next month, he was given eight months' detention for disobeying an order and malingering. Soon after he had finished his sentence, on 21 May 1916, his battalion was sent to France to serve with the British Expeditionary Force as part of the 143rd Brigade of the 48th Division. As such, Lightfoot was involved in the first day of the bloody Battle of the Somme on 1 July 1916. The next day he was wounded in the right eye and side. He was sent back to England two days later and was discharged from the Army in April 1917 as no longer physically fit for active service.[195] Henry Lightfoot died in 1936 aged sixty-three.

DEMANDING MONEY

In January 1896, a correspondent to the *Birmingham Mail* regretted that 'in spite of all the energy of the Birmingham police, the present time is a veritable reign of terror, owing to the conduct of the Professional Rough cum-Peaky Blinder'.

The reporter asserted that having one Peaky Blinder in a neighbourhood was enough to set the whole district in flame, as, 'He is sure to have a following, and young Peakies emulate his disorderly conduct and endeavour to act up to it when Saturday night darkness falls, and the knowledge of a numerous following seem to be propitious for their business.' That business was beating and robbing drunken market sellers and others. If by chance some of them were caught, according to the newspaper, they came up to court 'looking as harmless and dejected as possible, and wearing an unnecessary bandage. They plead that they are very sorry, but they were in drink, and with the aid of the Police Court lawyers are returned to their friends with a small fine.' Then they draw out a begging list to go round all the pubs within a mile, collecting for 'the poor so and so, who had got into a "little bit trouble" and woe betide those who do not contribute to this fund'.[196]

Pat Collins was a famed showman who was responsible for many fairs in the Midlands and he stood up to such crude protectionism when he took over Birmingham's Onion Fair in September 1890. Dating back to 1400, it had taken place in the city centre but, deemed a roisterous and vulgar spectacle, the council had abolished it in 1875. In response, Randle Williams, the king of showmen, moved it to the Old Pleck at the northernmost edge of Birmingham. Close to the border with Aston, it was cut through by St Stephen's Street and soon 'it became the happy hunting ground of toughs and gangs who exacted tribute from showmen in return for not molesting them'.[197] Owing to the trouble caused by the peaky blinders extorting protection, Williams sold the lease to Pat Collins. Stories were told that he smashed the gangs by the vigorous use of a knuckleduster, a tale he resented as he emphasised that it was nonsense to say that he had used any weapon. Instead, Collins recalled:

> I knew what I was up against. The gangs would come and demand money to leave the stalls alone – either 2s. 6d or, in the case of the peaky blinders, 'lads of eighteen or so who could mix it,' a shilling. I said I would take a lease and clean it up so that you could bang your watch and chain in the middle of the fair and find it again when you went for it. I asked Inspector McManus (later Deputy Chief Constable of Birmingham) for twenty policemen; he got fifteen, and the first of the gangsters to demand money he knocked down with his fist. The plain-clothes men came along with nasty looking sticks and we very soon had those gangs at heel.[198]

Terry Proctor was told how his grandfather dealt with peaky blinders who came into their butcher's shop at 89 Summer Lane demanding protection money. Edwin Proctor was a tough, adventurous man who was not going to brook intimidation, and ordered them to, 'Shift off quick, or else!' They did not and, according to Terry, 'Edwin grabs a large swivel meat hook of the back meat rail, swings it over the counter, hooks one of them around the neck, pulls him over the counter and beats the daylights out of him, then throws him through the open shop window. They never had any trouble with them after!'[199]

Small-scale extortion on shopkeepers was matched by bullying and intimidation. For example, in December 1896, a number of youths, 'belonging to a gang of ruffians, who have infested the neighbourhood of Ladywood for some time past', demanded tobacco from a clerk named Smith when he left his workplace in Sherborne Street at dinnertime. They made a rush for him, but he escaped back into the works. The manager, Josiah Griffiths, armed himself with a whip and accompanied Smith outside, but both were immediately set on by the gang. Griffiths had the whip taken from him and 'buckled-ended belts and knives were freely used. Eventually, a strong force of men from the works drove the ruffians off. Mr Griffiths, who was the most seriously injured, was removed to the hospital.'[200]

THE REIGN OF THE ROUGH

The fights of the slogging gang and assaults by peaky blinders in 1895 had once again drawn unfavourable attention to Birmingham, with the *Coventry Evening Telegraph* asserting that the city had too long been notorious for brutality. Scarcely a month passed 'but we have to record some shocking act of violence' and the infamous slogging gangs remained a terror in certain quarters.[201]

Although there were no major outbreaks of gang violence the next year, many citizens were still fearful of the peaky blinders. One correspondent to the *Birmingham Mail* accused the city's magistrates of ignorance about them because, to a large extent, 'those who administer justice in this city reside either in the fashionable suburbs, or in the country'. He urged them to pay an occasional visit to Summer Lane, Hospital Street, even the more respectable neighbourhood of Camden Street or Spring Hill on a Saturday sight. If they did so, they could form some idea of what the public put up with as Birmingham's street corners were 'infested with these human parasites, who seem to watch for the opportunity of a passing girl or woman and pour forth the filthiest language to pollute their ears'.[202]

In 1897, newspapers across the kingdom once again focused on the bad reputation of Birmingham with headlines such as 'The Reign of the Rough in Birmingham' and 'Birmingham Roughs on the Rampage'.[203] These were precipitated by the murder of Police Constable Snipe. Late at night, on Sunday, 18 July 1897 he, was on duty on Hockley Hill and, after the closing of the pubs:

A man named Kilrain under the influence of drink behaved so disorderly that Snipe, who was accompanied by Police-constable Mead, proceeded to arrest him. Kilrain offered strenuous resistance, and whilst the constables were engaged struggling with him, a man named Charles Alvis came up and joined in the attack upon them. A desperate scrimmage followed, during which a third man James Franklin threw a brick which struck Snipe on the head rendering him unconscious. It was found necessary to remove

Snipe to the General Hospital on an ambulance, where he died . . .[204]

The ongoing dangers faced by police constables are underscored by the fact that, over the previous six years, in the course of doing his duty, PC Snipe had been assaulted eight times.[205]

As with the murder of PC Lines in 1875, the killing of PC Snipe aroused outrage. A fund was set up for his widow and on the day of his funeral enormous crowds lined the streets leading to Warstone Lane cemetery.[206] Although Franklin was tried for murder, he was acquitted because of evidence indicating that another man had thrown the brick. This was George 'Cloggy' Williams, who was found guilty of manslaughter and sentenced to penal servitude for life. Four other men were sent to prison for lesser terms. Whilst PC Snipe was unconscious on the floor, he had been kicked in the head by Kilrain (also spelled Colerain), who had also kicked PC Mead. He was sentenced to eighteen month's hard labour. Thomas Hedges, Charles Edward Elvis and Thomas Moran were also convicted of unlawfully assaulting the two policemen and were given nine months' hard labour.[207] Thankfully, though, the reign of peaky blinders like these was soon to end.

Chapter Three

THE REIGN OF THE PEAKY BLINDERS ENDED

EPIDEMIC OF BRUTALITY

A bell tolls ominously as a lone rider gallops down a cobbled street. A big man, he is straight-backed and wears a bowler hat, an unbuttoned long coat, and a suit and tie. He pulls up at a row of mounted policemen, each with truncheon at the ready. Lined up threateningly across the street, they are the only people about. Behind them looms a big, ugly factory. Its presses pound, intensifying the gloominess of the setting and the sombre mood. The horseman speaks forcefully to the officers in a distinctly Northern Irish accent. They are to leave no stone unturned and to bring him every gun and bullet that they find for his inspection.

The mounted police ride down the street, each one turning at intervals to face the houses on either side. They are accompanied by a large force of caped constables who run along the street and stop two by two. Upon the signal of their leader, the policemen on foot smash through the front doors of each home and force themselves inside looking for communists. As police whistles blow, men are dragged out roughly. The sound of truncheons hitting flesh can be heard. Children run frightened down the street as women shout and are pushed aside.[208]

It is another vivid and absorbing scene from series one of *Peaky Blinders*. The man in charge of the attack on this street at the centre of the Shelby's power base is Chief Inspector Campbell. Physically imposing, he is full of guile and comes with a reputation for ridding Belfast of crime and corruption. Now he has been sent to Birmingham by Winston Churchill to recover a consignment of guns and other weapons that has gone missing from the BSA, the Birmingham Small Arms Company. The prime suspects are the Peaky Blinders led by Tommy Shelby, for whom Campbell quickly develops an intense hatred. He also loathes IRA Fenians and the Communists. Along with the Peaky Blinders, they are 'the three-headed beast' and he believes that it is his job to decapitate them.

Distrusting the Birmingham police, he brings in new men from Belfast, obviously Protestants like him. It is they who are his shock troops in the attack on the Shelbys' heartland. Campbell ultimately fails in taking down the Peaky Blinders. However, a Protestant police officer from Belfast did in fact play a leading role in ending the reign of the real peaky blinders and street ruffians of Birmingham. His name was Charles Haughton Rafter. He was appointed chief constable in 1899 following the furore over the 'epidemic of brutality' that was sweeping Birmingham.[209]

After the murder of PC Snipe, demands were made for the introduction of flogging for street violence, given that the law only allowed that punishment if an assault was accompanied by robbery. Chief Constable Farndale agreed and feared that he could do nothing more with the strength of the police force.[210] Complaints were also made against the perceived leniency of the magistrates in punishing assaults on police constables with fines rather than six months' imprisonment as the law allowed. In response, in August 1897, Arthur Chamberlain, chairman of the magistrates and brother of Joseph Chamberlain, asked his fellows 'to look at the cases from the point of view of the patient householder, and not from the offenders who went before them very penitent, but who, when in the streets on Saturdays and Sundays, were a most terrible nuisance to quiet people'. It needed to be made clear that offences against the person were more serious than those against property.[211]

Charles Anthony Vince was an academic, leader writer for the *Birmingham Post* and staunch supporter of Joseph Chamberlain, and, in his volume on the *History of the Corporation of Birmingham*, he strove to present the city in the best light possible. Yet even he admitted that in the 1890s public attention was drawn to the serious increase in crimes of violence. Popular feeling culminated in the demand for more drastic measures for 'the repression of this evil which was made after the murder of Police Constable Snipe'.[212] This widespread feeling reached a zenith in 1898. That year, according to Geoffrey Pearson, the word 'hooligan' made an abrupt entrance into the common English usage during the hot summer 'in the wake of an excessively rowdy August Bank Holiday celebration in London which resulted in large numbers of people being brought before the courts on charges of disorderliness, drunkenness, assaults on police officers, street robberies and fighting'.[213]

In Birmingham that year, the number of prosecutions for assaults on police constables reached a high of 623 – relating to a police force, including officers, of 700.[214] The attacks on the police in 1898 included that on Police Constable Leach, a twenty-three-year-old of 'fine physique from Cheltenham'. In taking a troublesome drunk to the police station, he was attacked by a gang of youths in Lister Street. One of them threw either a bottle or a brick at him. It struck him and fractured his skull, so that he needed a trepanning operation. Soon after, Detective Sergeant Brown and several constables arrested seven local men aged between seventeen and twenty-two.[215]

What distinguished peaky blinder gang members like these from other youths was their hairstyle and clothing. But much of that style was also adopted by roughs who were not necessarily in a gang. This meant that increasingly the name peaky blinder was also applied to a violent person fighting and causing damage in public places. As the *Daily Mail* informed its readers, 'Birmingham, like certain districts of London, has its Hooligans, though in the Midlands the ruffians are known by the euphonious name of "peaky blinders".' John Groves was such a young man. Described as a promising youth of eighteen, in May that year he had thrown a bottle at a police constable. The glass had cut the officer's left cheek badly and he had to be treated at the hospital. As Groves had no previous convictions he was sentenced to prison for three months' hard labour. Although no evidence was provided that he was in a gang, he was called a peaky blinder, one of those 'terrors who are accustomed to maltreat defenceless persons they meet in the streets'. This widening in the use of peaky blinder was accompanied by the appearance of two new terms to describe violent men and petty thieves – 'peaky types' and 'peaky class'.

THE COMING OF RAFTER

The epidemic of brutality in Birmingham led to growing demands to stamp out the dangerous element of 'Peaky Blindism'. As one commentator expressed it, the bell-bottomed fraternity 'had reigned far too long, and the assaults committed on the police and citizens have not been sufficiently met by the magistrates who have been far too lenient'.[216] The clamour for action grew louder and was heard nationally.

In January 1899, the *Globe*, a London newspaper, reported that 'not without good cause the citizens of Birmingham make bitter complaint of the brutal tyranny exercised by street ruffians'. It explained that some time back, the magistrates had imposed deterrent punishment instead of the 'absurdly lenient sentences they had been wont to pass'. The effect was immediately beneficial, they said, but latterly the justices of the peace had relapsed into their old merciful mood, so that ruffianism had again lifted its head. Recently, a gang armed with buckled belts and knives had pounced upon an inoffensive man as he was going home, and 'stabbed him nearly to death, besides beating him unmercifully'. A witness who gave evidence was attacked and badly stabbed by some of the gang as he was leaving the court. This was a case for exemplary severity but the ringleader was only given two months in prison.[217]

Three months later, Chief Constable Farndale resigned owing too ill health. Although he did so in the midst of the 'epidemic of ruffianism', some observers praised him. In particular, *The Owl*, a local publication, wrote that he was an admirable servant who had done much to curtail the spheres of influence of the slogging gangs.[218] This claim was debateable. Whilst large-scale battles between slogging gangs from different streets had declined, assaults on the police had not, and nor had the power of the peaky blinders in the back streets.[219]

It was Farndale's successor, the Northern Irish Charles Haughton Rafter, who was acclaimed popularly as the man who ended the reign of the peaky blinders. His death in office in 1935, after 36 years' service, was front page news locally and was headlined in the *Birmingham Daily Gazette* as 'Cleaned Up Black Spots'.[220] Rafter's funeral was a civic event attended by government officials and with a guard of honour of hundreds of police officers. But the real tribute to his life and work lay not so much in the official memorial service at St Martin's in the Bull Ring, and rather in the fact that the funeral 'filled the streets in the vicinity of St Martin's and the roads about Harborne Parish Church, with men and women with no official status who mourned the death of a man who was a man first and an official if necessary'. The average man and woman of Birmingham came from their homes and lined the streets in their thousands upon thousands in 'humble tribute to an official who, in addition to doing his job excellently well, had gained the affection of the people'. For the majority of law-abiding working-class folk, that affection had been won through Rafter's leadership in stamping out the peaky blinders and making the streets safe.[221]

Raised in a Protestant family in Belfast, he had joined the Royal Irish Constabulary as a cadet officer in 1882. It was a turbulent time when Ireland was increasingly divided between mostly Catholic Nationalists seeking an independent Ireland and mostly Protestant Unionists wishing to remain within the United Kingdom. He rose to district inspector and was given charge of the Ballinrobe area of Mayo, where the Land League was active. This was a popular campaign against landlordism – when bailiffs arrived to serve eviction notices they were met with huge demonstrations. Those forced from their homes were given succour by their neighbours and embargoes were placed on farms from which tenants had been thrown out, whilst those people who did not fall in with the land leaguers were ostracised.

Rafter was later involved in policing in Tipperary, where he gained the admiration of Count Arthur Moore, a Home Rule MP, who wrote a glowing testimonial for Rafter in his application to the Birmingham Watch Committee. Moore emphasised that so high had been the feeling in Tipperary during Rafter's tenure there that 'any want of tactic or judgement might have precipitated an encounter at a moment's notice between the two excited parties. During all that time, Mr Rafter kept a cool, clear head, and got well through the troubles of that eventful period, handling large numbers of armed and excited men with unfailing good temper and tact.'[222] Rafter was also known for his organisational ability and the thoroughness and skill he gave to his work.[223]

Out of 50 candidates for the position of chief constable of Birmingham, he was one of the eight shortlisted and was the only one to attend his interview in full uniform. Impressive though this was, more impressive was Rafter's obvious ability to deal not only with potentially violent situations in a calm and effective way, but also to oversee a reduction in crime. These were the very qualities needed to suppress the peaky blinders.[224] He began his job in 1899 'feeling with extreme caution', according to the *Birmingham Mail*. He thoroughly studied the town and its characteristics, whilst he was keen for his men to be smart, of good physique and to be knowledgeable as to the law under which arrests were made.

Rafter had shown his own personal courage in Ireland, and in his quiet and unassuming way he demonstrated this at meeting about the South African War at the Birmingham and Midland Institute. The meeting had pulled in a howling crowd and a menacing movement was made by some of them. As soon as that happened, Rafter left his unobtrusive spot in the corner of the room and went to the front of the platform, prepared to intervene if necessary. According to the newspaper, 'then came an ugly rush and some men got past the police cordon and made for the speakers. At once, Rafter singled out the leader and went for him, taking him by the collar.' Small of stature, he struggled in vain against the chief constable's clutch. Determined but not too vigorous in his hold, Rafter said something quietly but decisively and the man left.[225] In that incident was revealed some of the techniques with which the peaky blinders would be dealt with: through physical strength, resolve, bravery and determination. They would be needed as Rafter's early years were marked by ongoing violence.

CONSTABLE BAITING

In June 1900, and upon reports of disorder, five constables were sent to Barford Street. This was one of the streets associated with Birmingham's sloggers and street gangs since 1870. When they arrived and sought to arrest two brothers, PC Hurst was struck with a buckled belt by eighteen-year-old brass polisher Albert Harris. Percy Langridge, a sixteen-year-old polisher, then stabbed PC Barker in the back with a knife and also kicked the legs of constables Lawson and Watson, who were also assaulted by Fredrick Long, a fifteen-year-old filer. Finally, PC Macaulay was stabbed in the arm by Henry Attwood, aged twenty. All four offenders were described as the peaky blinder type. Harris was sentenced to three months and Long to one month in prison, both with hard labour.

Due to the seriousness of their charges – unlawfully and

maliciously wounding police constables – Langridge and Attwood could not be tried by magistrates and instead were sent to the assizes, the most important court in any county and which was held four times a year by a travelling judge. Born in Brighton, Langridge was 5 foot 5½ inches tall and had a number of tattoos. Both he and Attwood were given the long sentence of five years' imprisonment, in itself emphasising that the courts were now beginning to treat attacks on the police with severity. Following Langridge's release, aftercare was provided for him by the Discharged Prisoners' Aid Societies, which found him work as a striker in London.[226]

Reporting this case, the *Birmingham Mail* expressed the feelings of many people, when stating that 'the policeman's lot is not a happy one'. It was revealed that, in 1899, 585 prosecutions had been made for assaults against the police and, at that time, nine men were disabled because of assaults against them.[227] The next year, the police force totalled 700 men and there were 496 prosecutions for assaults on them. This figure was not as high as in 1898 but it remained obvious that there were still too many attacks, and in 1901 the figure rose to 507.[228]

Constable Bennett was one of those injured that year. In January 1901, the blade of a long pocket knife was plunged into his back. The wound was a very deep one and would have been instantly fatal if the blow had fallen an inch lower. PC Bennett was stabbed by Thomas Walters, who was one of a party of youths ejected from the Saltley Theatre for disorderly conduct and with whom PC Bennett remonstrated. Walters was sentenced to five years' penal servitude for malicious wounding.[229] Named as a peaky blinder in some newspapers, in others he was called a ruffian, and interestingly, a hooligan.[230]

The ongoing problems caused by the peaky blinders was emphasised in the summer of 1901, when a deputation approached the Watch Committee to seek a police station in the Garrison Lane neighbourhood because of rowdyism. They did not wish to exaggerate, they explained, 'but at the present time there is a state of terror and lawlessness as to constitute scandal to the city. Every night, and Saturdays and Sundays, the place was a veritable pandemonium, the peaky blinder and the rough reigned supreme.' So bad was the situation that recently one of the deputation had been made to fly for his life when he was seen by about 50 roughs who were pelting a works building with stones.[231]

My great uncle Wal told me of the notoriety of the gangs of Garrison Lane and Summer Lane. Born in Studley Street, Sparkbrook in 1897, he recalled that in his childhood, it was 'the practice to team up after a session of beer drinking, after getting equipped with knuckledusters, buckled belts, and other weapons, to make for the locality of the rival gang that had a "dust up" owing to them, when invariably it meant a set-to when no quarter was asked or given'.[232]

As the *Birmingham Mail* lamented in November 1901, 'still the peaky is with us, and the notion that the policeman exists only as a target for brick-ends has not yet been expelled from his mind'.[233] The violence directed towards the police was highlighted that year by a series of searing articles in the *Birmingham Daily Gazette* written by its leader writer, J. Cuming Walters. Called *Scenes in Slumland: Pen Pictures of the Black Spots in Birmingham*, its revelations about the extent of poverty and 'slum landlordism' in the 'best governed city in the world' caused an outcry. He drew his readers into what he perceived as the wretched streets of 'slumland', half of which were:

. . . crossed by the gloomy blue-stoned railway bridges over which the trains are continually passing with a roar, and these archways themselves are the finishing stroke to a dismal and unredeemed picture. A 'peaky' or two will almost certainly be found slouching about the corners, and in the less-frequented thorough-fares the menace they present is not to be disregarded. Police are not rare, though it would be thought they might be more readily encountered; but one fact not to be deemed insignificant is that they are almost always to be found in couples. Where a constable is regarded as a natural enemy, and his mere presence an affront to the mob, too much care cannot be taken. Ere now a lonely policeman has been half-murdered or maimed for life in this quarter of Birmingham in revenge for the arrest of an offender, and it has never mattered whether the revenge – which usually takes the form of bricks and belts – was inflicted upon the actual officer who had incurred resentment, or one of his colleagues. Next to constable-baiting comes the less exciting but very satisfying pastime of wife-beating, but the prosecution of the brutes who engage in it is seldom undertaken for reasons perfectly well understood.[234]

A few months after this dismal observation, another police constable was killed in the back streets of Birmingham. On the evening of 22 July 1901, George Fowles, a nineteen-year-old brass filer, along with Joseph Adey, 23, and John Davis, 33, both polishers, were drinking in the vicinity of Staniforth Street in the Gosta Green locality. Close to midnight, they began singing in the street. PC Gunter 'made the very reasonable request that they would move on and desist from disturbing the neighbourhood'. He then went to quell a domestic row nearby at the home of the Bruce family.[235]

At the inquest into his death, a number of witnesses from the neighbourhood gave evidence against the three men. They included Mary Ann Bruce. She stated that when PC Charles Gunter came into their house to quieten the quarrel he was followed by seven men, amongst whom was Fowles and Adey. Her cousin, Emma Butler, explained that as PC Gunter left the house, 'they all got round him'. When asked by the coroner what happened, she replied tersely, 'bricks went. About four. I should think.' More bricks were thrown from the direction of Fisher Street, and the constable was surrounded by about fifteen men. He fell to the ground.

Butler's mother, Fanny, said that William Willis, who had lodged with the Bruce family, told her that after PC Gunter had ordered the young men who were singing in the street to move on, one of them had said, 'Let's go down and do him in.'

What took place next was witnessed by Thomas Smallbone, the night watchman at the nearby large pen factory of Perry and Co. in Lancaster Street. He had seen a man in a trilby hat pick up a brick and break it on the kerbstone. A girl standing at the bottom of an entry called out, 'If you do, I'll blow you,' (inform the police), upon which she was struck by the man.

He was then joined by two men, one in his shirt sleeves and the other wearing a straw hat. They moved up the street a few yards. One of the men threw something and the police officer fell. Smallbone ran from the works and found the constable lying on the ground, bleeding from a wound to the forehead. The next morning a police sergeant went to where PC Gunter had fallen and found that it was strewn with brick ends. That day, another local witness, Alice Lee, heard Fowles telling his wife that he had been in a row and had 'broken a brick or two'.

Constable Gunter was admitted to the General Hospital on 30 July. He went on to have eight fits and was operated on, but he remained in a critical condition and was paralysed on the right side and unable to speak. Three more operations were carried out, in each case for an abscess in the brain. After the fourth operation, PC Gunter's condition improved but he suffered a relapse and died on 26 October due to meningitis caused by a cerebral abscess set up by the wound in his forehead.[236] He left a wife and child and was taken back to Carmarthenshire for his funeral. His body was escorted to Snow Hill Station by 100 police constables and officers. They were led by Chief Constable Rafter.[237]

The jury at the inquest had given a verdict of wilful

murder, but at trial of the three accused they were found guilty of manslaughter – to the surprise of the judge, Justice Bigham. He sentenced each to 15 years' imprisonment, hoping and trusting that this 'would be a warning to the people of your class in this town, who don't know how to control their passions and who through drink or other causes allow themselves to be carried away, so that they carry out violence'. The passing of the sentences created a sensation in court and several women became hysterical – although the *Birmingham Daily Gazette* fulminated that the men should have been sent down for life. It also vilified the neighbourhood of Staniforth Street as 'the haunt of the accursed "peaky blinder" a savage beast in human form'.[238]

Constable Gunter was killed in the parish of St Laurence, an area widely condemned as one of the blackest spots in 'Blackest Birmingham' and yet his memorial service was held at that church in that very parish. Gunter had worshipped there, having been based at the nearby Duke Street police station. So many people attended the service that an overflow had to be held in the school rooms.[239] And it was the witnesses from this supposedly low and rough neighbourhood who provided the testimonies that were vital to the convictions of the three men accused of his murder. They did so despite intimidation. It would be the brave support for the police by poor people such as these, angered and weary as they were of the reign of terror of the peaky blinders and street ruffians, which would be a crucial factor in bringing an end to the back-street gangsterism.[240]

Soon after the death of PC Gunter another brutal attack

on a police constable shocked and disgusted Birmingham. In January 1902, PC Ernest Blinko 'was struck down and mercilessly hacked with a chopper [small axe] to the point of death'. His assailants were two brothers, David and Frank Cherry, who were noted as of the 'peaky blinder' persuasion.[241] The previous day, Constable Blinko had accompanied PC Stevens in serving David Cherry with a police summons. It seems that he and his brother sought revenge for this, as before the attack the brothers were seen prowling about the district in a suspicious manner as if they were looking for someone.

When PC Blinko appeared, the brothers ran up Sherbourne Road and followed him down Longmore Street. Overtaking the constable, David Cherry pulled a chopper from his pocket, and 'struck him a severe blow on the head which felled him'. Whilst the defenceless constable was on the ground, he was again struck by Cherry with three or four heavy blows on the head. His brother, Frank, was present throughout and, according to a lad called Thomas Steadman, he said to his brother, 'Come on, you've done him in.' This account was corroborated by other witnesses.[242]

The screams of women who had seen what had happened brought a number of men to the scene, and the two brothers fled, whilst their victim was rushed to hospital in a cab.[243] He was unconscious and losing a lot of blood. Only once did he recover to speak, stating, 'Raise me up: I am going.' By now, parties of police were seeking the brothers. They had no difficulty as many people had seen them, conspicuous as they were because one of them was carrying the chopper.

Eventually the brothers were found in the George pub on the Ladypool Road, Sparkbrook. There was a struggle to arrest them, which ended when Frank Cherry remarked, 'We will go quietly. David. We are beat to the wide.'

The Cherry brothers were found guilty of malice and aforethought with intent to kill and murder. Justice Bigham pronounced that if not for the skills of Dr Jordan Lloyd, who had saved the life of PC Blinko, they would have been hanged. He went on to stress that, 'There seems to be a disposition in Birmingham for men in your position of life to hunt policemen to death. So I am going to do my best by the punishment I shall inflict upon you to stop it.' The Cherrys were each sentenced to life imprisonment. It was an announcement greeted by applause at the back of the court, whilst the *Birmingham Daily Gazette* hoped that these exemplary sentences would check the 'unruly hooliganism which exists among the peaky type' and which led to unprovoked and murderous attacks upon the police.[244]

THE PEAKY BLINDERS' DISAPPEARANCE

Initially, it seemed that the sentences passed on the killers of PC Gunter had not been effective. Prosecutions for assaults on police constables did drop by 91 in 1902, and although this was a 'a gratifying decrease', the high number of other violent offences led the *Birmingham Daily Gazette* to announce that, 'The result is not conducive to any hope that the peaky-blinder has been tamed and the hooligan robbed of his most characteristic attributes.'[245] The figures seemed to support this conclusion as then, in 1903, prosecutions for assaults on the police rose dramatically to 459 and reached 487 in 1905.[246]

Despite this, on 13 September 1905, the *Birmingham Daily Gazette* announced that, whilst the city was known as the abode of the peaky-blinder:

> His palmy days when he flourished in triumph, and disgraced the city's record by his outrages, have long since passed by. The 'peaky' of today, fortunately, is living upon his past reputation, and thanks mainly to the exertions and vigilance of the police he has practically retired from active service. Nevertheless, periodical outbreaks of ruffianism occur to remind us that the spirit which animated the Birmingham roughs of other years is liable to occasional revival among the present day city hooligans. Our news columns today contain evidence of this spirit of lawlessness in the city, but we need not be alarmed at the prospect of a return to the old days of street rowdyism and ruffianism. The police assure us that Birmingham is a well-conducted city, and is in no danger of lapsing into bad ways. The magistrates can materially help in the work of suppressing the Birmingham rough by passing exemplary sentences.[247]

A week after this positive report, on 20 September 1905, William Lacey, a member of a slogging/peaky blinder gang, shot one of the Summer Hill Gang. He died five days later.

Both men and their associates were declaimed as belonging to 'a class of which no city could be proud, roaming the streets in gangs, constantly meeting rival gangs, and entering into conflict with them, more especially on Saturday nights'. Nevertheless, the *Mail*'s piece was perceptive as such gang fights were increasingly rare and the days of the peaky blinders had indeed passed, with not much longer to go before they were retired from active service.[248]

The next year, 1906, the number of prosecutions for assaults on constables dropped dramatically by 150 to 337.[249] There is reference in the *Birmingham Daily Gazette* to a 'hooligan outrage' in Newton Row in January 1907 – which had formerly been a peaky blinder stronghold – when three men of the peaky blinder type savagely attacked and robbed a businessman late at night, but there appears to be no mention of assaults or fights by peaky blinders after that.[250] Their disappearance was so complete that in 1912 the paper could write that, 'There was once a time when a midnight walk from Birmingham through Slumland to any of the suburbs was an adventure fraught with danger. Dark deeds were done in side streets, a warfare waged by the notorious "Peaky Blinders" made night wanderers fearsome.'[251]

CLUBS, SPORT AND THE PICTURES

What had led to the rapid disappearance of the peaky blinders? In 1898, they were rampant and seven years later, they were still inflicting serious injuries on policemen and civilians alike. Yet, by 1907, they were beginning to be referred to in the past tense and by the 1920s they were only a memory. There were a number of contributory factors to this phenomenon, as there was with the disappearance of the scuttling gangs of Manchester and Salford. In his deeply researched book on the gangs there, Davies has noted that the gang conflicts diminished between the late 1890s and the outbreak of The First World War. This coincided with a change in attitudes towards 'Outcast Manchester', 'Blackest Birmingham', and 'Squalid Liverpool'. There were fears that in the polluted and overcrowded big cities, poor youths were suffering as a result of their dismal environment, becoming physically unfit and unwell due to the poor conditions in which they lived. An important response was the development of clubs for working lads. These had begun to gain momentum from the late 1880s, but it would be a decade before they would make a significant contribution to the development of more peaceable pastimes amongst the rising generation of youths.[252]

Gooderson discerned a similar process in Birmingham, focusing on the work of Arnold Pinchard, a High Church of England clergyman in charge of St Jude's from 1896. This church was in Hill Street, one of the poorest parts of Birmingham and close to where the Navigation Street Riot had occurred in 1875. Pinchard started a club for 'budding peaky blinders' and street-corner loafers aged eighteen to twenty with a subscription of a penny a week. It was open every evening and Pinchard was helped by his curate, a layperson and a Church Army captain. Boys could play draughts, dominoes and cards but, as Gooderson recognised, 'more important were two pairs of boxing gloves'.

Recognised as a hard hitter and clever boxer himself, Pinchard was able to hold a boxing competition within two months of starting his club – 'although there were no ropes, so the boxers fell into the laps of the front-row spectators'. The boys fought in ordinary dress of flannel shirts, corduroy trousers, belts and heavy boots for a first prize of a suit of clothes and a second of a pair of boots. The winner was called Copestick and he had 'a peaky fringe shown to best advantage'. Pinchard also provided a recreation club for girls, and a Church Lads' Brigade for those under eighteen who were drilled as if in the military and taught gymnastics.[253]

Known nationally for his clerical efforts amongst the peaky blinders, Pinchard was of the same ilk as the celebrated Father Jay, the vicar of Holy Trinity in the Old Nichol, decried as the most infamous criminal area in Late Victorian London.[254] After he took over the parish in 1886, he set up a gymnasium and boxing ring in the basement of his church. By then, boxing was an important part of East End mission work to the poor. This was because, as historian Sarah Wise has indicated, charitable and university settlement outreach workers 'had come to realise that the best way to engage poor men was to formalise an already existing passion; so street prize-fighting – often, horrifically, undertaken with bare knuckles, and leading to serious injury – was transformed into a disciplined, structured, and therefore more "moral" pursuit'. What distinguished Father Jay's efforts was his coup in removing boxing from the pub so breaking the association between the sport and alcohol.[255]

Boxing to the Queensbury Rules – a code that enforced the use of gloves – was a new sport which had a deep and a positive impact, particularly on those youths who might have been more prone to becoming peaky blinders. In an insightful article on them from 1899, one writer acknowledged that, despite the work of many organisations, he knew 'of no existing agency ready to go in and win over the Peakies to decent manhood and law-abiding citizenship' other than one city church which had been successful in its mission. This was undoubtedly Pinchard's church of St Jude's, the success of that was 'obtained through the medium of the gymnasium and the gloves'.[256]

Boxing did indeed have a constructive effect on many young men, inculcating most with a respect for fair fighting rather than dirty fighting. The Birmingham Amateur Boxing Club began in 1881, but it was based in the centre of town and catered mainly for skilled working-class young men and as such did not reach out to poor youths as did Pinchard's club.[257] But from the early twentieth century, smaller-scale boxing clubs began to open in working-class neighbourhoods. They included the Sparkbrook Amateur Boxing Club. Founded in 1906 by Albert Smith in Main Street, within two years its membership had reached about 80 and it had to move to larger and more suitable ground floor premises in Sampson Road North, close to Camp Hill.[258]

Like Jay, Pinchard was an Anglo-Catholic, and upon his death in 1934, the *Birmingham Daily Gazette* drew attention to his pioneering work in the city: 'the founding of a "Boxing Club", the institution of a club for girls who had worked all day in a factory were perhaps new departures in Christian philanthropy, but the Vicar knew his people, and what was of more importance the people got to know their Vicar'.[259]

Sister Beta, later Mrs Hornabrook, was another person from a well-off background who worked for the wellbeing of poor youngsters. The daughter of a Wesleyan minister, she became a Wesleyan Sister attached to the Central Hall Mission in Corporation Street. She worked there for six years and 'started several enterprises – a Saturday party for the little boys who in those days sold matches and evening papers in the street, and a club for the Aston "peaky-blinders", young hooligans who greeted her first appearance in their midst with a shower of stones, but afterwards thought better of it, and formed themselves into a bodyguard to protect her as she walked the roughest districts'.[260]

The biggest and most successful club of this period, however, was that started in July 1889, by the Kyrle Society when it opened a boys' club in Lawrence Street. This experiment was sited in what was deemed as Birmingham's Seven Dials – at the time a notorious London rookery.[261] Soon after, a girls' club was begun and in 1893 new premises were opened nearby in Sheep Street.[262] Kyrle Hall would have a long-lasting and positive impact and become famed for its boxing club. In 1911, it was given to the Birmingham Boys and Girls Club Union. This had been started five years before by Canon Carnegie, Rector of Birmingham Cathedral, who had been he upset when he had arrived in the city to see barefooted lads in ragged clothes touting newspapers at the station. Determined to help them, he set up a club where they could have a chat, drink a cup of tea and play games. Within two years, he had eight clubs, and from 1909 there were also clubs for girls.[263]

However, despite this success, only a small number of lads joined the clubs, and it was hard to involve those who were regarded as the roughest. In Birmingham, the Street Children's Union was formed expressly to help the large class of boys and girls 'whose occupations or bad home conditions cause them to spend most of their lives on the streets'. Yet, by 1914, the Union had only 400 such boys over the age of fourteen in its eight senior clubs, whilst the numerous other clubs in the city appealed to boys from a more 'respectable' working-class background.[264] Still, as Davies maintains, it is possible that the indirect influence of the clubs was more important in that they encouraged active participation in sports. This rose significantly in the 1890s, a decade which also saw the massive growth in popularity of association football, especially on the streets. Importantly, in Manchester and Salford, street-based teams gave a new outlet for territorial rivalries, other than violence.[265]

In Birmingham, association football was as popular. School teams were competing in leagues from the later 1880s, whilst by early in the twentieth century, teams based at factories, churches, chapels and also pubs in the back streets were involved in leagues such as the Small Heath and District League.[266] In addition, many working-class lads played ad hoc games on an almost daily basis.

'H. V.' was one of them. He kept a diary for one week as part of a detailed investigation in early 1914 into the conditions of 'boy labour' in the city. This was carried out on behalf of the Council by Arnold Freeman. He focused on a carefully chosen sample of 71 boys aged seventeen that was believed to be 'typical of the mass of uneducated boy labour in Birmingham'. Each weekday dinnertime, H. V. revealed that he went home to eat and then played a short game of football with the other lads before starting work again. Then on the Saturday morning, he and his workmates talked about football, as they always did, and after dinner he and his pals 'went to a football match with our shop and Cape Hill Mission'.

'K. L.' also took part in the survey. In his diary he wrote in detail about the Birmingham City match against Preston North End which he watched on the Saturday. After breakfast on the Sunday, he got ready and went out for his friends at 9.50. They played football on some waste ground until about 2pm. Later that afternoon, he says, 'We gathered together and saw some lads who live in the other end of our street and asked them if they would play us at football.' They agreed and K.L.'s team won 8–5, after which they all went to the coffee house.[267]

The cinema was another form of popular entertainment that had a positive effect, emerging as it did as the peaky blinders and scuttlers were declining. From 1900, Pat Collins was showing moving pictures at his fairgrounds and his example was soon followed by other entrepreneurs who put on cinema shows in theatres, halls and meeting rooms, some of which were converted into 'penny gaffs'.

These were cramped and uncomfortable, with the patrons prodded by the cane of the usher or barker to crush together on tightly packed wooden benches. Little wonder that they were called 'the penny crush', or else the 'flea pit' because of the unhygienic press of people. Then from 1910, the Cinematograph Act ensured that 'the pictures' had to be shown in permanent premises that were licensed and subject to inspection.

As Davies made clear with regard to Manchester and Salford, senior police officers were 'grateful to see so many lads and lasses spending as many as three or four evenings a week in picture houses rather than on the streets'.[268] Cinema going proved so popular, that in his study, Freeman said he 'gave up asking the lad if he went to the Cinema because the response was invariably in the affirmative'. Each boy went to one of Birmingham's 46 picture palaces about twice a week, spending practically the whole evening there.

Freeman identified one other factor which, in his opinion, had a positive influence on youths – schooling. Because of the reforms of the New Liberal government of 1906, schools had been partially transformed into organisations concerned not only with the education of children but also with their medical treatment, feeding and even housing. If this great influence on the lives of the nation's children were taken away then, Freeman believed, 'we should be manufacturing a race of hooligans'. Instead, schools rescued children from a hundred sinister influences and imperfectly yet steadily and forcefully shaped them productively into good workers and capable citizens.[269]

CAN THEY FIGHT

For all the importance of social forces, the putting down of the peaky blinders depended on three other causes. First, the stronger sentencing on violent men from the turn of the century. Second, the support of working-class people for the police and against the peaky blinders. And third, forceful policing. All three factors were interconnected. Chief Constable Rafter initiated the stronger policing, which gave confidence to working-class people to support the police, and it was also he who pushed the magistrates into taking a tougher line with offenders who assaulted the police.

In its article on the peaky blinders in November 1901, the *Birmingham Mail* drew attention to the stern action recently taken by Mr T. M. Colmore, the stipendiary magistrate, against roughs of the peaky blinder class. The sentences passed on them 'could scarce be complained of as unduly lenient'. He sent to prison without the option of a fine even those offenders against whom there was no record of rowdyism.[270] The local newspapers had been calling for this shift in approach for many years and it came about because of Rafter.

At his instigation, the prosecuting solicitor had asked Mr Colmore to inflict exemplary punishments of substantial terms of imprisonment upon those convicted of attacks on policemen. The aim was to make it possible for a police constable to do his duty unmolested.[271] Magisterial confidence in Rafter and his police force was matched by that of working-class people, some of whom were now emboldened to take a stand against the peaky blinders.

Following the Navigation Street Riot of 1875, the police had the utmost difficulty in securing witnesses because of the 'terrorism exercised by the roughs in the quarter'. It is not surprising, given the attack on Mary Ann Bell. Suspected of having given some information to the police, she was brutally assaulted by a number of people, headed by the mother of one of the accused, and suffered blackened eyes and severe cuts to her scalp.[272]

The peaky blinders were as vengeful and vicious. Ministering in one of the poorest areas in the city, Reverend T. J. Bass gained widespread notice for his parish in 1898 through his pamphlet, *Everyday Life in Blackest Birmingham: Facts Not Fiction*. The district was:

. . . the home of the 'Peaky Blinder', and awful is the vengeance of this blackguard king to those who refuse obeisance. These thoroughfares constitute his little kingdom, and the terror of his anger is manifest on all hands. His methods of repaying a distasteful act are unpleasant – to use a very mild expression. A blow or a stab in the dark, the total destruction of your windows, and a hundred petty tyrannies are exercised in so ingenious a manner as to defy detection. Even were he discovered in some illegal act, a rapid retreat to the intricacies of the courts with which he is familiar, renders pursuit not only difficult but practically unavailing.[273]

Yet within a few years, some working-class people were no longer paying homage to blackguard peaky blinders, rather they were acting against them and in support of the police. This was made plain in May 1901 when a gang of ruffians paraded Bromsgrove Street, jostling and assaulting everyone who came across their path. A doctor was hit by a piece of offal and then punched; a labourer who went to help him was struck on the head with a buckled belt, knocked down and kicked about the face, and another man was hit on the face and had a tooth knocked out.

A young woman called Harriet Chaplin, who lived locally in Hurst Street, witnessed what happened. Unheeding of the violence meted out by the gang, she followed them and told the police what had happened and where the attackers were. James Thornton, aged twenty-four, was identified as the one who had struck the doctor and labourer. He was sentenced to two months' imprisonment. The magistrates then thanked Harriet Chaplin for 'her courageous conduct in following the men and recommended that the chief constable should make her some allowance'. Her bravery was all the more remarkable given that the offender, Thornton, also lived in Hurst Street.[274]

Four years later, in March 1905, there was an 'exciting struggle between the police and three peaky blinders' at Key Hill. PC James Smith found James Brough drunk in Park Road, Hockley. Aged twenty-two, he was a polisher from St Mark's Street in Ladywood. He resisted arrest and, after knocking down the constable, kicked him about the body and face. Other officers appeared but then two of Brough's friends tried to drag James Brough away. They would probably have succeeded 'but for the prompt assistance rendered by several bystanders, who clung tenaciously to the prisoners and rolled over on the ground with them'. In particular, a Mr Tiller 'displayed conspicuous courage, and it was mainly through his instrumentality that the prisoners were handcuffed, after an hour's struggling'. PC Smith was unconscious and had to be taken to hospital, as was James Brough, whose clothes were almost torn off him. He and Mullis were each given a month's hard labour, whilst William Brough was fined 20 shillings or a month's hard labour. The chairman of the magistrates complimented the members of the public who had rendered prompt and valuable assistance to the police.[275]

The willingness to actively help the police was facilitated by the strong policing enforced by Chief Constable Rafter. From the beginning of his office, he was acutely aware that he had insufficient men for the needs of a city the size of Birmingham. Fortunately, this view was quickly confirmed by Her Majesty's Inspector of Constabulary. In 1900, Captain the Hon. C. Legge declared that the Birmingham was much under-policed and recommended the addition of 220 men, as the beats were undermanned by about 200, whilst the detective department was understaffed and overworked.

The Watch Committee was convinced by these representations, but still did not ask the council for 'the full augmentation suggested at one blow'. Probably influenced by ongoing cry for action against the peaky blinders and ruffianism, in February 1901, the council 'assented without demur to an immediate increase of one hundred, to be followed by six annual increments of twenty men each'. This was to take the force to a strength of 920 by 1907.[276]

This marked rise in the number of men under his command ensured that Rafter could end the practice of single officers walking the beat. Working in pairs, the police were more able to defend themselves and fight against the peaky blinders. Rafter understood that there were 'some parts of the city where police patrols literally carry their lives in their hands, and where the Hooligan looks upon it as his privilege and amusement to assault anyone who wears a policeman's uniform'.[277] Still, local newspapers were concerned that PC Gunter had been on his own when he was attacked, but as Rafter informed the Watch Committee, the constable had been joined by PC Heeley until ten to midnight, when everything seemed quiet. The murderous assault happened shortly after they had parted. Rafter also revealed that there were fourteen beats which worked double that night, and when PC Gunter blew his whistle it was heard by three other members of the force as well as other people in the neighbourhood. Moreover, the division in which PC Gunter served had already received its full quota of 100 men, authorised by the Watch Committee, whilst 'the acquirement of the men was being proceeded as rapidly as it was possible for the training of staff to deal with the recruits'.[278]

According to a tradition in the city's police force, Rafter asked three questions of his recruits: 'Can they read? Can they write? Can they fight?' An advertisement from the *Sheffield Daily Telegraph* of October 1901 suggests that the qualities he sought did include literacy and physical strength. It invited applications to join the Birmingham City Police from young men of good character and some education, who were at least 5 foot 9 inches tall and had a chest measurement of 36 inches. Nine years later, recruits were sought from 'smart intelligent men of good character, physique, and education; single; age twenty-one to twenty-six; height, 5 foot 10 inches; chest measurement, 37 inches'. Wages were 25 shillings a week, rising to 33 shillings.[279]

Recruits who were not prepared to fight were not welcomed. In September 1903, a singular case of cowardice was brought before Rafter. A police constable had gone to arrest two youths for gambling, when he was assaulted violently by another man. The officer had been accompanied by a young recruit who had 'not only failed go to his senior's assistance, but, it is stated, he took to his heels to save his own skin'. The older constable was severely maltreated and was in hospital for over a week, whilst the recruit was dismissed.[280]

The belief that Rafter's tall and well-built constables used physical force to put down the gangs is supported by the memories of Chief Inspector James McArdell. Hailing from Berkshire, he joined the Birmingham Police in January 1896 and 'soon afterwards was mixed up with the notorious "Peaky Blinder" gangs which terrorised Birmingham. Month after month he was engaged in the repression of this hooliganism', and recalled that 'often we had to fight for our lives with these gangs'.[281] Looking back on these years in 1955, a reader of the Birmingham Weekly Post, R. W. Hawkins stated that it was recognised that if a member of a peaky blinder gang was arrested he should resist the police and 'the gang would endeavour to rescue him. As the police of the period were mostly big and stalwart, and the tykes (as they were called) were usually short and tough, the gang usually had the worst of the deal.'[282]

There is a little official evidence for this claim that the police were willing to seek out physical fights with the peaky blinders, however, in the summer of 1900, certain police officers were found guilty of unjustifiable violence towards civilians and were punished.[283] Two years later, on 1 May 1902, the Police Order Books recorded that complaints had been made to the chief constable by the justices of the peace regarding 'certain cases where prisoners had been brought to Police Stations and complain of having been assaulted by the Constable arresting them, no memorandum of such complaint is made by the Reserve Sergeant or the Constable and no report on the subject is made to the Superintendent of the Division'.

It was ordered, therefore, that the superintendent would take steps to ensure that in future all such complaints would be noted down by the reserve sergeant and reported in due course. The chief constable also stressed that self-defence was the only circumstance in which policemen could use their staffs – and then only in the case of absolute necessity. Moreover, it was forbidden to strike anyone on the head with a staff, and they could not be used on prisoners who had to be treated with no unnecessary violence.[284]

From the late 1880s, the staves used by the police had been made of lignum vitae, a hard wood. However, in 1890 there was an outcry in the press as several of them had broken when constables had been using them against violent offenders. As a result, tests were carried out and, from 501 staves, 157 either snapped off short or cracked such a way as to be unfit for further use. It was said that, if properly cut, the staves should be almost unbreakable, but most of those that broke had not been cut with the grain of the wood, and in almost every case they snapped off short at the tapered portion above the grip.[285] Given this evidence, the Watch Committee decided to arm the police with new staves made of hickory wood. This was chosen because it was tough but pliable, did not break readily, and a good sharp blow could be dealt with it.[286]

My great-uncle Wal told me that before the First World War, some of Rafter's police, though, preferred another weapon to fight with:

They were nearly all Irish coppers at the time. Charles Haughton Rafter was Chief Constable and his recruits come from Ireland and they were all big, broad Irish blokes. They could carry out a job that he wanted them to; a bit of order . . . They used to come round, a couple of 'em if they found a disturbance at the Gate or any other pubs and they used to wear a cape rolled up on their belt. They'd find out who the culprits was and give 'em a warning, get 'em out the road and say, 'Off home!' If they didn't comply with the coppers' orders, they used to set about them. They hadn't used to use their truncheons, they used to use their capes.[287]

The police cape was usually made of Melton cloth, although in Birmingham it was of wool serge.[288] Thick, solid and hard-wearing, it made a hefty weapon that was easy to use and quick to hand, rolled up as it was on their belt.

Interestingly, former Royal Irish Constabulary men were not accepted by Rafter as, despite his own background, he did not believe in having ex-policemen in his force.[289] Moreover, in February 1901, it was reported that he would only take on former soldiers if they had been discharged with a character of very good or excellent, but preferably the latter. It was also noted that most of the applicants for the force were Irishmen.[290] This led to suggestions that the city's police was becoming 'Hibernianised'.[291] But, as was explained in the *Birmingham Mail* in October 1901, a large number of applications were continually received from young men in Ireland because the rate of pay for the police was better in England, whilst there was a lack of English applicants because of the good state of trade.[292] In reality, the Irish made up a small but significant minority of the Birmingham police force. In 1909, its actual strength was 950 men and they included 832 English, 64 Irish, 45 Welsh and nine others.[293] The Irish made up almost 7 per cent, at a time when only 1 per cent of the general population was Irish.

One of the leading Irish policemen in Birmingham was Michael McManus, Rafter's deputy chief constable, and the man who had knocked down a peaky blinder with his fist in defence of Pat Collins, the fairground showman. McManus had an outstanding and remarkable career. Brought up in Newfield, Mayo, and formerly a labourer, he joined the force in 1873, retiring in 1918. For several years, he was attached to the Duke Street Division, in what was deemed the roughest part of the town. A tough and determined man, he started his career when 'there was good deal more lawlessness than there is to-day – when it was unsafe for policemen to venture singly into some of the streets in the slum quarters of Birmingham'. One of his earliest experiences was 'a scrimmage with a crowd of roughs, one of whom struck him on the head with a brick necessitating his detention in hospital for five weeks'.[294] On another occasion, McManus took on a gang of highway robbers on his own. Kicked, stabbed and beaten with belt buckles, he was mauled severely, but 'he had some consolation as the ruffians had to accompany him to hospital'.[295] Well known for riding a large white horse around Birmingham, McManus and many other Irish police officers passed into local working-class folklore.

Tough policing was also evident in Aston. Here, the police fightback against its feared slogging gangs was led by Superintendent H. A. Walker, who was appointed to his position in 1882. Upon his retirement in 1900, he emphasised that ridding the streets of these infamous bands was easier said than done. The sloggers 'resented any interference on the part of the police, and in the course of the crusade which ensued a large number of officers were not only badly maltreated, but some of them so seriously injured as to be practically incapacitated from further service'. At the start of Walker's campaign against the sloggers, heavy fines were imposed in the hope that these would have an effect. They failed as the gangs had collections for their members so punished. Fines were replaced by short terms of imprisonment, but they did not have the desired effect. The sloggers continued to flourish and 'the police were daily flaunted and frequently brutally assaulted'. Then magistrates began to impose the maximum sentence of six months for each separate offence and the sloggers slowly disappeared. But it is apparent that the Aston police also fought fire with fire, breaking up the gangs with 'severe repressive measures'.[296] One policeman who was especially feared by the sloggers was 'Big Jimmy', PC Hodson, who never hesitated to tackle the gangs, no matter how threatening their attitude'.[297]

WHAT HAPPENED TO THE PEAKY BLINDERS?

Outbreaks of ruffianism did occur in Aston after Superintendent Walker's retirement, but the reign of the slogging gangs was almost over in the district. Within a few years, the peaky blinders in Birmingham had also been put down. So what happened to them? In 1915, the *Birmingham Mail* reported that, 'like the rigorous young vagabonds who preferred a roving life to one in which work formed a part', many peaky blinders had joined the Army and made good soldiers, too. Others had found respectable jobs with employers prepared to engage unskilled workers. It was emphasised that, 'No one is more delighted than the local police, to whom these young "peaky blinders", as they used to be called, were a never-ending source of trouble.'[298]

Reminiscing forty years later, Hawkins, the letter writer to the *Birmingham Weekly Post*, agreed that the First World

War saw the end of the gangs: 'Many were in the old militia and were called up and many joined the Regular Army. Few returned and they were older and more disciplined and settled down.'[299]

Henry Lightfoot, the first man to be specifically called a peaky blinder, exemplifies the perceptive observations of Hawkins. So too does George Hickling. Hickling was one of the notorious Ten Arches Gang of Aston, named after the railway viaduct crossing the Birmingham to Fazeley Canal at Holborn Hill, and first mentioned in 1883.[300] In May 1900, George Hickling and his brother, Thomas, 'two young men of the peaky type' were charged with having thrown stones and brickbats that broke a window at the Church Inn on the Lichfield Road, where a man they disliked was drinking. The brothers were found guilty and jailed for one month as they could not pay the damages, fine and costs required of them.[301]

Fifteen years later, George Hickling joined the Army, but as he was temporarily unfit he was transferred to the Reserve before he re-joined the colours with the Royal Berkshire Regiment in May 1916. Just five feet, 4 inches tall, he was aged thirty-nine and a bill poster. Soon after, Hickling married Clara Timmins at St Mary's, Aston Brook. They had been cohabiting for seventeen years and had two illegitimate children. Living in a back house in Powell Street, they wed so that, presumably, Clara and their children could receive a separation allowance. Later, Hickling was assigned to the 17th Company, the 3rd Labour Battalion. It included men who were medically rated as below the 'A1' condition required for front line service. Hickling was BII. He was discharged in March 1919 with a 20 per cent disability of deafness and a pension for 26 weeks of 5 shillings and sixpence a week. His character was given as good.[302]

The peaky blinders continued to be written about, but now in the past tense. In 1925, in an article on the improvements in Birmingham, it was stressed that one important positive change was in the keeping of the peace, for the 'bell bottom trousered and outrageously capped roughs who were a real source of annoyance, if not danger, to the general public and authorities a few decades ago' had gone.[303]

The ridding of the city of the peaky blinders was further emphasised in 1929, when the *Birmingham Daily Gazette* informed its readers:

A slight on Birmingham by a London newspaper was refuted by returns the Chief Constable (Sir Charles H. Rafter) submitted to the Birmingham Watch Committee, yesterday. In a recent article the newspaper in question declared, 'Three British cities are notorious for crimes of violence: Birmingham, Sheffield and Glasgow.' Sir Charles Rafter, in presenting a return of crime in Birmingham from 1899 to 1928 said the article in question gave the city an extremely bad name, and so far as its remarks applied to Birmingham, they were wide of the truth. The returns would show that the city was in a comparatively happy state in regard to crime; instead of there being an increase, there had been a considerable diminution.

The chairman (Councillor W. E. Lee) said there were a few comparisons in the returns which were worth singling out. Comparing the position in 1913 with that in 1928, it would be seen that assaults on police had fallen from 387 to 123; common assaults from 877 to 484. All these decreases had taken place notwithstanding the fact that there were 120,000 more people in the city in 1929 than there were in 1913. The peaky blinder of 1899 had disappeared long ago, and so had the gangs.[304]

Of course, not all violent men suddenly became peaceful and the police still faced violence, albeit markedly less so. In September 1910, two constables asked a crowd of men to move on from outside a restaurant in Essex Street. Very filthy language was heard from one of them and, as the policemen moved towards the offenders, Robert Daly swung a military buckle belt in his hand and crashed it through the helmet of PC Clark and cut his head. He and his colleague were then both hit. Daly ran away but was caught by PC Clark and was 'felled to the ground with his staff'. He remained on the ground for two minutes and then rose up and further assaulted the officers. By now the crowd had become hostile and bricks and bottles were thrown at the two policemen. Daly was sentenced to two month's hard labour.[305]

Some small gangs also continued. In June 1920, six young men were each given six months' hard labour for assaulting Robert Graves and Albert Woodin by kicking and striking them in Dale End. Whilst the *Birmingham Daily Gazette* called the offenders hooligans and street terrorists, the chairman of the magistrates named them hooligans and sloggers. It is suggestive that they were not called peaky blinders. This occasion appears to be the last use of the term 'sloggers' and came fifteen years after the previous mention of slogging gangs in the newspapers.[306] Yet, and as with any big city, there were plenty of other hard men in poorer working-class neighbourhoods, some of whom had been peaky blinders in their youths and some of whom were bullies.

Notable amongst the latter were the Kirbys. In March 1927, James Kirby, aged twenty-six, and Frederick Kirby, twenty-four, were sent to prison for two months for a brutal assault on a policeman. They both lived in Tower Street in the Summer Lane neighbourhood, and in court Inspector Shereston said the district had become so troublesome that extra police had been drafted in.[307] Three years later, the Kirbys and two others were described as the 'most notorious men in the city' and people in the Newtown Row neighbourhood 'dare not come to court to give evidence against them'. Convicted of breaking into a factory, James Kirby was sentenced to twelve months' hard labour. His brother was already in prison for violence after the Birmingham races and was give fifteen months' hard labour.[308]

Importantly, though, no concern was raised about a revival of peaky blinderism or hooliganism in the Birmingham newspapers following the 1920 case or the reports about the Kirbys. As for the Garrison Lane/Watery Lane neighbourhood, in which the Shelbys and their gang are originally based in the *Peaky Blinders* series, no available working-class accounts from or relating to the 1920s make mention of peaky blinders.[309]

THE GARRISON LANE NEIGHBOURHOOD

In common with other poorer neighbourhoods, though, this area of Bordesley on the borders of Small Heath did have a family that was feared – the Harper brothers. Beattie Hamill was born in Artillery Street in 1907 and lived at number 44. As a teenager in the 1920s, she worked at the fish shop in Garrison Lane, and recalled, 'When they got drunk they used to come in there, you know, and play up they would, and of a Friday night you could always expect 'em to come in drunk'. On one particular Friday night, the brothers arrived blind drunk and Billy Harper wanted to swap some oranges for fish and chips. Hamill told him that she could not do that. 'Any road, the gaffer come in from the living accommodation and told 'em to clear orf and of course they started to get rough then, and they was throwing the oranges at him and one went into the pan of fat.'

At that, Hamill went 'through the back of the house and come down the entry to look for the night policeman, which you would always find, either in Gordon Street or Wolseley Street or somewhere, 'cus they tried every door'. The constable came and had to use his truncheon and handcuff the brothers. Billy was remembered as the biggest terror of them all, and he, his brother, Wagger, and their mates used to stand at the corner of Wolseley Street and Gordon Street, where they went into Garrison Lane. After they came out of the pub, the men would stand there singing, and it was here where they used to pitch their pennies. The gang, of which they were leading members, was named the Five Ways Albion.[310]

Born in 1915, and raised at 312 Garrison Lane, Victor Andrews wrote an evocative account of his younger days in the neighbourhood. Their house was 'on the hill', opposite St Andrew's, the Birmingham City ground. Behind the ground's terrace was a tip for industrial waste in the old clay pits. The digging out of millions of tons of red clay had made an enormous gash in the hill. Although it was fenced off, local people found ways of getting in, and for children it was 'a forbidden land of excitement and danger'. And for the local unemployed men it was a place of seclusion and escape from the attentions of the police when they played at tossing coins.

Although harmless, it was illegal and police raids were frequent. Andrews was offended by the police action against poor men seeking solace and release from their miserable existence and wondered how the police justified their operations instead of apprehending 'some gang of dangerous criminals'. One raid on a quiet Sunday morning in 1926 was etched into his memory. He was sitting on the doorstep to his house, watching other children play hopscotch, when:

A Black Maria van crossed over the tramlines from the other side of the road and braked sharply to a halt at the corner of the cul-de-sac leading to the clay pit. Another police van carried on down the hill and stopped at the other cul-de-sac by the railway bridge. The rear doors of the vehicles were thrown open and dozens of uniformed men erupted out. Some ran up the roads towards the pit, whilst others clambered over the railway bridge parapet to drop down onto the railway banking. I learned later that all the exits had been covered in this operation involving over fifty policemen. The 'bag' was about thirty men. They were bundled into some cars that had appeared. Some angry mothers, wives and sisters had by this time emerged from their parlours and kitchens and were giving the constables an earful of screamed abuse. The sight of the gleaming black batons in the fists of the officers deterred any thought of attempted rescue. Their passive, sullen menfolk were taken away. The wives later donned their outdoor coats or shawls and set off, some to try to raise bail money from sympathetic relatives or friends, others to go to the police station to give moral support to their imprisoned husbands.[311]

In the later, nineteenth century, such a police raid would have provoked a violent response from local sloggers and peaky blinders. Yet though the peaky blinders had gone, not all of them settled down and become peaceful citizens. A few went on to become part of the notorious Birmingham Gang that terrorised the racecourses of England, whilst other became involved in a bloody and long-lasting feud that became known as the Garrison Lane Vendetta. It was fought between a man called Billy Beach and his allies against a violent and vengeful family called the Sheldons, who have a connection with the fictional Shelbys of *Peaky Blinders*.

Chapter Four

ILLEGAL BOOKMAKERS AND A VENDETTA

ILLEGAL BOOKMAKING

Honoured for gallantry in the First World War, Tommy Shelby is a complex character. Handsome, intelligent and charismatic, his Special Branch file records that he is also a gangster, racketeer, armed robber, leader of the Peaky Blinders and bookmaker operating from his base in Small Heath. In an early scene in episode one of the first series, he walks through the family's house and, after pulling back a heavy curtain, opens the door and walks into big, noisy betting shop bursting with activity. In the foreground, a clerk is dragging on a cigarette and entering bets into a book, whilst in the background John Shelby stands on a platform facing a wide and high black board. It is filled with the chalked up names and odds of the horses for the forthcoming races as well as the results for those already run.

As the younger brother puts up the latest betting, men look at the *Winning Post* sporting paper, choosing their fancy, whilst a voice calls out for them to get their bets in for the 2.30 at Kempton. A ticker tape machine relays information from the racecourses whilst the punters (bettors) place their bets on scraps of paper in top hats on a table in the laying of bets area. Two pairs of hands tally up the coins as cigarette smoke curls upwards. An excited John Shelby then shows Tommy the book, the ledger in which the bets have been recorded.[312] It is a vivid, atmospheric scene and, as the BBC publicity put it, the overall aim of the sets in the first series was 'to bring the streets, homes and gambling dens of the time back to life'.[313] Yet there were no such gambling dens in back-street Birmingham in the 1920s as betting was a street activity.

Betting for cash away from racecourses in premises had been outlawed in 1853 by the Betting Houses Act. Those who were found guilty of keeping them were subject to a penalty not exceeding £100, or else they might be imprisoned for six months. The advertisement of betting houses was also prohibited, and if a place was thought to be in contravention of the law, then it could be broken into and those inside arrested, whilst any documents which related to racing and betting could be seized. In Birmingham, some bookmakers sought to evade the law by setting up large-scale standing markets outside on waste ground, whilst a few publicans defied the legislation by encouraging betting on their premises. Police action was taken against both but the demand for off-course betting for cash remained and bookies began to stand on the streets, collecting bets from punters as they passed by.

They were prosecuted under existing council by-laws for street obstruction but this action was ineffective. So too was a by-law passed specifically in 1900 stating that 'no person together with another shall assemble in any street or public place for the purpose of betting'. The maximum penalty was five pounds. Similar by-laws elsewhere also failed to stop street betting and concern over its growth nationally led to the Street Betting Act of 1906. This made it an offence for any person to frequent or loiter 'in streets or public places, on behalf either of himself or of any person for the purpose of bookmaking, or betting, or wagering, or agreeing to bet or wager, or paying or receiving or settling bets'.

First offenders could be fined up to £10. This amount was doubled for those convicted twice, and for third or subsequent contraventions, law-breakers either could be levied a maximum of £50, or else they could be imprisoned for no more than six months with or without hard labour. Furthermore, the police were empowered to confiscate any articles which related to betting and which were found on those whom they arrested. Finally, in a crushing denial of the rights of individuals and in an abrogation of the much-vaunted principle of British freedom, officers of the law were empowered 'to take into custody without warrant any person found committing an offence under this Act'. [314]

Because it exempted credit betting and cash betting on racecourses on race days, the new legislation was regarded by many as an unjust class law aimed specifically at stopping the cash betting of working-class people. As such, it has been argued that the Street Betting Act was part of efforts made in the late-Victorian period to extend police power into working-class areas and to control space there. Moreover, at the time of its passage, senior police officers regarded street betting and bookmaking as social evils and believed that both could be eradicated.[315]

Initially, their faith in putting them down seemed to be justified. According to Charles Vince, the more severe fines imposed by the Street Betting Act provided a strong deterrent in Birmingham because, compared to the previous seven-year period, between 1907 and 1914 the number of convictions dropped substantially by over 50 per cent to 1883.[316] However, Chief Constable Rafter accounted for this fall because 'the difficulties of the police had largely increased owing to the ingenuity of the betting men who adopt many devices to elude the law'.[317] Those difficulties were exacerbated after the First World War because street betting expanded noticeably – as is reflected in the series *Peaky Blinders*.[318]

This trend was highlighted in Rafter's annual report for 1919. He remarked that there had been a startling number of convictions for street betting, which had risen from only 97 in 1918 to 535. He also revealed that 'over 109 betting "pitches" have come under the notice of the police, which are watched by "scouts" of the men who frequent them'.[319] A pitch was the place on the street where a bookmaker took bets. Over the next decade, the number of pitches increased and in 1932, Rafter told the Royal Commission on Lotteries and Betting that practically the whole of this pitch betting was 'carried on in the working class districts and industrial areas'. He observed that its location was usually an entry, such as the narrow passage-way which connected the street with a courtyard of back-to-back houses.[320]

PITCH BOOKIES

The popularity of taking bets in an entry was explained by Harry Vokes. He noted that his neighbourhood in Aston 'gave a rabbit warren impression of entries, yards, back alleys, all getaway runs for the bookie's touts, takers, runners and punters'.[321] Touts, takers and runners all took bets for the bookie in some capacity. The advantages outlined by Vokes were enhanced by communal buildings such as 'miskins' – outhouses which were built for the deposit of rubbish and which sometimes went across two yards. Consequently, if the police were sighted, a bookie or his taker of bets could flee into them and escape into the next yard. Other shared facilities were as useful and sometimes the bookie moved away from the entry and took bets hidden behind the door of the brew 'us, the communal washhouse in a yard. Another feature in poorer neighbourhoods were 'double knacks'. Most yards of back-to-back houses had only one entry into them but some had another leading elsewhere into the street or else into a different street. These double knacks were invaluable to a bookie who was fleeing capture by the police.

Some illegal bookmakers had several pitches, but most worked one either in the street where they lived or else close to that location. My granddad, Alf Chinn, was such a local bookie. He started up in 1922 in Studley Street, where he and his family rented a back-to-back house, taking over the pitch vacated by 'Nack' Carey and his cousin, Bill Preston. Granddad stood on a double knack, leading from Studley Street to the Olympia picture house on the Ladypool Road, where he could get lost amidst the crowds of shoppers if he were chased by the police. Like the fictional Tommy Shelby, my granddad, Nack Carey and Bill Preston were veterans of the First World War.

Many other back-street bookmakers were former soldiers. They included Sid Clamp of Highgate, as remembered by his daughter, Hetty Bradbury:

> When my father was demobbed from the 1914 war, he started this bookmaking business at the house where we lived, which was No. 50 Darwin Street, only one room downstairs with scullery, one bedroom, and one attic. The business flourished and we moved to a larger house across the street, No. 165. We had some very hectic times there. The regular man would stand at the entrance to the entry and another two men would stand on street corners one above and one below. As soon as one or other of them saw a policeman they would signal down to Dave (the taker) and he would run up into the house. Once inside a very thick plank of wood was placed in two iron brackets across the door.[322]

This system of a taker, called a teker in Brummie speech, actually taking the bets from the punters on the street and then handing them over to the bookmaker in his house or in a rented front room had emerged before the First World War. It was adopted by most back-street bookies, some of whom carried it on until legalisation in 1961. This method was implemented because if the bookie or taker were arrested, they would be charged under the Street Betting Act, which incurred a much lower fine than under the Betting Houses Act.[323]

The takings of most street bookies were supplemented by runners in nearby factories. These workmen were paid on a commission basis. So widespread was this practice that by 1923, it was stated wearily that 'there is scarcely a works in the country employing more than 20 workmen where one is not a bookmaker's agent'.

Bets were also collected by children.[324] Indeed, Steven Knight has said that as a youngster in 1920s Small Heath, his mother was a bookies' runner. In an interview, he noted that bookmakers used children because they were less likely to be arrested – although they still needed to resort to subterfuge. As he pointed out: 'the kids would walk down the street, sometimes with a basket of washing, and people would drop in coins, wrapped in piece of paper with the name of the horse they were betting on. The kid would take all the bets and deliver them to the bookies'.[325]

There were two main street bookmakers in the Small Heath area. One was Charlie Wright, who had a pitch in Arthur Street, as well as another nearby run by his brother and sister-in-law. The other was Tucker Wright, whose territory was on the other side of the Coventry Road. Called by his initials, T. K., his main pitch was in Green Lane, but he also had one in Victoria Street and several others in the Garrison Lane neighbourhood, all of which were worked by runners. Albert Judd, a renowned character in Birmingham, recalled Tucker Wright as a gentleman and 'a right nice bloke'. The most notable bookie locally, he always had a flower in his coat.[326] This positive view was reiterated by a Mr A. T. Richardson, who affirmed that 'Tucker the Bookie' was 'well liked all around Small Heath because he never failed to pay out'.[327]

George Langham grew up in Wright Street, Small Heath in the 1920s and was eleven years old when he had his first bet – which was when he started taking bets for Tucker Wright, from the neighbours in his family's terrace of back-to-backs and elsewhere in Wright Street. Mr Langham remembered that:

> I was paid 2/- a week every Saturday night by the bookie, Tucker Wright. I was late for school many times while I was taking my bag of bets as the bookie's runner would make a dash to escape the copper. That meant I had to hang about till the runner came back. In those days, anyone having a bet had to trust the bookie being honest and you had not got a copy of your bet like you have now.

Street bookies like Tucker Wright got the racing results from the later editions of the local evening newspaper and, like my Granddad, many paid out winnings in the local pub – a procedure that was not illegal. With his wages from Tucker Wright, tips from winning punters and another two shillings a week for taking coal out for Granny Plumley who ran a coal yard in Wright Street, Mr Langham was able help his mother by giving her about seven shillings a week.

DOG OUTS AND GREASING COPPERS

George Langham also recalled that 'the coppers used to get up to all kind of tricks to catch the bookie's runner'. [328] In such circumstances, lookouts, known as scouts, touts, dog-outs or narkers, were vital so that illegal bookmakers could carry on their business, as Harry Vokes explained:

In a place of advantage, usually the corner, stood a look-out reading a paper or smoking a fag, generally minding his own business, but really sharp-eyed. All unlikely strangers were suspect, in some areas discouraged. Hat raising, head scratching and such like were danger signals to the lookouts outside the bookies house who also blocked anyone looking suspicious from handing a bet through the door which opened only a crack at the special knock. The betting slips were a piece of paper that came to hand, envelopes old and tatty, anything capable of being written on and wrap money inside. No names appeared on a slip, only a nickname. Black Jack, Charley Chase, Lobby Lud all sorts of strange things. The amount of toing and froing was something to see. Neighbours

and everyone else took it as part of the normal scene
until the lookout who knew all the coppers gave the
warning. Then the real fun would start with the police
trying to catch the taker like grabbing a piece of soap
in the bath.[329]

Punters needed to include a name with their bet so they
could be identified by the bookie if their horse came in, but
they could also be arrested if they used their real name and
the police captured the taker or runner, so nicknames, or
monikers, provided the necessary anonymity.[330]

Uniformed police constables working to a beat system
were easily spotted by lookouts. Mr A. T. Richardson was
born in 1919 and grew up in Cattell Road, Small Heath,
close to the Birmingham City ground. As a youngster on
Saturdays and in the school holidays, he and a couple of
school pals watched for the bookie's runners working
for Tucker Wright. They used to sit on their bikes on the
corner of Cattell Road and Templefield Street keeping an
eye out for when the policeman passed on his rounds. If
he was spotted, they would 'ride up the street and shout to
the bookie's runners, who would then dash up the entry by
the side of the bookie's house with the bets in a little bag
and go to the back door which would be open. He would
throw the bag in and then jump over the garden fence and
into another house quite a distance away.' These young
look-outs were given thrupence or sixpence. Winning bets
were usually paid out in the bookie's house. The runner
would stand at the bottom of the entry and let the winning

punters go up it 'so long as we were on the corner on our bikes giving them the all clear. This again usually meant another 3d if we did this after school, but 6d if we did it all Saturday afternoon.'[331]

To try and evade the look-outs and capture the tekers and runners, uniformed police officers were assigned to plain clothes duty and used deceptions to carry out their task. Mr Ebury's father was policeman in the Balsall Heath area in the 1920s and on one occasion his sister saw him 'all dressed up in women's clothes. She ran up to him and said, "Eh, Dad? What are you doing?" And what he was trying to do was some form of disguise to catch the street bookie. They used to wait in entries to catch the street bookie and they would spend a couple of days or so trying to catch him.'[332]

Another ploy was reported as novel and successful in the local press in 1928. A constable stated that he was concealed in a large basket carriage beneath articles such as those that might be on the way to the laundry. He was then pushed along the road by another officer in plain clothes. The hidden constable jumped out when he got to the place where the bookie was taking bets. He initially managed to run away, but was then captured, and said, 'It's all right; it's a fair cop.'[333]

The difficulties of catching bookies, tekers and runners were heightened by the general support for them in their neighbourhoods. This was recognised in 1932 both by Rafter and John Maxwell, Chief Constable of Manchester, who affirmed that this backing was based greatly on an abhorrence of what was widely decried as a class law. As a result, both legislation and police action had failed in eradicating street betting.[334] Disillusioned, many policemen came to an accommodation with their local street bookie, such as my granddad. My great-uncle Bill told me that 'he used to grease 'em with a bit of silver, half a crown, something like that'.[335]

'Big' Horace Foster was a bookmaker nearby in Kyrwicks Lane, Sparkbrook. His daughter, Mrs V. G. Pullin explained how her father would occasionally have a clandestine meeting with the plain clothes officer to confirm the day when a raid would be made to arrest his taker. He could then drop his regular man for that day and 'find another man to stand on the step who would be arrested, hauled before the magistrates and fined, which Dad used to immediately pay after generously reimbursing the criminal for his good deed. Life would get back to normal until the next time.'[336] Such 'dummies' or 'stooges' were given a few bets and a small sum of money.

This system benefited bookmakers in three ways: firstly, it meant that they paid a lower penalty if their stand-in was a first offender; second, it ensured that their regular taker was protected, meaning that they did not have to lay him off because he had incurred a higher fine for a second offence; third, it did not interfere with business as the police could simply stand on the pitch if they wanted to prevent the bookie from taking bets. On the part of the local police, the understanding was satisfactory because it kept up their arrest figures for a known pitch; it did not bring them into conflict with the community, and for those who accepted bribes, it added to their income. Finally, the 'dummy' or 'stooge' was happy because he had received a significant sum of £2 or £3 for his services, and if he were unemployed, as most were, then that extra income was welcome.

ILLEGAL BETTING SHOPS

Neither betting nor bookmaking were gendered activities. Many women placed small bets, whilst others became pitch bookies – and in some respects the latter resembled Aunt Polly, the matriarchal figure in the series *Peaky Blinders*. She takes a leading role in the business affairs of the fictional Shelby family. Strong, intelligent, independent and assertive, she is a forceful personality who is important both to her relatives and her community. So, too, was Rose Pickering, a popular bookie in Darwin Street, Highgate. Her daughter, Olga Packer, explained that her mother had a fish and chip shop with a little room at the back where she used to take the bets:

> Well, it was in a yard and there was four of us in the yard. There was the pork butcher's, there was us the fish shop and next door there was Elliot the barber's and then next door to that was Ingram's the butcher's and we was all in this one yard, and being a butcher he had a fridge in the yard. So he had two great big doors put on the yard so that it was all private and there was a little door cut in the big door and of course they used to put their bets in there and of course you used to have a man on the door because of the police, it wasn't legal then and that's how they used to just give the

man the bets behind the door and he used to put them in a bag and we used to bring them in the house and Mom and Dad used to do 'em in the house.

The double gate used to be closed at 12 noon until 2.30pm for the taking of bets, and Pickering also paid a tout on the nearby corner to look out for the police. If he saw a plain clothes policeman, he would skip onto the pavement and walk away. That was the sign to bolt the little door on the gate until the all clear.[337]

With another pitch operated by her son, Richard, in Bristol Street, Pickering reckoned up the winning bets of punters and was also a popular figure within her community. In common with other street bookies, bets were only taken in the dinner hour of the factory workers. This ranged between 12 noon and 2pm according to the workplace, although usually bets were taken until 2.30 to allow for stragglers. Thus there was no race-by-race betting as seen in the series *Peaky Blinders*. The racing results were taken from late editions of the *Birmingham Mail* or *Evening Despatch* and not a ticker tape machine. In common with other street bookies in the early 1950s, and encouraged by her son, Pickering finally installed such a device in the house behind the fish and chop shop. This drew in groups of punters to the yard behind the double gate, allowing her to take bets throughout the day.

In the mid-1950s, the butcher's shop on the corner closed and, because their kitchen came into the yard, the Pickerings took it over. They knocked down the kitchen and put up a wooden shed with benches all around it. As the results came in on the ticker tape they would be put up on a piece of paper on a board.[338] The Pickerings had now moved from the street and were running an illegal betting shop something like that shown in the series *Peaky Blinders* – but over 30 years later. My family was amongst the other street bookies making that shift. It was a move overseen by my father, Alfred 'Buck' Chinn, but it was a slow change and one that was reactive rather than proactive, as he explained.

On a Saturday, there would literally be dozens of people around the pitch:

> So we used to employ a chap to have very likely twenty pounds' worth of change, thirty pounds' worth of change in a day, and he used to be in this avenue which was about ten feet wide and it narrowed down to about six feet wide, but it was the length of the shop so that the customers could go up there and write the bets . . . and by then we were putting a box on the door and in the window we used to put the actual time of the race . . . we was then giving the results because by then we got the ticker-tape in and we were trying to give the service to the customer so we used to have a little effort in the window and in it we'd have 'the next race is' and we'd put the time 2 o'clock, 2.15 and 2.30 so that we'd take that box off and then we'd stamp each of the bets in that box for the 2.30 race.

However, so many punters were congregating around the pitch, that this position became unsatisfactory. So, in early

1958, and with the belief that the legalisation of cash betting away from the racecourse was imminent, Dad bought a nearby outdoor (off licence) on the corner of Alfred Street and Queen Street. He transformed it into a proper betting shop with racing papers on show, a ticker-tape machine and race-by race betting. This development increased the turnover of the business spectacularly to £2,000 per week.

A few months after the shop started taking bets, it was raided by the police. There were two inspectors, a sergeant and four constables. They charged my dad and his brother, Wal, for using an office at 48 Alfred Street, Sparkbrook 'for the purpose of betting with persons thereto contrary to Sections 1 & 3 of the Betting Act, 1853'. Each was fined £75. My great uncle Bill was also working in the shop but he was not charged because of his age.[339]

INCORRIGIBLE ROGUES: THE SHELDONS

The Shelbys are making much of their money as illegal bookmakers in series one of *Peaky Blinders*, and Steven Knight has explained that his father's maternal uncles were from 'a family called the Sheldons, which in fiction became the Shelbys. They were bookmakers and were known to him, and everyone else in the area, as Peaky Blinders.'[340] One family story about the Sheldons stood out especially. Knight's father was sent to his uncles with a message on a piece of paper. When he went into their house about eight men were sitting around a table. They were 'immaculately dressed, wearing caps and with guns in their pockets. The table was covered with money – at a time when no-one had a penny – and they were all drinking beer out of jam jars because these men wouldn't spend money on glasses or cups.' That evocative image of 'smoke, booze and these immaculately dressed men in this slum in Birmingham' struck Knight with the thought – 'that's the mythology, that's the story, and that's the first image I started to work with'.[341]

Three of these Sheldon brothers were notorious criminals in Edwardian Birmingham and were involved in riots, shootings, brutal attacks and the worst gang war in the city's history until the more recent feud between the infamous Burger Boys and Johnson Crew.[342]

The Sheldons belonged to a large family raised by Samuel and Rosehanna. Both were from Dudley and in 1871 they were living a poor part of the town with their two oldest sons, John aged four and Samuel, two.[343] Another boy, Thomas, was born in Dudley, as was the oldest daughter, Mary, however the next child, Joseph, was born in Birmingham in 1879.[344] The family's move was pushed by a severe downturn in trade in the Black Country. Battered by unemployment, low wages and an unsteady future, many folk left the district looking for work in Birmingham, the city of a thousand trades.[345]

The Sheldons rented a back-to-back in Glover Street, Deritend, and thereafter lived in the same vicinity. By 1891, they had moved the short distance across Watery Lane to Garrison Street, Bordesley. Their house backed on to Witton Street, at the other end of which was the real Garrison Tavern. The family had now increased by four, with the births of Lizzie, Anna, Edith and Arthur.[346] Their father died in 1910 and, a year later, his sixty-eight-year-old wife was recorded in the census as the head of the household at 6 house, number 2 Court, Allcock Street, Deritend – round the corner from where the first named peaky blinder attack had taken place. Living with her were two nieces and her single daughters.[347]

Of the five brothers, Thomas became a gas stove grinder and later an agent, and by 1911 he was living with his wife, Mary Ann, four children and a niece at 686 Bordesley Green.[348] There is no evidence to suggest anything but that he and his younger brother, Arthur, were honest. The lives of John, Samuel and Joseph Sheldon, however, were in sharp contrast.

In 1881, aged fifteen and having previously been charged with felony, John, the oldest brother, was imprisoned for one month's hard labour for stealing a small quantity of timber. He gave himself as a brass caster, but it was one of many occupations he would say that he was engaged in. A year later he was jailed for three months as a reputed thief, the same term that he was given in 1883 for stealing a basket, a knife and other items. In between these two offences, he was handed summary convictions for vagrancy and obstruction.[349] Then, in 1884, he was described as one of three bad characters who were each fined 10 shillings and costs for travelling on a train without paying their fares.[350]

John Sheldon was not only a petty thief but also a vicious and vindictive man. That was made clear in November 1895 when he and William Green made an unprovoked attack on Thomas O'Neill as he was coming out of the Great Western public house in Allcock Street. Sheldon shouted, 'I have been looking for you!' and struck his victim with a blow to his head. O'Neill tried to fight back and closed with his assailant but was then hit on the head with a heavy buckled belt by Green, who claimed that he had done so accidentally. Margaret O'Neill, the victim's daughter, disagreed as she had seen the belt swung at her father and had appealed to his attackers not to beat him. Green then pulled her to the ground by her hair, and whilst she was lying there, Sheldon had kicked her so that she was badly bruised. Both men were found guilty of assault and were sentenced to six weeks in prison with hard labour. Aged twenty-nine, and living in Palmer Street, in court, Sheldon was disapproved of as a loafer – an idle, good-for-nothing. The next year, he was convicted for nine months for uttering – knowingly tendering – counterfeit coins.[351] He had done so at several public houses in Warwick, in the company of four men from his neighbourhood.[352]

Younger by two years, Samuel Sheldon was cast from the same mould as his elder brother. Brown-haired and of sturdy build, he was green or blue-eyed, according to different police descriptions. Quite small at just 5 foot 1¼ inches, for all that he quickly gained a reputation for violence.[353] In June 1886, and aged seventeen, he and Michael Carroll had thrown stones at a cyclist and knocked him down in the Digbeth area. Carroll later threw stones at two police officers and was arrested. Sheldon did the same thing. In court, both youths were described as 'a perfect nuisance in the streets'.

They were sentenced to three months' imprisonment having been convicted previously for similar offences.[354]

Undeterred, within a year, Sheldon committed the same crime. One evening in May 1888, he was amongst a group of youths who were loitering in Glover Street. When a policeman requested them to move on they refused and threw two stones at him. One hit the constable on the right cheek and the other on the chest. For committing a very serious assault, Sheldon and another youth were sent to prison for three months with hard labour.[355]

Of course, stone throwing was associated with the slogging gangs, some of the earliest of which had emerged in Deritend where Sheldon lived. It is apparent from the record of his crimes that he was a slogger and it is highly likely that he became an early peaky blinder given that he always wore their headgear of a billycock and that he was a violent man who hated the police.

He proved that in 1888, when he was charged with assaulting two police constables. On the night of 4 November, in Heath Mill Lane, they had been 'in a fierce combat with a gang of roughs', which was reinforced by Sheldon and others. The constables managed to arrest some of the ring leaders but were then 'assailed more violently than ever'. Sheldon pelted the police with stones, but realising that he was recognised, ran off. A day or two later he was hunted down and arrested by a constable. In the meantime, he had joined in another attack on the police and had stoned one constable, 'behaving with a violence which knew no bounds'.

Though young, Sheldon had already been convicted a

dozen times for assault and was now sentenced to four months' imprisonment with hard labour. The *Birmingham Daily Post* was pleased that such a rough had been severely punished, but it did not act as a deterrent.[356] In August 1889, he was given two months in prison as one of a gang who had committed a violent assaulted.[357] Weeks after his release, Sheldon and eight or nine other roughs went to the house of a woman in their neighbourhood. They smashed the windows then followed her upstairs where they 'committed a most disgusting assault'. The unfortunate sixteen-year old girl raised the alarm and a police constable rushed to the scene and arrested Sheldon and two others. He was now sent to prison for six months for aggravated assault.[358]

It is apparent that violence coursed through Sheldon's being and in July 1890, he was convicted of a breach of the peace after assaulting a man in Curzon Street.[359] Five years later, he was sentenced to six months for wounding, which was to run consecutively with twelve months for shop breaking. His wife, Ellen, was involved in the latter crime.[360] They had married in September 1890 at St Laurence's, the parish church of one of the poorest districts in Birmingham and where PC Gunter's memorial service would be held in 1901. Ellen signed her name but Sheldon made only his mark, indicating that he could not write.[361]

A year after their marriage, Sheldon was back in his home neighbourhood and he and his wife had a general grocery shop in Little Barr Street.[362] In February 1900, Ellen Sheldon and two other women were charged with attacking Charlotte Nolan, a neighbour, after she had given evidence against Samuel Sheldon. Once she had left the court, Nolan was abused, her eyes were blackened and she was disfigured after she was kicked on the ground. The prosecuting counsel proclaimed that the three women came from 'the most lawless part of Birmingham'. Ellen Sheldon was fined five shillings.[363]

A year later, Samuel Sheldon was living in Glover Street with his nine-year-old daughter, also called Ellen, a boarder and a housekeeper called Ella Maria Small, aged twenty-seven. His wife was not with him.[364] It is evident that they had separated as she went on to live elsewhere.[365] In 1917, Sheldon, now a widower, married Small. This time he was able to sign his name and had a general store in Montague Street.[366]

Over the previous 30 years, Samuel Sheldon had given his occupation variously as a labourer, wire drawer, tube drawer and nailcaster, but it is clear that in reality he was a criminal.[367] Indeed, by the turn of the twentieth century, it was also likely that he was one of the notorious racecourse ruffians from Birmingham who travelled the country picking pockets, as in January 1902, and under the alias of Samuel Small, he had been sentenced in Manchester to three months as a suspected person.[368] Such an offence came under Section 4 of the 1824 Vagrancy Act, which allowed the police to arrest every suspected person or reputed thief frequenting streets, highways and places adjacent to them and who had the intent to commit an arrestable offence.[369] This section was regularly applied with regard to pickpockets.

Confirmation that Sheldon was a racecourse pickpocket

is provided by his arrest in late May 1905, after a meeting of Hall Green Races, which were held close to the Horse Shoes public house on the Stratford Road. He was one of several men who were charged with having frequented the area with intent to commit felony. After racing had finished, a crowd of 1,000 had gathered in the large space in front of the pub, where the landlord had erected a temporary bar. The only officer present was Sergeant Hall, who was in plain clothes, and as he knew Sheldon he watched his movements and those of his three companions. They were 'working in and out in the thickest part of the crowd, throwing their arms about' and the prosecuting solicitor told the court that without the slightest hesitation their purpose was the picking of pockets.

Superintendent Sherriff of Sparkhill arrived and shortly afterwards arrested Sheldon. He was very violent, so much so that Sherriff and Hall were bustled backward and forward across the road for some minutes. The crowd around them was hostile, consisting as it did of 'the biggest lot of roughs seen together for long while', forcing the policemen to take Sheldon into the pub until a vehicle arrived to fetch them to the Sparkhill police station. Because it was necessary to prove that Sheldon was a suspected person, it was revealed in court that he had as many as 30 convictions against him for theft, loitering and shop-breaking, as well as other offences such as using obscene language, obstruction and drunkenness. On this occasion, he was sentenced to three months for loitering.[370]

Two years later, describing himself as a hawker of Great Barr Street, Sheldon was sent to Wakefield prison for five years for uttering base coins. When giving particulars relating to Sheldon's career, Inspector Meson said that 'he was a most notorious character' who was a constant associate of thieves, and he 'would not like to say how many thieves he had made. He had been convicted 35 times, and there was not a crime committed in Birmingham in which Sheldon had not a finger.' [371]

By now, he was marked by the many fights in which he had taken part. He had two large scars on his head and others at the back of his head and hands as well as on his stomach, chest, various fingers, one shin, wrist and an elbow. Sheldon also had tattoos: two dots on the back of one forearm, two marks on a wrist and three marks on the back of one arm.[372]

He and John Sheldon had been followed into a life of crime by their younger brother, Joseph. Born in 1880, by the age of nineteen he had received eight summary convictions for assault and obstruction and had been imprisoned five times for petty theft, such as stealing a pair of boots, four pounds of sweet meats and two silk handkerchiefs. In 1899, though, he committed a more serious offence when he broke into a premises and stole eleven pounds, two cash tills, eleven bottles, sixteen pints of rum and other articles. He was sentenced to four and half years in prison, which he served at Dartmoor.[373] At 5 foot 3½ inches, the younger Sheldon was fresh-faced and had light brown hair and blue eyes. On his right forearm were tattoos of cross flags and the words 'Cab', 'Box', 'Lizzie' and 'Nellie'; on the back of his right hand was 'Love': and on his left forearm were an anchor and a heart and the words 'Ivil' and 'Mizpah'.[374]

Not long after his release, he was imprisoned for 12 months' hard labour for uttering base coins – a family trait.[375] Once again, he was not free for long, as in May 1905 he and two other men broke into a house in Handsworth and stole £50 worth of jewellery and a quantity of cigars. This time Sheldon was sentences to five years.[376]

Whilst he and Samuel were in prison, their brother John became a leading figure in what became known as the Garrison Lane Vendetta. A bloody and bitter gang feud, it was also called the Dartmouth Street Vendetta, the Garrison Street Vendetta and the Watery Lane Vendetta. The Sheldons were violent individuals who had previously acted independently, but the Vendetta would bring the three brothers together as the leaders of a vicious gang prepared to use any weapon against their enemies.

THE GARRISON LANE VENDETTA

By the early twentieth century, John Sheldon was living with his wife, Ada, in a back-to-back in Glover Street. They had no children. According to the 1901 census he was a fender grinder, but it is apparent that, like Samuel, he was a full-time criminal and racecourse rogue, as within a few years he was calling himself a commission agent.[377] This was a favourite 'catch-all' term used by the pickpockets, thugs and fraudsters to disguise their felonious activities and to give them a semblance of legitimacy by suggesting that they were legal bookmakers. In reality, however, men like Sheldon preyed upon legitimate bookies and punters on racecourses.

His true calling was made plain in September 1919, when he was one of three Birmingham men arrested at Derby racecourse for fleecing others through a fixed gambling game. He was fined 40 shillings, and the *Nottingham Evening Post* reported that 'he was particularly well-known to the police, there being seventeen previous convictions against him'.[378]

Of 5 foot 6½ height, with thinning hair and blue-eyed, John Sheldon had a tattoo of woman on his left forearm, a sailor on his right forearm and a dot on his wrist. Scarred in the centre of his forehead, under his left eye and on his left eyebrow, he was a man for whom violence was a way of life and who was prepared to do anything necessary to win a fight.[379] In early 1906, he was charged with attempting to shoot Police Constable Thomas Mooney. Mooney stated that on Boxing Night, Sheldon had obviously been drinking and was using obscene language in Glover Street. After he was told that he would be reported for a summons, it was alleged that Sheldon put his hand in his overcoat pocket and Mooney then felt the barrel of a revolver against the side of his forehead. 'Take that, then,' said Sheldon, and the revolver hammer clicked.

Fortunately the chamber was not loaded and so the constable closed with Sheldon, but he got his hands round Mooney who again heard 'the ominous snap of the hammer, which once more fell on an empty chamber, this time at the back of his head'. A tussle followed, the revolver fell to the ground, and Mooney managed to throw Sheldon. Picking up the heavy five-chambered 'bulldog', the constable marched his prisoner to Moseley Street police station and there 'discovered that in the very next chamber was a bullet, the only one in the revolver'. In his defence, Sheldon explained that he had been drunk, that he did not know that the revolver was loaded and that he had actually offered the weapon to the constable. His evidence was supported by two companions and the case was dismissed.[380]

Soon, Sheldon would be discharging a revolver in earnest in a feud with Billy Beach. Born in 1879, Billy was the oldest of four children who grew up in a back-to-back in Palmer Street, in the same neighbourhood as the Sheldons.[381] The family history research of his descendent, Janice Jackson, has revealed that in 1898, Beach was married, worked in a tube works, and was a part-time soldier with a militia battalion (6th) of the Royal Warwickshire Regiment. According to his attestation papers, he weighed 119 pounds and had a chest measurement of 31 inches. Fair of complexion, he was brown-haired and blue eyed, and he was just over 5 foot 6 inches – although later military records indicate that his height was 5 foot 8 inches.[382]

Margaret Beale's mother was Beach's niece. She was told that her great uncle always wore a white silk scarf around his neck, in the fashion of the daff of the peaky blinders, and that whilst her grandfather was:

. . .over 6 foot tall and slim, his brother Billy was shorter and much more heavily built. He could remove his shirt collar (as they did in those days) without undoing it as his neck was as wide as his head. He was always very kind to Mum and her brothers and sisters when they were children. My grandfather was a travelling salesman so wasn't at home much and not involved [in the feud]. One tale that the whole family know is that Arthur, my grandfather, was drinking in a pub with his friend Sam when he knocked a man behind him and spilt some beer. The man was about to start a fight and confront Arthur, but Sam said to him, 'Do you know who this is?' The man replied that he didn't care, he was going to see to him, but when Sam said, 'It's Billy Beach's younger brother,' the man apologised and bought them beer all evening.[383]

Mr Beasley actually knew Billy Beach. He was born in 1914 and lived in Palmer Street as a youngster, the street which was Beach's home during the inter-war years. Beasley's mother had moved into the neighbourhood as a young teenager, whilst his father had grown up in Ivy Lane off Great Barr Street and both knew Beach well. He was remembered as 'a very polite man. You'd see him touch his hat to any ladies, to women'. However, although he was thought to be 'alright when he's not had a beer but if he's had a beer he's a bit nasty'. He could then be 'a vicious man, a tough little bugger'. A loner most of the time, if Beach's enemies wanted to do him 'they'd wait till he'd had a few jars of beer, see, and then they'd get stuck in'. But someone always informed him who had done him in and, as Mr Beesley expressed it, he would go around the pubs and 'he used to wait till there was one on his own or two, he didn't matter about two' and sort them out.[384]

According to Beach's grandson, Ray Lewis, the feud with the Sheldons began over something to do with the racecourses, whilst his great-grandson Terry Lines was told that the fight started over a gambling debt.[385] This belief is supported by a statement in the *Birmingham Gazette* of 1912, explaining that the vendetta had originated over a betting transaction.[386] Beach himself later admitted that the two of them had been involved in a dispute in early 1908, and it was said that he had fought and beat John Sheldon. With a fearsome reputation, Sheldon was not prepared to let the matter rest.[387] On the afternoon of 21 June, shots were fired in Watery Lane and Beach was treated in the General Hospital for a bullet wound in the neck. He refused to name his assailant to the police, but added that he had given him a good thrashing 'and was apparently well satisfied with taking the law into his owns hands'. It was reported that Beach and the unknown man were leaders of two rival gangs that had been at war for several weeks.[388]

In a unique handwritten account from July 1908, an acting superintendent in the Birmingham City Police detailed what happened next. Late in the evening of 28 June 1908, Charles 'Coaly' Jones, alias Craley, James Thorne and Joseph Gannon used firearms against Beach in Montague Street. This use of firearms was most unusual in gang fights in Birmingham. When the police approached the men, all but Beach got away. He was locked up for being drunk and disorderly. The other three were arrested soon after and charged with unlawfully assembling in Montague Street with others for the purpose of a breach of the peace. Beach and

Jones were later charged with intent to murder each other with the earlier shooting on 21 June. With convictions for drunkenness, assault, burglary and theft, Jones was another disreputable and violent man.[389] Despite the seriousness of the events, on 9 July all those involved were bound over to keep the peace for six months.[390]

They did so until 2am on 1 January 1909, when violence again erupted. Beach had arrived at his home in Lower Dartmouth Street shortly after midnight. He ate his supper and went to the door to empty the leaves from the teapot, when he saw a number of men in the yard. It was the Sheldons and their gang. One of them said 'that's him; there's the – on the steps.' A shot was fired at Beach who threw a paraffin lamp at the group. He was then struck at the back of the ear with a bullet, whilst another shot went through an upper window in his house and grazed the head of his daughter aged ten. Despite his injury and the numbers against him, Beach took on the men. He was admired locally for fighting on his own, unlike the Sheldons, and Beasley remembered that his enemies 'used the three or four timing when they wanted to set about him 'cus they needed two or three blokes'.[391] On this occasion, John Sheldon was mob-handed. Even so, Beach fronted them and when asked in court if it was a free fight, he replied, 'If you call ten to one a free fight.'

As he struggled with the attackers, his wife ran to fetch the police and the assailants ran away. The yard was a shambles. There was blood everywhere, and in the snow the officers found 'a six-chambered revolver, containing six spent cartridges, a pickaxe, a coal hammer covered with blood, another hammer, and a number of broken bottles'. One of the attackers, Charles Loone, was also found lying unconscious on the ground, having been knocked out in the struggle. When Sheldon was later searched, an empty six-chambered revolver was found in one pocket and a knuckleduster in another. After he was charged, he said to the police, 'I wish you people would let us settle our own affairs, and we would soon do it.'[392]

Along with Sheldon and Loone, 'Coaly' Jones was arrested for the attack on Beach. The three of them were found guilty of unlawfully and violently assembling to disturb the public peace and making 'a great riot and disturbance to the terror and alarm of His Majesty's subjects'. Sheldon and Jones were each sentenced to twelve months' in prison with hard labour. Loone only had convictions for drunkenness against him and so was handed a term of eight months. In court, Inspector Moxon declared that the two factions were as bad as each other and they were involved in private feuds which had started twelve months ago. They had a code of honour amongst themselves and would not incriminate each other. That was why Beach would not say all he knew.[393] But even if he would not 'grass' to the police, he was swift to avenge the attack on him.

Late on the evening of 5 January 1909, five days after he had been attacked and before the trial of his enemies, he was joined by Arthur Morris, Thomas Lane and nine or ten others at the Lodge public house on the Coventry Road. They then marched down Watery Lane to the house of Edward Pankhurst, a friend of Sheldon and a petty thief and suspected pickpocket.[394] Pankhurst and his wife, Sarah, lived at 35 Court, Deritend, and on arriving there, Beach and his gang smashed in the door. They rushed inside, giving Sarah Pankhurst and their lodger, Kate Coley, a terrible fright. Brandishing revolvers, they demanded to know where Pankhurst was, but although he was in, his wife bluffed that he was out. At that, one of the men remarked, 'When we catch the – we will kill him.' After breaking furniture, the gang left, and when the police arrived, Sarah Pankhurst was almost in hysterics. Thence Beach and his men went to Glover Street, where Sheldon and Jones lived on opposite sides. The mob knocked violently on the door of Sheldon's house, but getting no reply they went across to the house of Jones. His wife told the court that she was:

> . . . in bed with my husband when I heard a hammering at the door. I listened, and heard the door forced open. Some men rushed into the house and began to smash the furniture, while shots were fired up the stairs. I threw up the bedroom window and shouted 'murder'. A man in the roadway shouted to another 'Shoot that –', and the man spoken to fired a revolver shot. The bullet smashed a pane of glass in the window, but did not hit me. Police whistles were blown, and all the men ran away.

Mrs Jones could not say who it was that fired the shots as his features were screened by his cap. However, Mrs Sheldon

Above: The real Garrison Tavern in the 1950s, on the corner of Garrison Lane and Witton Street, on the right. Now closed, it was a small back-street pub with the bar in the corner. The Sheldons lived in this vicinity for most of their lives.

Below: Numbers 5–10 in Number 36 Court, Deritend. All the men involved in the Garrison Lane Vendetta lived in back-to-back houses like these.

Above: Samuel Sheldon in 1907, when he was sentenced to five years' imprisonment for uttering counterfeit coins. He is wearing a billycock like that of the original peaky blinders.

Below: Glover Street in the 1920s. This street and its immediate neighbourhood were where John and Samuel Sheldon lived much of their lives.

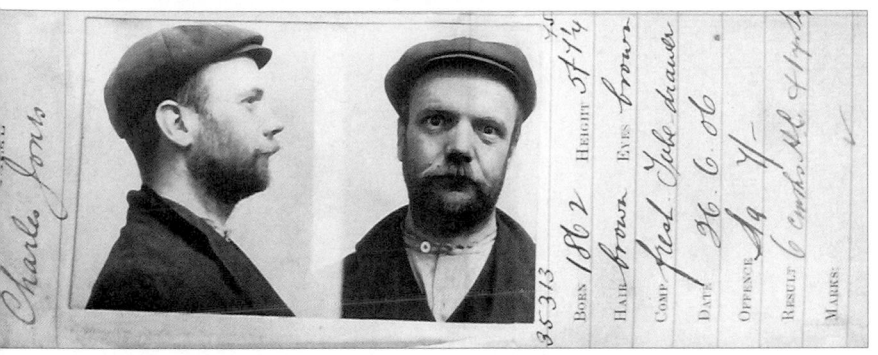

Above: Charles 'Coaly' Jones, one of the leading members of the Sheldon Gang and a very dangerous man.

© West Midlands Police Museum

Below: Edward Tuckey was a leading member of the Birmingham Gang. In the photograph on the right, taken in 1906, he was aged twenty-two. On the left he is with his wife, Florence, and daughter, Violet, in about 1920. Tuckey's criminality paid well and his great-grandchildren, Lesley and Robert Staight, were told that his daughter 'was positively spoiled! Piano lessons, ballet. Both she and Florence had very nice clothes. Florence had fur stoles. They had a gramophone and a piano. Teddy, Florence and Violet lived in a new house on Perry Common Road with a bathroom and kitchen – very nice for those days.'

© Lesley and Robert Staight (left) and © West Midlands Police Museum (right)

The infamous Billy Kimber as a young man.

Left: Maud Kimber, née Harbidge, Billy Kimber's first wife, bouncing on her knee her daughter, Maud, born in 1900. © *Juliet Banyard*

Below: John Garnham, wearing a waistcoat, at his china stall on Chapel Market, Islington in 1951. John was a close friend of Kimber and led a small gang. © *Tommy Garnham*

THE CHAPEL MARKET TRADERS DO NOT KEEP IT A SECRET!

They shout out loud their welcome to FAMILY SHOPPERS

THE GAUMONT ISLINGTON WITH

"THE SILENT VOICE"

WELCOMELY REVEAL

"THE FAMILY SECRET"

WEEK COMMENCING JUNE 9th.

Above left: A betting ticket for Sydney Lewis, whose real name was Simeon Solomon, the younger brother of the real Alfie Solomon.

© Carl Chinn Bookmaking Archive, Cadbury Research Library, University of Birmingham

Above right: Alfie Solomon at Hurst Park racecourse in the 1920s. *© Brian McDonald*

Below: Martino Changretta is the man in the middle of this photograph taken at the demolition of Elmdon Hall in 1921. *© BirminghamLives Archive*

Above: The Sabini Gang in 1920. Second from the left is Joe Sabini and seated is Harry Cortesi. To his right and without a hat is Angelo Gianicoli and to Cortesi's left is Darby Sabini in a flat cap and collarless shirt – looking very different to the elegantly-dressed fictional Darby Sabini. Next to him is Gus Cortesi and peering behind him on the right is 'Harry Boy' Sabini.   *© Islington Local History Centre*

Below: A day out for the gangs in 1919 before they came to blows. On the back row, on the charabanc: Harry 'Boy' Sabini is fourth from the right; second from the right is the burly figure of Billy Kimber; next to him on the right is Bert McDonald; whilst Joe Sabini is third from the left. On the front row, second from the right, is Darby Sabini with Wag McDonald to his left. Wal McDonald is fourth from the left wearing a billycock hat, whilst Enrico 'Harry' Cortesi is last on the right of the four men wearing straw boaters. His brother, George Cortesi is wearing a similar hat and is fifth from the right.   *© Brian McDonald*

These are the real heroes of Birmingham: from the mothers of Deritend, one of the poorest parts of Birmingham (*above © BirminghamLives Archive*), to a group of men from the Stag's Head Inn on the corner of Summer Lane and Brearley Street heading off on a day trip (*below © BirminghamLives Archive*). These people suffered hardships daily, yet, for the most part they were honest, law-abiding and hardworking, striving to stay clean and respectable, and forming strong relationships in the neighbourhoods where they lived.

had been watching what happened through her bedroom window and she was certain that it was 'Nugget' Morris who had fired.

Morris and Lane quickly left Birmingham, but Beach was arrested an hour or so after the attacks. On the way to the station, he told Inspector Bennet:

> I wish Sheldon would fight me and settle it. It's killing me going on like this. The quarrel's between me and him, and I should like to fight him even if I get put through it. Sheldon always wants to win. He does not back losers and will win at any price. I sent a pal round to get the whole dispute settled but Sheldon only wanted me to apologise, which I would not do.[395]

Beach was charged with the same offences as Sheldon, Jones and Loone. Whilst they all awaited trial, Jones and Beach met in the Crown public house in Newton Street, across the road from Birmingham's Law Courts. According to the acting superintendent's account, 'during a melee, Beach was seriously assaulted. A warrant was issued against Jones for inflicting grievous bodily harm, but when he was sentenced for riotous assembly the Recorder ordered that the warrant should not be enforced.' Soon after, Beach was stabbed in Steelhouse Lane 'no doubt by Joseph Sheldon', who was now out of prison. Again, Beach declined to give information to the police.[396]

His supporters, Morris and Lane, were later arrested on the same charges of riot. The latter was found not guilty but

Morris was sentenced to twelve months' imprisonment. He was thirty-six and supposedly a bricklayer, but was in fact another hardened criminal. When he had been thirteen he had been sent to industrial school for five years because he was an associate of thieves and he went on to be convicted many times for assault, theft, wounding and other offences.[397] As for Beach, he was imprisoned for eight months.[398] It was revealed that although he had five summary convictions, he had none for theft or loitering – unlike the Sheldons. Furthermore he was still a tube worker, as he had been all his life, whilst the Sheldons were career criminals.[399]

Shortly after John Sheldon and Beach came out of jail, there was a disturbance in Fox Street at about 10 o'clock on the evening of 18 September 1910. Interestingly, one of the few stories passed on to Beach's grandson, Ray Lewis, was that his grandfather's gang had set fire to one of the Sheldon's houses, and during this disturbance Beach and three other men broke into the house of a woman and ran upstairs with a paraffin lamp.[400] It was reported that one of the men said, 'Go on, Bill, set the house on fire.' The woman became hysterical when she realised that some of the contents of the attic had been ignited, after which the men ran off. The fire was put out by neighbours.

It is apparent that this event had something to do with the vendetta, as an hour later, Beach was walking with his cousin along Lawley Street when they were set upon by a crowd of men and youths at the railway bridge. Revolver shots were heard 'followed by screaming and cries for help, and it is also asserted by some that knives were brought into play'. Beach was rushed to hospital. He had a fractured skull, severe scalp wounds and a wound to the shoulder and had to be operated on.[401]

John Sheldon, his brother Joseph, 'Coaly' Jones and Edward Collins were arrested for the attack. In court, Beach said that they and another man had surrounded him and pointed revolvers at him. Jones fired at Beach, who dashed through the crowd. As he did so, Sheldon struck at him with a large knife and missed. At Portman Terrace, Beach saw a man on the doorstep and ran towards him, but the door was shut in his face. Cornered, he turned round in a fighting attitude. He was slashed across the face by Sheldon with his knife, struck on the head with a hammer by Collins and shot at by Jones. Asked whether he had many enemies, Beach replied that he had many friends but no enemies apart from the 'prisoners' crowd'.[402]

Found guilty of feloniously and unlawfully wounding Beach with intent to kill him, John Sheldon hoped for leniency from the judge 'because all this trouble had arisen from Beach'. However, Mr Justice Bucknill noted that he was the captain of the gang and that 'the murderous weapon', an old sword bayonet, had been found in his possession. Although Beach was as bad, Sheldon was a dangerous man. His brother, Joseph, had made himself a prominent member of the gang, whilst Jones was also dangerous and had 'openly boasted that he would not work for his living'. Each of them was sentenced to five years with hard labour. As for Collins, he was a new member of the gang 'but was spoken of as a very violent man'. He told the judge that he had an old mother dependent upon him, to which the reply was that this was 'a constant cry of men who come here, criminals of the worst description, but why didn't they think of that before. It was the mothers, wives and children that suffered'. Collins was sent down for three years.[403]

The Sheldons were now severely weakened by the imprisonment of so many of their gang, but in March 1911, Billy Beach was sent back to prison. Beasley's recollections that Beach was nasty in drink were well founded. He had gone into the Mogul pub in New Bartholomew Street where he had a row with three drunken women and was said to have wounded all three of them with a pen knife.[404] In court, he insisted that he had not done so and that he did not have a knife at all, whilst the women were drunk and falling 'all over the shop'. He had been pushed and a general melee followed. Inspector Moxon informed the judge that he had known Beach for many years and that the police had never known him to use a weapon before, but despite this he was found guilty of unlawful and malicious wounding under provocation and sentenced to fourteen months' hard labour.[405] Justice Hamilton accepted that Beach fought the Sheldon gang with his fists while they used weapons, but now he was found using weapons, and against women.

Beach and Samuel Sheldon came out of jail early in 1912, and the Garrison Lane Vendetta flared up once again when Beach summonsed Sheldon, Thomas Ingram of Heath Mill Lane and Edward Tompkins of Floodgate Street for assault. In turn they cross-summonsed him. Beach alleged that on the evening of 12 March, he had been drinking in Lawley

Street in the Village Inn. When he left, the three men were waiting for him and he was attacked by Sheldon with a chopper. Beach ducked, but was cut on the cheek. He closed with Sheldon and they struggled on the floor. The other two men tried to help Sheldon and Ingram stamped on Beach's eye as he was on the ground. As the prosecutor pointed out, no police officer was nearby and nor was there anyone to give independent and impartial evidence. Moreover, 'It was a remarkable thing that despite the feud which existed between these two gangs they sank their differences before they came to court, and it was impossible to get at the truth of things.'

However, it was believed that Beach was going to Canada, and if he did so, it was likely that the strife between gangs would come to an end.[406] He did go to Canada. As Beasley recounted it, the story went that the local police 'come and took him. They were wonderful to him. Eventually, they all clubbed together 'cus they could see he was getting a bit past it.'[407] Apparently, the police raised the money to pay for Beach's emigration because they respected him for fighting so many battles on his own with his fists, whereas the Sheldons always fought in numbers and with weapons. Support for this story is found in Inspector Moxon's opinion of Beach in 1911.

Unfortunately, Beach's move did not end the vendetta. Instead it made national news after another shooting. On 15 October 1912, the *Manchester Guardian* reported a revival in the feud in Birmingham between rival gangs of roughs resulting in a number of serious cases of wounding. The police declared that the local people lived in a state of terror and that 'it is almost impossible to persuade them to give evidence against the offenders owing to their fear'.[408] It was reported that although Beach had emigrated, he had left behind lieutenants, and on the evening of 5 October they had been involved in a fight with Samuel Sheldon and Ingram in the King's Arms public house in Great Barr Street, the main meeting place of the Sheldon Gang.[409] A day or so afterwards, one of Beach's lieutenants, Charlie Franklin, confronted Sheldon with a revolver, saying, 'I hear that you and Tommy Ingram are going to set about me. I have a shooter here and I thought about blowing your — brains out.' Sheldon managed to take the gun from Franklin, whose face was later slashed in a fight with Ingram.[410] In revenge, Franklin went in to the King's Arms on Friday, 11 October with a revolver and shot at Ingram.[411]

The next night, at about 9.30pm, Franklin, his brother-in-law Albert 'Buck' Broome, Charlie Connor and Sammy Morris confronted Samuel Sheldon in the King's Arms.[412] He was alone as his ally Ingram had just left. As reported in the *News of the World*, Connor told an acquaintance, 'You had better clear out; it's going to be on.' He then turned to Sheldon and said, 'Hello, Baggy, we've got you now.' Sheldon replied, 'You haven't come here for a row, have you?' Whereupon, Connor hit him on the head with a life preserver, a metal cosh. Morris and Franklin had revolvers in their hands and as Sheldon fell forwards, Franklin put his over Morris's shoulder and fired two shots at Sheldon. One bullet went through his billycock hat and hit the wall behind him and the other struck him in the side of the head but did not kill him. The four assailants then ran out.[413] Sheldon fell to the ground in a pool of blood and was rushed to the General Hospital.[414]

His assailants were swiftly arrested and, on 30 October, were fetched before the magistrates. Sheldon appeared with his head in bandages. He was shown a blood-stained bowler hat with two bullets in the crown and said that he had been wearing it on the night of the shooting.[415] At the trial for intent to murder, at Birmingham Assizes early in December, Detective Collins spoke of the periodical outbreaks of shooting between the gangs and explained that no matter how serious the injuries, no side sought assistance from the police. He also added that the defendants, all of whom lived near to the Sheldons, 'had the best of characters as regards to their work': Morris was twenty-eight and a tin worker; Broome was thirty-one and a labourer; Franklin was thirty-three and a rubber worker, and Connor was thirty-five and a tin stripper.[416]

In passing sentence, Mr Justice Scrutton explained that in 1910, Mr Justice Bucknill had handed long terms of imprisonment to the Sheldons to give 'the inhabitants of the neighbourhood a warning that unless they halted their ways heavier sentences would be passed until they were induced to become law-abiding subjects of the King'. This warning had not been heeded and so now Franklin, who had served fourteen days for burglary in 1899, was imprisoned for ten years. Morris was given four years. Broome, who had only one conviction for obscene language, received a sentence of three years. And Connor, who had no previous convictions, was sentenced to five years, although on appeal this was reduced to three years for wounding.[417] Previously, however, he had been found not guilty of intending to cause grievous bodily harm after he had shot at another man in 1905. Although described then by the police as 'a steady, sober and most respectable young man', Connor had been shot in the neck two years previously and had been involved in a number of fights since then.[418]

Thus ended the notorious Garrison Lane Vendetta. It was also regarded by some of the end of the peaky blinder gangs.[419] Thereafter, John Sheldon continued to live as 'a racecourse pest'.[420] By contrast, in 1914, upon the outbreak of the First World War, Beach joined the 13th Battalion of the Royal Highlanders of Canada.[421] His attestation papers indicated that he was in Montreal working as a bridge builder whilst his wife was living in Lawley Street, Birmingham. Ruddy of face, he had a long scar through both his upper and lower lip and another under his right jawbone.

During the Second Battle of Ypres, in a fierce counterattack by the Germans on his battalion's position on 24 April 1915, Beach was shot on his right forearm. He then spent some time in the 1st Southern General Hospital at the University of Birmingham and at the 1st Birmingham War Hospital Rubery. In early 1918, and after several operations, he was discharged as medically unfit for further service because of a compound fracture in his arm and ankylosis – the abnormal stiffening and immobility of a joint due to the fusion of the bones. This latter condition made it difficult for him to walk.[422] Beach returned to Birmingham in 1920 to live with his wife in Homes Buildings in Palmer Street. He led a quieter life and died sixteen years later aged fifty-six.

However, one of Beach's allies, Charlie Franklin, would become a fighter in Billy Kimber's Birmingham Gang in the 1921 racecourse war with the London gangs of Alfie Solomon and Darby Sabini.[423] The Sheldons, however, did not become part of the Birmingham Gang. Aged fifty-three when that conflict erupted, Samuel Sheldon moved to Charles Henry Street, Highgate, in the mid-1920s and became a hawker.[424] He died in 1943 aged seventy-five.[425] His older brother, John, continued to live in Glover Street with his wife, Ada, and in 1939 he gave himself as a retired gun polisher.[426] He died two years later.[427]

Chapter Five

THE REAL GANG LEADERS OF THE 1920S

THE REAL BILLY KIMBER

Tommy Shelby's plot to fix a race so that he would clean up on the bets laid in his illegal betting shop enrages the powerful gangster Billy Kimber in episode two, series one of *Peaky Blinders*. Waxing wealthy through his control of the legal and illegal bookmaking sites at racecourses across the country, he confronts the Shelbys in their headquarters, the Garrison pub. Flanked by two armed minders, Kimber strides assertively through the bar. The drinkers are silenced by his intimidating presence and then he calls out for a man named Tommy Shelby. He shoots his revolver into the air, at which Shelby leads his brothers out of the snug. Telling the customers to go home, he sits at a table facing Kimber. A Londoner by his speech, Kimber is short of stature and smartly dressed. He shouts that he is the boss, that the Shelbys fixed a race without his permission and that he runs the races. As he is leaving, Kimber threatens Tommy

Shelby, who then offers a deal that is worth listening to. He tells Kimber that he admires him because he had started with nothing and built a legitimate business – something that Shelby desires.[428]

The real Billy Kimber was indeed a gangster who made his money on the racecourses by way of protection rackets and pickpocketing and he did go on to become a legitimate businessman. But he was not from London and nor was he short. He was a burly Brummie from the Summer Lane neighbourhood. Powerfully built, strong and charismatic, he feared no man but many feared him. A tough fighter himself, he was the leader of a group of vicious and frightening thugs called the Birmingham Gang. As such, he was one of the first major gangland figures in England.

Kimber was born in 1882 at Number 55 Court in Summer Lane, although the family later moved nearby to a back-to-back in Hospital Street.[429] His mother was the daughter of Irish parents and a laundress, whilst his father was a brass founder from Birmingham.[430] There is no suggestion that either of them was dishonest, but from an early age their second oldest son broke the law. In 1894, and aged twelve, he was given four strokes of the birch for stealing a glass cutter. This was made of a bundle of robust birch twigs bound at one end with wire. Its strokes were given over the bare buttocks of the offender, who was made to lie face down on a 'horse' with legs and arms strapped. As a punishment it was usually given to boys under sixteen convicted of petty theft and it was administered to discourage further offending. It was ineffective on Kimber, and over the next three years he was given summary convictions for assault, gaming and vagrancy.[431]

The Summer Lane district was of course noted for its peaky blinders at this time, and although Kimber is not specifically named as such, it is most probable that he was one because of his violence. As with so many peakies, he was also a petty thief, and, in October 1900, he was sentenced to six months' imprisonment, which he served in Birmingham Prison at Winson Green, for trying to break into a restaurant through its roof.[432] Though only eighteen, by now he was regarded as a habitual criminal. He was described as having a fresh complexion, brown hair and blue eyes. He had the words 'W Kimber' and 'S Birch' tattooed on his left forearm and a cross and 'Love' on the back of one hand. His height was given as just over 5 foot 8 inches but given, the two-inch discrepancy regarding the height of Billy Beach in official records, Kimber may have been an inch or two more, as he was recalled as a taller man.[433]

His occupation was given as a brass caster, but it was not a job he carried on, as in August 1901, he was imprisoned again for assaulting a police constable – another reason to think he was a peaky blinder.[434] Kimber was now a father. His oldest child, Maud, was born in July 1901, and a year later he married her mother, Maud Beatrice Harbidge, who was living nearby in Howard Street. She was a bedstead ornament worker aged twenty and signed her name, however, Kimber could only make his mark.[435] It is not known how she and Kimber met, but her great-granddaughter, Juliet Banyard, was told that, 'Maud had a lovely singing voice and earned money singing in the pubs in Brum.' Juliet's grandmother was Kimber's second child, Annie, who was born in December 1903. Juliet explained that her mother, Sheila, who was Annie's only child, said that, 'Annie was Billy's favourite. He was not much bothered with Maudie and she didn't care for him either. Maudie used to say, "You owed our dad money, you paid with your life."' [436]

By 1908, Kimber had received another summary conviction for assault on a police officer and two others for drunkenness, whilst he had been found not guilty of the burglary of a house.[437] It was now obvious that he was also travelling the country as a criminal. In January 1906, he was one of a four burly built youths each fined a guinea (21 shillings) with the alternative of month's imprisonment for travelling from London to Birmingham on a train without paying their fare, and with altering the date on their ticket. All of them bore a bad reputation and it is suggestive that one of them stated that he was a bookmaker's clerk – meaning that he worked on the racecourses.[438]

The belief that Kimber was now a racecourse 'pest', as pickpockets and other ruffians were often termed, is substantiated by his arrest at Hall Green Races in May 1907. He was charged under the Prevention of Crimes Act with loitering with intent to commit an offence, punishable on summary conviction. He gave himself as a dealer, a description that covered a wide range of activities, as did his older brother, who was prosecuted as a suspected person found loitering at the race meeting with intent to commit a felony. In evidence, Detective Sergeant Wright of the

Birmingham City Force stated that he had seen the brothers acting in a suspicious manner and going into several crowds. William Kimber had attempted to snatch a winning ticket from the hand of a punter who was holding it up to a bookmaker for the payment of a bet. Kimber rushed out of the crowd when he saw Wright.

When arrested, Kimber became violent and tried to get away. Harry Kimber was 'covering' his brother and ran in a different direction but was arrested by another detective. In court, the arresting officer said that he had known William Kimber for ten years and that he was 'an associate of dangerous racecourse thieves, and no doubt made a living by following races'. He was sentenced to six months' imprisonment with hard labour.[439]

At some time in the next three years, Kimber abandoned his wife and their two children and, in 1911, he was recorded on the census as a single man boarding at a house in Saltord.[440] His great-grandson, Justin Jones, believed that Kimber 'went to live with a woman called Florence Brooks, who I think was a relation of Ellen Brooks who lived with another gang member, George "Brummie" Sage'. As for his wife, 'Maud went back to live with her parents in King Alfred's Place with her two children, my beloved aunty Maud who gave me sweets every week, and grandmother, Annie, whom I never met, unfortunately.'[441]

It must have been tough for Maud with two young daughters to care for and with ageing parents. By 1920, she was living in a back-to-back in Charlotte Street on the edge of the Jewellery Quarter. It was a big yard with thirteen houses and she remained there until she died, aged just forty-three in 1926.[442] Her granddaughter, Sheila, once tried to find the grave, but the records showed that Maud had a pauper's funeral and so there was no grave – something which angered Sheila as she knew that Billy Kimber had money at this point.[443]

Kimber did have money by the time that Maud died, but before he abandoned her, he had much in common with the Sheldons as a petty thief, violent man and racecourse pest. And in 1911, he described himself as a commission agent – as did John Sheldon.[444] But unlike the Sheldons, who remained in the back streets of Birmingham, Kimber became a gangland leader with a national profile. He achieved this position because of his leadership of the Birmingham Gang. This was not a firmly organised criminal outfit like that of a mafia family, with a don, captains and soldiers; it was rather a loose grouping of fighting men that could occasionally be brought together into a formidable force.

The Birmingham Gang had emerged from the Brummagem Boys – the collective name for the small bunches of ruffians and pickpockets from the city. They had terrorised racegoers in the Midlands and the north of England from the mid-nineteenth century, when they took advantage of the development of the railway system. There were similar rogues from elsewhere, but the Brummagem Boys were the most notorious. This was emphasised in 1898 by the *Daily Telegraph* which announced that the largest number of racecourse roughs and thieves 'come from Birmingham, and some of them are of the lowest type possible. The "Brums", like the rest of their fraternity, work in gangs of six, seven and eight – never separating.' This organised ruffianism made it hard to deal with. The criminals surrounded and tripped up their victims to rob them, or snatched purses, watches and chains; whilst on the way to and from the racecourse by train, they worked the three-card trick upon gullible fellow passengers.[445]

Kimber belonged to one such gang. In January 1913, the *Derby Evening Telegraph* reported that for a recent football match, the local police had placed officers at the railway station to watch out for known lawbreakers arriving by train. Amongst a group of eight men, they recognised William Kimber, his younger brother, Joseph, and a George White who were 'expert travelling pickpockets and hotel thieves'. The police followed them, but they were spotted by the men who ran off. Chased by the police through several streets, both the Kimbers threw something out of their pockets into the snow and escaped down different entries to various houses.[446]

Joseph Kimber was a longstanding thief, and in 1912 he had been imprisoned for pickpocketing at Doncaster races. He was then sentenced to three months in August 1913 after he was arrested as a suspected person at the Maze Races in Belfast.[447] In the 1920s, he would describe himself as a commission agent.[448] As for White, that was an alias and his real name was Thomas MacDonald. He was also known as Thomas McDonagh and he would become one of the most notorious fighters and bullies in the Birmingham Gang.[449] It was through the support of the likes of men like him that Billy Kimber, himself a hard man, gained some form of control over the pickpocketing gangs and racecourse roughs from Birmingham.

But his power also arose from his friendship with feared fighting men from London. They included George 'Brummy' Sage, who became leader of the Camden Town Gang in North London, but whose nickname arose from his closeness to Kimber. Another thief, Sage was regarded as 'a stand-in, toe-to-toe fist fighter' by Wal McDonald of the Elephant Boys gang and another London friend of Kimber who also revelled in his reputation as a top man. Brian McDonald is his nephew, and he explained that Wal's brother, Wag (Charles) was a major south London gang leader, who later had a significant presence in the West End, where he was an early nightclub protector. By 1909, he had been joined by his four younger brothers and was controlling a number of illegal street betting pitches. Additionally, Wag hired himself as a 'bodyguard' to racecourse bookmakers to protect them from gangs extorting money from them and obtained 'favours' from other bookies.[450]

Through these latter activities, he had met Kimber, who was travelling the country in his pickpocketing gang. The two men became firm friends. Brian McDonald's uncle Jim described Kimber as 'a big, jovial, well-liked fellow, respected as a settler of disagreements and disputes. He could fight and was a natural leader.' [451] Because of his friendship with the McDonalds, it seems that – whilst still maintaining his strong links with Birmingham – Kimber moved to London. Brian McDonald notes, 'Kimber lived for a short while with my family at 116 York Road, Lambeth, before moving to

Warren Street (now Grant Street), Islington.'[452] And in the summer of 1910, Kimber joined the McDonalds in fighting a rival gang.[453]

Three years later, Sage and Kimber were arrested after a fight in a pub in Whitechapel in the East End. When a constable arrived at the scene, Kimber and Sage were throwing chairs at another man. When told to stop, they ran into the street where another policeman arrested Kimber. The man they had attacked came up and said, 'I charge Kimber and Sage with doing this' – and pointed to his face which was bleeding freely having been stabbed. On the way to the police station, Kimber dropped a brass harness buckle. When charged with cutting and wounding, he stated that he was a wardrobe dealer whilst Sage gave himself as a bookmaker.[454] They were later discharged as the publican's daughter stated that she could prove that the stabbing had been done by another man known as the 'Kidderminster Kid'.[455]

It seems more likely that Kimber and Sage were the guilty parties and that the licensee's family were frightened of them – justifiably so, as the man assaulted was in the London Hospital in a serious condition from stab wounds to the face and neck. This case first appeared in the *Illustrated Police News* on 20 February 1913 and, elsewhere in that edition, 'Brummy' and Kimber were noted as 'well-known on racecourses and in the boxing-ring'.[456]

By 1914, Kimber had established himself both as a racing man and a vicious fighter in London, where he had also forged an alliance with the Garnhams of Chapel Street Market in Islington. An intriguing article from April that year highlighted that connection. It was reported that a conflict had taken place in Dunstable between the police and a party of Londoners in a car returning from the Towcester race meeting. The defendants included Anna Kimber aged forty-three, of the New Cut, Lambeth, in South London, who was charged with being drunk and disorderly on the highway, and her husband, William, a china salesman aged thirty-two, who had assaulted two policemen in the course of their duties. Anna's identity is mysterious, and she could not have been his wife as Kimber was still married to Maud. The other two defendants were Thomas Garnham, a china salesman from London, and his wife, Eliza, both of whom were charged with obstructing one of the officers in his duty. The Garnham family would play a prominent role in the rest of Kimber's life. All of the defendants pleaded guilty and Kimber's counsel said that this was his first appearance in a court of this kind – a blatant lie. The defendants were fined a total of eight pounds and six shillings.[457]

A few months afterwards, the activities of racecourse rogues like Kimber were curtailed as, following the outbreak of the First World War, racing was severely restricted in Britain.[458] Kimber joined up but, as recalled by the Birmingham racecourse bookmaker Denny Green, he deserted and went to Dublin, where horse racing continued until late in 1917. Green stated Kimber was attacked on a bridge over the River Liffey by four men, whom he put away. The Birmingham gangster was remembered as 'a game un, a fearless fighter who fought fairly with his hands and did not use knives' – although of course, he had done so.[459]

In May 1917, Kimber and James Cope, another prominent member of the Birmingham Gang, were arrested in Dublin. They were charged as suspected persons found frequenting at Kingsbridge (now Heuston) Railway Station for the purpose of picking pockets on the day of the Limerick races, and also with having frequented the nearby Harcourt Street Railway Station on the day of the Leopardstown race meeting. Kimber described himself as a dealer living at New Cut, in the South London heartland of the McDonalds. As for Cope, he was also a notorious pickpocket.[460]

It is interesting that the chief clerk of a major racecourse bookmaker called Thomas Henry Dey appeared in court, explaining that Kimber was employed to collect large sums of money owed to the bookie. In so doing, he always acted honourably and 'racing being quiet in England, some of the people owing debts to Mr Dey had come over Ireland, and Kimber crossed over from Liverpool to meet those people'. Dey's clerk added that he had 'full knowledge of the past career of Kimber who had been honest man for the seven last years', and that Mr Dey was prepared to keep him employed and give a substantial sum for bail for his good behaviour. This was set at £50.

Kimber did not stay free for long, however. He was charged with having been a deserter from his role as a driver in the Army Service Corps since 11 June 1915,[461] and in October 1917, he was tried and sentenced to six months' detention.[462]

Kimber's relationship with Dey is intriguing. Dey was one of Britain's most notable and wealthy bookmakers, winning the staggering amount of £84,000 in one year alone, and as such he took huge bets in cash on the racecourse and on credit through his office in New Bond Street, London. Amongst his credit punters there were those who did not pay up when they lost and there were others who resorted to cunning deceptions to try and swindle him.[463] It seems likely that as a very hard man, Kimber not only collected debts for Dey but had also acted as his minder on the racecourses.

With the end of the First World War, racing resumed and, as with other sports, attendances soared in the short post-war boom. They peaked in 1919 and 1920, but thereafter remained much higher than before 1914, until dropping significantly from 1925 as the British economy struggled.[464] The rise in spectators was matched by much higher spending on betting. According to Tom Divall, a former chief inspector at Scotland Yard employed to keep order at various racecourses, people flocked to them and their pockets were full of money.[465] This is emphasised by the story of Bud Flanagan, who later became a bookie. In 1919, his bets on four races at Ayr 'disposed of the whole of his gratuity earned in three-and-a half years of soldiering'.[466]

Such outlays meant rich pickings. Megging mobs, as they were called, fleeced all and sundry with the three-card trick; card sharps swindled unwitting travellers on their way to meetings on trains; whilst gangs of pickpockets and thieves preyed upon spectators, beating up any who retaliated. Bookies were also victimised. A favourite dodge of the gangs, or 'boys' as they were called, was to go round with a bogus subscription for 'poor old Bill', and 'dear old Charlie', who had hit hard times – or for a fatherless family on the brink of starvation. Another scam was to shout out a bet to a bookie. If the horse won then the gang would expect to be paid out, but if it lost they held on to their money.

Those bookies who stood up to the gangs paid a heavy price. In June 1919, *The Times* recounted how three men had demanded money from bookmakers at Windsor. Several paid up without demur but when one refused to hand over £1 he was knocked off his box, from which he called out to the punters, and his satchel filled with money was grabbed by another rogue.[467]

Under the leadership of Kimber, the Birmingham Gang ruled unopposed in the Midlands, the West Country and the north up to Newcastle. He himself was no longer a pickpocket because now he oversaw the racecourse protection rackets in a more organised form. At the bigger meetings, he controlled the most prominent five or six pitches, the places which took the most money in bets and which were thus the most lucrative. London racecourse bookmaker Sam Dell remembered that Kimber either put his own men on these pitches or allowed bookmakers to run them for a return of 'ten bob in the pound' – fifty per cent of the profit. As for the other bookies, to get their pitches they had to arrive at a meeting 'early in the morning to stake a claim and be prepared to be blackmailed or prepared to fight . . .'[468]

Most bookies did not fight – they paid for the right to set up their joints in specific places. Controlling the allocation of pitches was lucrative, but that that was not the end of the scams for making money. Another leading member of the Birmingham Gang was Andrew Towie, and he either came up with or developed the idea of selling dots and dashes cards for each race. This was a simple operation whereby a card representing each horse was pricked with symbols to alert bookies to its form and chances in the race. In fact, this supposed 'service' told the bookmaker nothing more than he knew already and it was merely a means to extort money.[469] Then there was the calling out of the numbers of the horses in each race once that information became known shortly before the 'off', whilst bookmakers were 'encouraged' to pay for 'tools of the trade'. Included among these were the tissues, the lists of runners for each race; pieces of chalk with which to mark up the prices of the horses on their blackboards; water and sponges with which to rub them out; the calling out of the names of the jockeys; and stools on which to stand.[470]

Dell recalled that, in the 1920s, 'it was the Birmingham mob that used to run the stools at Cheltenham and places like that. And they used to have to cart the stools from track to track and they used to have a big van to do it in. And then when they got there, they were collapsible stools, used to have to bang the legs in, and they used to have to set all the stools up.'[471] Exorbitant prices could be charged for the use of a stool, as if a bookie did not have one then he was at a disadvantage to others as he would not stand above the crowd.

Bookies usually paid two shillings and sixpence for each of the 'services' provided by the gangs. This was handed over each race and over six races or more it added up to a lot of money. At a big meeting like Doncaster, there could be more than one hundred bookmakers, meaning that something like

£300 to £400 or more could be paid to the gangs – although obviously, the sum was a lot less at smaller meetings. To these sums could be added the more crude protection money extorted from bookmakers for being allowed to set up their joint – the spot on which they operated.[472]

An example of Kimber's power, physically and personally, was given by former Chief Inspector Divall. In 1919, he was in charge of one the rings of spectators at Doncaster – a very popular and important racecourse. There was a large crowd and a dangerous situation arose over a disputed bet. The course officials and police lost control as 'high words and ugly threats passed between some miners and bookmakers' runners'. Divall feared an awful scrimmage and then 'up came Billy Kimber, a host in himself among his fellows, and he soon settled the disturbance'. What would have happened without his most timely help could not have been imagined as there were thousands of men about, most of whom were of the roughest class. Divall had no doubt that Kimber was 'one of the best'.[473]

In the more prosperous south of England, with its large number of racecourses, there was a more anarchic scenario in the years immediately following the First World War. A variety of gangs were active, often on the same racecourse on the same day. In particular, the thugs of Dodger Mullins from Bethnal Green and of Alf White from Hoxton and King's Cross plagued racegoers, before, during and after a meeting.[474] They soon drew national attention and on 18 October 1919, the *Daily Mail* carried a report on 'Racecourse Gangs', asserting that 'robberies with violence were said to be increasing'.[475] In the summer of the next year, *The Times* called for immediate action against the rogues of the racecourse.[476]

In the event, it was Kimber who took that action, as he saw an opportunity to extend the Birmingham Gang's operations onto the more lucrative southern racecourses by running off the other gangs. Brian McDonald believed that Kimber's involvement was facilitated by the racecourse authorities who realised that they could not deal with the gang problem just with their own stewards and the police. Importantly, Kimber had major back up from London: the McDonalds and the Elephant Boys; George 'Brummie' Sage and the Camden Town Gang; and Freddie Gilbert, formerly a member of the Titanic Gang from Hoxton and now leader of the Finsbury Boys.

Kimber and his allies succeeded. The Bethnal Green and King's Cross gangs fell out and were expelled.[477] W. Bebbington, later appointed as Senior Jockey Club Supervisor of Recourse Detective Personnel, affirmed that in the early post-1918 period, the Birmingham gangs 'held the whip-hand all over the country and ruled with a rod of iron'.[478] This 'mob law' seems to have been accepted by London bookmakers because it brought some semblance of order. Ali Harris, a racecourse bookmaker from London, praised Kimber as a 'pretty well respected bloke', as did Dell.[479]

However, there was another racket with which Kimber was involved, as explained by Tommy Garnham, the grandson of Thomas Garnham, the china salesman who had been arrested with Kimber in 1914 in Dunstable. By the early 1920s, Garnham's son, John, was running a crock stall in Chapel Street Market in Islington but he was also the leader of a small team that worked for Kimber on the racecourses of southern England. Garnham and his men looked out for pickpocketing gangs that had not been authorised by Kimber and who had not paid 'tribute' to work the course. His son, Tommy, recounted, 'Dad used to say you look for the boss, the main man and give him a good hiding in front of the others. "This is your boss look what I've done to him," and all the others'd go. That's if Dad could handle it, if not they called in Billy and they wouldn't take him on.'

John Garnham recounted many stories of Kimber's fighting prowess. On one occasion, he and his friend known only as 'the Wizard' were on a train going up to a race meeting. They started gambling in the compartment with a couple of big hard men and as Tommy Garnham was told:

They had a game of cards and Dad and the Wizard took all their money. They went up overnight and the blokes said, 'We want our money back.' The Wizard said you won't get your money back so they said, 'We'll see you at the track.' That's where they were all going and when they get in there, Dad and the Wizard went straight over to Bill. 'See them two over there. Took their money off them last night and they want their money back.' 'Alright,' said Bill Kimber. Bosh, bosh. And they were both carried out, both. Bill Kimber on his own did them.[480]

But the control of Kimber and his allies on the racecourse rackets in southern England was soon challenged after some of the Elephant Boys and Birmingham Gang began to terrify East End Jewish bookies and blackmail them for money in addition to that which they were already paying Kimber for protection. As Divall put it, if they 'did not shell out, they were cruelly assaulted and badly damaged'.[481] One of those so treated was the real Alfie Solomon.

THE REAL ALFIE SOLOMON

Named as Alfie Solomons in the series *Peaky Blinders*, he is portrayed wearing the clothes of Hasidic Jewish men: the wide-brimmed black hat worn on weekdays, a long black overcoat, black trousers and a white shirt. The members of the gang led by Solomons are depicted as Orthodox Jews, wearing yarmulkes and tzitzit –the fringes or tassels worn on traditional or ceremonial garments by Jewish men. By contrast, the real Alfie Solomon was a secular Jew whose family had been settled in England for decades and were not recent immigrants fleeing the pogroms in the Russian Empire.

Born in 1892, Solomon was the third oldest of the ten children of Elisha and Elizabeth Solomon. His father had been born in the Strand in the City of Westminster, whilst his mother had been born in a poor part of the East End. Elisha Solomon was a fruit merchant employing people, and in 1901 he and his family were living with a servant in Long Acre in Covent Garden. A decade later, they had moved nearby to New Street. By now, two of their six sons were clerks to bookmakers, working on the racecourses, and one each was a fruit salesman, clerk and hat maker. Although he was aged nineteen, no occupation was given for Alfie Solomon and it was recorded that he was 'at home'.[482]

In January 1915, however, he recorded that he was a horse driver when he volunteered to join the Royal Field Artillery and became a driver. He was 5 foot 6 inches tall with a waistline of 35 inches. Weighing 125 pounds, his physical development was good. Fresh complexioned, his eyes were blue and his hair brown. Solomon went on to serve for over three years in France, from June 1915, winning the 1914/15 Star and receiving the British War Medal and the Victory Medal.[103]

Unlike Kimber, Solomon was not a pickpocket and had served his country loyally. It is obvious, though, that he was interested in gambling. In August 1907, he was one of four youths fined for frequenting premises used for betting on horse racing, and, in April 1916, whilst in the Army, he was given seven days' detention for gambling with dice.[484] His only other misdemeanour was one charge for insubordination to a non-commissioned officer.[485] Then, after he left the Army in January 1919, Solomon was bound over for betting. Importantly, though, there is no evidence of violence from him until the racecourse wars.

With the coming of peace, Solomon became a bookmaker, as had his youngest brother, Simeon 'Simmy' Solomon, who took bets as Sydney Lewis. In 1987, he indicated that anti-Semitism was the reason he did this, telling me, 'If I'd put up as Simmy Solomon as a bookie I wouldn't take a penny.' In his view, the racecourse war began because, 'The Birmingham mob began to come down here. We were not up the north, they came down here. If they'd have stayed up north there would have been no problems. They didn't and it became us against them, them against the south.'

At the Sandown Park Military Meeting, on 12 March 1921, the Birmingham Gang turned up in numbers and one of them brutally assaulted Alfie Solomon, as his brother recalled.[486] Edward Greeno, a former detective chief superintendent in the Metropolitan Police, stated in his memoirs that Solomon (whom he termed 'Bernie') was knocked down and kicked in the teeth.[487] Boxing referee Moss Deyong actually saw the attack, though referring to Solomon as Lewis, the betting name of his youngest brother. One of the gangsters shouted out a bet but Solomon refused to take it, knowing that he would not get paid if the horse lost. It won and the mobster came up for his money, insisting that Solomon had taken the bet. He stood up to the threats and refused pay. Deyong graphically described what happened next:

> Suddenly the mobster swung his race-glasses, heavy and solid, into the bookmaker's face. Down went Lewis, and the assailant promptly stepped on his unprotected face as he lay on the ground, immediately afterwards slipping away into the crowd. Lewis was picked up, his face a bloody mass and with several teeth missing. From that moment the gang wars between the North and South opened up in earnest.[488]

Tragically, another Jewish bookmaker died of the injuries caused when he was also hit on the head with a pair of field glasses. His assailant was Thomas Armstrong, a leading hard man in the Birmingham Gang who was almost certainly the man who had beaten up Solomon. Armstrong was later found not guilty of manslaughter.[489]

Brian McDonald stressed that Alfie Solomon had a gang before he was attacked and that Kimber had a hatred for him 'as one of the scum that threatened racecourse bookies at the edge of a razor'. Given Kimber's long record for violence it rings hollow for him to take the high moral ground.[490] However, Solomon's brother claimed, 'My older brother's involvement with Darby Sabini came after he was beaten up by the Brummie mob.'[491] Whether or not Solomon did have his own men before he was attacked, he was later described in a police report as 'nothing better than a member of a gang of thieves who blackmail bookmakers for a living'.[492] But if he did lead a gang, in early 1921 it was not strong enough to take on Kimber and his allies, so Solomon sought the support of a powerful man called Edward Emanuel.

Born in 1880, he was one of eight children and his family was also well established in England, unlike the recently arrived Yiddish-speaking immigrant families from Eastern Europe.[493] His father, Alfred, was born in Aldgate and his mother, Adelaide, in Spitalfields, but from the late 1870s they were living south of the River Thames in Bermondsey, running a greengrocers.[494] By 1901, they had moved back across the water to the boundary of the East End. Edward Emanuel was now a fruit porter.[495] The next year, he and another man were discharged from maliciously wounding a Cornelius Haggerty and assaulting a Metropolitan police officer.[496] Then, in 1904, he threatened to shoot an Islington street trader and was charged with the possession of a loaded revolver. The magistrate declared that Emanuel was 'a dangerous fellow' and imposed a high surety of £250 or twelve months' imprisonment.[497]

He was indeed a very dangerous man, as John McCarthy found out. In 1908 he was found guilty of unlawfully wounding Emanuel, intentionally but without malice. Both men had been drinking in the Lord Nelson on the evening of 15 July 1908. Emanuel had gone there to have a row with McCarthy over a dispute with some of his friends. McCarthy explained that Emanuel had bought him several drinks before calling him 'a dirty little closet' and challenging him to fight. McCarthy refused because Emanuel was too big for him but at last he did. Emanuel got hold of his throat, threw him across a barrow and nearly strangled him. Somehow McCarthy got away and pulled out a revolver that he had brought with him to frighten Emanuel. But the bigger man kept on rushing forward with a sharpened tin-opener. McCarthy then pulled the trigger and ran away as he was in fear of his life. Although suffering from a bullet wound in the chest, which had gone through his body, Emanuel ran after the frightened McCarthy. The surgeon who operated on Emanuel explained that the wound was about six inches long and that he was a very strong man.[498]

Despite being a terror, Emanuel was intelligent and ambitious, and by 1911 he was no longer a porter, having become a retail fruit salesman. Married to Elizabeth, née Prudon, they had two children and were living in a five-roomed house in Thrudon Road, Bethnal Green.[499] But Emanuel's main living was as a proprietor of spielers, or illegal gambling clubs.[500] In January 1912, he and two other men were charged with keeping one in Whitechapel. When it was raided, fifty-seven other men were arrested, most of whom were described as foreigners. Playing cards were strewn about the room and there were boxes full of pennies. Emanuel was fined £40, and £12 and 12 shillings costs.[501]

He incurred the much heavier fine of £300 and 10 guineas costs in September 1917 following a raid on another spieler he ran in Whitechapel in which over 100 men were arrested. Occurring during the First World War, this raid gained wide publicity as a 'Recruiting Scandal'. The club was 'patronised mostly by Jews', many of whom were of military age and were noted as 'aliens'.[502] The inference was that, given they were of an age to be eligible for conscription, they had actively avoided recruitment to the war effort. This clear anti-Jewish prejudice in the newspaper coverage would be even more pronounced in the racecourse war that would soon erupt.

As well as a gaming house keeper, Emanuel was named as a bookmaker, for in addition to 84 packs of cards found in the 'gambling den' there was a large number of betting slips and racing cards.[503] However, Emanuel had ambitions to become a legitimate businessman, as recalled by Lou Prince, an East End racecourse bookie with a Jewish father. He saw the Birmingham team 'take liberties' when they came down to the southern racecourses and told me that, as a result, the Jewish bookies turned to Emanuel for help because he was 'a financial power'. Prince explained that Emmanuel then set up the Portsea Press printing company, and it was through providing bookmakers with a better service for the lists of runners for each race and other printed material that he aimed to move away from criminality.[504] But with Kimber controlling the racecourse rackets he was not able to do so – that is, until the brutal attack on Alfie Solomon gave him the opportunity to act.

According to Arthur Harding, a notorious East End terror and pickpocket, Emanuel 'governed the whole the East End Jewish underworld. He was the Jewish Al Capone, everything was grist to his mill'.[505] Through this powerful position, he could forge an alliance of London gangs to force the Birmingham Gang off the racecourses of southern England. With them removed, the bookies would have no option but to buy their printed material from him and he could cease his illegal activities.

Emanuel 'had a group of Jewish terrors' who he could send in to help Alfie Solomon and, as Prince emphasised, 'The Jewish team found their power in strength and gameness. They wouldn't be dictated to.' Still, they did not have the numbers to take on the Birmingham Gang and their London allies. So, because 'Emanuel was pally with the Italian push' – the Sabini Gang – he called them in for more backup.[506] Importantly, there was another influential and powerful figure in the background who aided this alliance. When his club had been raided in 1917, it was revealed that behind

Emanuel was a man of means – but it had not been possible for the police to charge him.[507]

That man was Walter Beresford. In 1891, he was a short-hand reporter living with his widowed mother, a prosperous publican in Hackney Marsh.[508] A decade later, he was married, had a house in Leyton and was a commission agent – someone who took bets and placed them on a commission basis. He also employed others.[509] But he was also a gaming house keeper, and in May 1902, he and others were charged with using the New Savoy Club in the Strand for the purpose of unlawful gaming and betting. He was fined the large sums £200 and £50 respectively.[510] This was over four years' wages for an unskilled worker.

By 1921, when Solomon was savagely attacked at Sandown, Beresford had an office in Bond Street and was a prominent and respected racecourse bookmaker, noted as the first person to start betting at a meeting and from whom the other bookies took their prices.[511] As such, he would have been keen to end the protection rackets of the Birmingham Gang, and, through Emanuel, he had influence over the Sabinis. This was confirmed by the writer and conman, Netley Lucas. In 1926, he wrote that this gang was 'backed and upheld by one of the best known and most powerful bookmakers on the turf. A member of all the racing clubs, a man who pays out thousands after each big race, and retains twice as much, he has a smart flat in the West End, several expensive cars and a still more expensive wife.'[512] This man was Walter Beresford and the gang he backed up and upheld was led by the formidable Darby Sabini.

THE REAL DARBY SABINI

The fictionalised Darby Sabini of the series *Peaky Blinders* is depicted as a 'violent and volatile Italian crime boss' controlling the gambling 'on the racing tracks of the South, as well as various bases around London'. And he has the police on his books, which has given him the freedom to do as he pleases.[513] Immaculately dressed, his appearance highlights his Italian identity, adhering as it does to the aesthetic notion of '*bella figura*' – showing care for outward appearance and elegance.

Bella figura features in films on the Mafia such as *The Godfather* series. Applying this look to Sabini in *Peaky Blinders* implies to the viewer that he is a mafia-style boss. In crime mythology he was, and that mythology has been accepted as historical fact. In 1963, crime writer Norman Lucas wrote that Sabini 'reputedly was a member of the notorious Mafia', whilst in 2005, the *Telegraph* described Charles 'Darby' Sabini as the 'leader of a Sicilian "razor" gang'.[514] In her book on the London underworld, Catharine Arnold went further by asserting that Sabini had imported over 300 henchmen from Sicily to act as enforcers and that he had taken on the role of a Mafia godfather in his neighbourhood. As such, he dispensed justice, resolved internal conflicts and protected the honour of young women.[515]

This characterisation of Sabini gained traction from the biography by Edward T. Hart published in 1993 and entitled *Britain's Godfather*. Hart was a crime correspondent in Fleet Street in the 1950s and 1960s, and his information was gleaned from people in the world of Sabini, 'club-owners and bouncers, boxers and jockeys, bookmakers and their bruisers, robbers and racketeers'. Unfortunately, there is no evidence of any recordings or transcripts of Hart's interviews, whilst the book itself is written in a novelistic style. It includes long verbatim conversations and thoughtful musings from Sabini, who had been dead for many years, as well as vivid 'first-hand' descriptions of bloody battles between gangs.

Throughout Hart's book, Sabini's Italian identity is accentuated. His voice was 'an odd blend of Southern Italian and Bow', and he had fashioned his gang upon the Mafia of Sicily. After he had supposedly knocked out a leading fighter with the Elephant Boys, who had insulted an Italian woman, the men of London's Little Italy in Saffron Hill, Clerkenwell, made their way to Sabini's house to offer allegiance to their new leader as if he were a don. And when he and Billy Kimber met at Sabini's home to try and end the war between their gangs, they sat at a table laid in the Italian tradition with a freshly baked loaf, great chunks of cheese, and a carafe of anisette.

According to Hart, Darby Sabini's wife was called Maria and the descriptions of her drew on media tropes of Italian emigrant wives.[516] In fact, she was a local woman, Annie Emma Potter, who had been born in Clerkenwell.[517] She married Sabini in 1913, not in the Catholic church of St Peter, which was deeply associated with the Italians of Saffron Hill, but in the Anglican church of St Philip, Clerkenwell. Their oldest daughter would be christened Church of England.[518]

Sabini himself would later stress his Englishness, declaring that 'England is the only country for me', whilst his only son, Ottavio Harry, was killed fighting for Britain in August 1943.[519] Crucially, I could find no links between Sabini and Sicily, and so reports that he imported Sicilian knifeman unlikely. Although he came from London's Italian Quarter of Saffron Hill, from 1876 to 1915, most of those who settled there originated from Lombardy and Emilia in the north of Italy, or from Tuscany or Campania – the region between Naples and Rome. Of those, the main area of emigration was the Apennine region south of Parma, from where it is believed that the Sabinis originated.[520]

In the early years of the Italian community, most of the newcomers were young men and they tended to marry women from the locality.[521] From 1875, whilst increasing numbers of wives were Italian women or first generation London-born daughters of Italian couples, mixed marriages continued. They included Sabini's father, Ottavio, who married Eliza Elizabeth Handley in 1898 at the Anglican St Paul's church in Clerkenwell. It is apparent, however, that they had been in a long-term relationship, as fourteen years before, Ottavio Sabini was involved in a serious affray with other Italians in a pub and Eliza Handley said that he was her young man.[522] Four years later, in July 1888, their son Ottavio was born, although his birth was registered under his mother's name of Handley.[523]

Better known as Darby, this nickname is thought to have arisen from a term for a south paw boxer. He had two older brothers, Frederick and Charles. Their births were also registered as Handley and they were named after two of their mother's brothers.[524] Contemporary news reports often referred to Darby Sabini as Charles, which has led to confusions over his real identity by historians, including myself. Sabini later acknowledged that he also called himself Frederick Handley, after his mother's maiden name, but pronounced clearly that 'my name is not Charles Sabini' and that 'my real name is Ottavio Sabini'.[525]

By 1891, his parents were living in Mount Pleasant, Clerkenwell with four children.[526] Darby Sabini was not with them, but the previous year he was recorded as attending the Drury Lane Industrial Day School.[527] Set up in 1895 for children whose school attendance was irregular, it was like a half-way house before a youngster with criminal tendencies was sent to a residential industrial school.[528] Still, no evidence has been uncovered indicating that Sabini was a habitual criminal like Kimber and other racecourse rogues, and as Heather Shore remarked, he seems 'to have steered remarkably clear of the law'.[529]

At his wedding in 1913, Sabini recorded that he was a carman, and three years later, at his daughter's christening, he said that he was a railway porter.[530] He was a porter but not on the railways – instead, he worked at a nightclub in Drury Lane, as he admitted in 1926. It is likely that as such he was a protector of some sort.

After the outbreak of the First World War, the club closed down. Sabini said that he was rejected for Army service and then became a bookmaker and a runner. It is probable that he was the latter as he stated that he used to collect betting slips. Then, in 1918, he was again engaged as a porter, at the

White Horse Club in Stepney Green, earning £3 a week. Two years later, in May 1920, he was bound over not to frequent gaming-houses – so it would seem that it was through his work in clubs and spielers that Sabini became acquainted with Emanuel.[531]

By then, Sabini had become the leader of a major gang. Shore has suggested that, like the other London gangs of the 1920s, it may have had roots not only in the territorial street fighting gangs that had long been a feature in areas like Clerkenwell, but also in forms of defence against incursions from other local youths.[532] There is evidence to support such a suggestion, for in 1898 there was 'another case of revolver firing by the Clerkenwell War Gang' in which Alfred Smith shot at an Augustus Sabini.[533]

This suggests that the Sabini Gang may also have been rooted in the violence of older kin. Darby Sabini's father had a brother, Giuseppe, and cousins in Clerkenwell.[534] Two of the family were accused of wounding with knives in 1883 and 1888, whilst Sabini's father was fined for assault in 1895, having been stabbed the previous year. All these fights took place between Italians.[535] Younger Sabinis were also violent, and in June 1909, Darby's older brother, Charles, was charged with assaulting two men with a hammer.[536]

Six months later, a Vincent Sabini and George Cortesi were accused of maliciously wounding. Sabini was found not guilty, but Cortesi was sentenced to two months' hard labour. The latter had other convictions for assault and theft, and he and one of his brothers would become key figures in the Sabini Gang.[537] Born in France, they now lived in

Clerkenwell.[538] So too did Angelo Gianicoli.[539] Later calling himself George Langham, at fourteen he was discharged for malicious wounding, then a decade afterwards, in 1913, he was given six months' hard labour for unlawful wounding.[540] He would become a main enforcer for Darby Sabini.[541]

Bound together by a shared background and neighbour-hood loyalty, the ties of the Sabini Gang were strengthened not only by personal relationships but also by blood, for as Shore has discerned, 'The most enduring "structure" connecting with the Sabini Gang was family and kinship.'[542] So it was, and the gang also included Darby's two youngest brothers, Joseph and Harry, or 'Harry Boy', as he was known. Yet it was Darby who became the leader. Unostentatious in his dress, unlike the *bella figura* of the fictional Sabini, he wore a flat cap, a suit with a waistcoat and usually a collarless shirt. For all that, he had a commanding presence. The bookmaker Prince remembered, 'He was the gentleman of the mob but he feared no one.' It was the fearless Sabini who would lead the fight against Kimber's Birmingham Gang and its allies.[543]

THE RACECOURSE WAR OF 1921

The Sabini Gang had come together by 1919, when a photo was taken of a group of well-dressed men about to go on a charabanc trip – presumably to the racing. This was before the racecourse war, and, amongst other gangsters, the photograph shows Darby, Joe and Harry 'Boy' Sabini and two of the Cortesi brothers, along with Billy Kimber, the leader of the Birmingham Gang, and Wag and Wal

McDonald of the Elephant Boys. It is noticeable that Alfie Solomon is not amongst them, even though he had been discharged from the Army by then. This could be because he was not yet involved in gangsterism, but it is also telling that no Jewish men at all are on the photograph. There can be little doubt that anti-Semitism infected the Birmingham Gang and its London allies.

The cordial relations between Kimber's alliance and the Sabinis broke down, however, in the spring of 1921 over the chance to make big money. Through their strong connection with Emanuel and Beresford and attracted by the large sums to be made from the 'services' to bookmakers, 'the Sabinis took up the cudgels', as Divall expressed it, in defence of the East End bookies.[544] They were supported by Alfie Solomon and Emanuel's Jewish terrors as well as by Alf White's King's Cross Gang.[545]

But Kimber was not prepared to back down in the face of the new alliance, and on 21 March Darby Sabini was surrounded by a mob at Greenford Trotting track. Cries of 'Shoot the —' and 'I'll murder him' were heard before Sabini pulled a revolver and fired shots. He was rescued by the police. The gun was loaded with blank cartridges, although Sabini was found to have a cut-throat razor on him.[546] This was a favourite weapon of the racecourse gangs and it inflicted terrible wounds. Greeno once broke up a fight in which a bookmaker was attacked by some of the Bethnal Green mob, but the victim's face was 'criss-crossed like a lace curtain'.[547]

When Sabini was remanded over the shooting incident,

he was granted bail and was able to pay the large amount of £200 himself, whilst two other men each paid sureties of £100.[548] The charge of shooting against him was dismissed but he was fined £10 for being in possession of a gun without a licence.[549] Brian McDonald suspected that 'money changed hands' for the favourable police report that led to Sabini's acquittal for the main offence. His belief would seem to be corroborated by Arthur Harding, who recalled that Emanuel had 'the police buttoned up' and could get criminals out of trouble.[550]

Whether or not that was the case, it was apparent that both sides were matched evenly and so Kimber agreed to a meeting at Sabini's house in Collier Street, Kings Cross, on the evening of 27 March to discuss splitting the country's racecourse rackets between the gangs. Kimber was accompanied by George Sage and Wag McDonald, whilst Sabini had invited other racing men but not Solomon. It may be that an agreement was reached but, after some drinking and singing, Kimber and his friends went to leave. According to the only witness, as they moved into the passageway, they spotted Solomon, and 'one of the men turned round and said, "What do you want, you Jew!"'[551]

Shots were fired and Kimber was later found unconscious on the pavement. He had suffered a wound in the side and was rushed to hospital.[552] Solomon then went to the police and said that he had shot Kimber by accident after the head of the 'Birmingham gang of terrors' had shouted, 'What are you doing here, you Jew? Get out or I'll shoot you!' Solomon then knocked a revolver out of Kimber's hand and in the ensuing struggle, the weapon went off. Frightened, Solomon ran away. In court, when he was committed to trial, Kimber stated that he did not know who had shot him, declaring that if Solomon 'said that he shot me then he is a coward. Only cowards carry revolvers. I would rather blow out my brains than use one on anyone.'[553] Although Solomon was charged with unlawful wounding, Kimber refused to say anything thereafter, and at the trial at the Old Bailey, the judge directed the jury to return a verdict of not guilty.[554]

There followed six months of violence on the racecourses of southern England and in London. On 4 April, at Alexandra Park, there was fighting between the Sabini Gang and their Jewish allies and the Birmingham Gang, one of whom was later acquitted of attempted murder. Then, on 2 June 1921, there took place what *The Times* declared was 'The Epsom Road Battle'.[555] Originally believed to be a Sinn Fein riot, in fact it was a vicious attack after racing by a large number of the Birmingham Gang on Leeds bookmakers. Mostly Jewish, the latter were thought to be changing allegiance from Kimber and were thus targeted. Twenty-two men were found guilty of causing grievous bodily harm. They included hardened criminals who had been convicted for manslaughter, robbery with violence, unlawful and malicious wounding and attempted murder.

In a separate case, two other members of the Birmingham Gang were jailed for demanding money from bookmakers with threats at the Epsom Meeting. They had made a lot of money, obtaining £1 each from 50 bookies. One of them was

Charles Franklin, of the infamous Garrison Lane Vendetta, who was sentenced to three months' imprisonment.[556]

Kimber was obviously weakened by the loss of so many fighting men, but in August 1921, he led an attack on London bookmakers and their workers at Bath Races. Amongst them was Alfie Solomon. As he and his clerk, Charles Bild, were walking to the course, a crowd of roughs closed round Bild and 'blows were rained on him from hammers, sticks, iron bars, and finally a sandbag'. Covered with blood and almost senseless, he managed to escape and reached Bath's Pump Rooms, where a maid tore up a sheet to bandage his wounds and from whence he was taken to hospital. As for Solomon, he had been knocked out by a hammer. Four wounds were inflicted to his head and, as he lay bleeding, he was violently kicked and hit. His assailants then headed off and he was also taken to hospital.[557]

Solomon's brother, Harry, was another victim. During the meeting he was chased by a gang of men. Frightened, he produced a revolver and directed it point blank at his pursuers. One of them knocked it out of his out of his hand and another struck Solomon. As he lay prostrate on the ground, he was hit on the head with a hammer. Saved by the police, Solomon was charged with carrying a revolver and ammunition without a licence and with intent to endanger life. He appeared in court with a bandage around his head and was sentenced to one month in jail.[558]

Kimber was one of two men charged with the unlawful wounding of Charles Bild, who did not turn up in court and the case collapsed. However, it was announced 'that there would be no more trouble of this kind' as the feud between certain sections of the race-going fraternity had been amicably settled.[559] It had because Kimber had been outwitted. In August 1921, Beresford and Emanuel had formed the Bookmakers and Backers Racecourse Protection Association (BPA), becoming president and vice-president respectively.[560] Within a month, they had appointed eight stewards, at the high wage of £6 a week, to protect southern bookmakers from the Birmingham Gang and their allies. Among these stewards were Darby Sabini and some of his men and Philip Emanuel, a relative of Edward Emanuel.[561] Despite this connection to gangsters, the new association was welcomed by the Jockey Club, which ran many of the leading racecourses in England.[562] Emanuel and the Sabinis benefitted from this legitimacy, which made it difficult for them to be challenged by Kimber and his men.

With both sides at a stand-off and with the press demanding action from the police against the 'hooliganism' and 'ruffianism' on the turf, a meeting was held at Beresford's house. In effect, it was agreed to divide England into spheres of control for the racecourse protection rackets. Those in the north, Midlands and West Country would be run by the Birmingham Gang, which had new leaders; those in the south and East Anglia by the Sabinis and their allies. Most of the Birmingham Gang still lived in the city and they were satisfied. The truce with them held but Kimber and his London friends were angered and a new racecourse war broke out between them and the Sabini Gang and its allies.[563]

AFTERMATH

Stabbings, razor slashings, shootings and even an attack with a machete made the news.[564] In a fluid and rapidly changing scene, there were also disputes between allies and in September 1922, the BPA dispensed with the services of their stewards. This action followed complaints that included an allegation that they had demanded a royalty of a shilling on every set of lists that they sold to the bookies.[565]

Then on 20 November 1922, there was a violent confrontation in Little Italy itself when Harry 'Boy' and Darby Sabini were shot at by two of the Cortesi brothers in the Fratalanza Club.[566] They had also been stewards of the BPA and had apparently fallen out with the Sabinis over the selling of the racing lists to bookmakers. In giving evidence, Darby Sabini publicised the large sums of money that could be made. Each list was sold for five shillings and as much as £100–£200 a day could be made, giving an annual income of £3,000–£4,000. He added that the lists were now sold by the Association, but they were not.[567] Printed by Emanuel, who was on the way to legitimacy, they were sold by the Sabini Gang.

Dave Langham was the son of one of its enforcers, George Langham (Angelo Gianicoli) and he emphasised the amount of money that could be made from these sales. By the early 1930s, his family had moved from Saffron Hill to a house with an indoor bath and his father would come home from the races with money bags filled with silver. So many coins were there that they had to be poured into the bath, from which they could be divided up with his associates.[568]

No longer supported by the Cortesi brothers, in 1922 Darby Sabini had also lost his brother, Joe, who was sentenced to three years' imprisonment for shooting with intent to murder.[569] A few months later another major ally, Alf White, leader of the King's Cross Gang, was jailed.[570] Then in 1924, Alfie Solomon was sent down for three years.[571] He had been playing cards in the Eden Club, fictionalised in series two of the *Peaky Blinders* as the opulent jazz club owned by Darby Sabini. In reality, Brian McDonald described it as 'nothing more than a spieler occupying two floors above a garage, with a bar, card tables and a roulette wheel'.[572]

Solomon was in the company of his *éminence grise*, Emanuel, against whom another customer called Barney Blitz had a grudge. A former boxer and hard man, he argued with Emanuel who threw a drink over him. Blitz then hit Emanuel 'so hard with a glass that he lost all reason'. The two men were separated but Solomon seized a knife from a table and plunged it into Blitz's head, inflicting a fatal wound. Another man who tried to wrench the knife away was wounded. In his defence, Solomon stated that all he could remember 'was seeing Emanuel bleeding like pig from his head. I thought Blitz was going for him again.'[573]

Although the coroner's jury had delivered a verdict of wilful murder, the defence team stressed the violent character of Blitz, secured testaments of good character from the Jewish community and produced Solomon's medals and Army discharge papers in court.[574] As a result, he was fortunate to be was found guilty of manslaughter.[575] When first charged, he was described as 'a young man of

Jewish appearance who was smartly dressed in a long blue overcoat, grey hat, and brown shoes'.[576] In the Metropolitan Police Records he was documented as 5 foot 6½ inches, fair-complexioned and blue eyed with brown hair. Scars on his right wrist, left thumb, at the back of his neck, and on his upper lip were evidence of attacks by Kimber and others. Solomon also had tattoos. His left arm featured a shell, a lion and a Japanese woman with a fan, and on his right arm he had another Japanese woman.[577]

Despite the imprisonments of Solomon and others, the Sabini Gang continued to intimidate bookmakers. Darby Sabini, though, continued to escape conviction and in 1923, on the one occasion when he was charged with attacking a bookmaker with a knuckle duster, the case was dismissed.[578]

Yet soon Sabini himself was in trouble. Though he was adept at steering clear of arrest he made an error of judgement when he sued the *Topical Times* for alleged libel for naming him as the leader of a gang of blackmailers who terrorised bookmakers and carried revolvers. A weekly newspaper with a high sports content, the publication was owned by DC Thomson. In March 1924, under the headline 'How We Outwitted a Rival Gang', it revealed Sabini's criminal activities in a first-person piece by a gang member.[579]

Realising that the publication had too much evidence to show that he was a gangster, Sabini sought to end the action. In December 1925, he failed to turn up to the hearing. For their part, the defendants said that Sabini was associated with a gang of racecourse pests and their words were true in substance and fact, whilst they had voluminous particulars to support them. Judgement with costs was entered for them.[580] Sabini now owed D. C. Thomson over £700, but he did not attend a first meeting of his creditors on 10 June 1926. His address was unknown although he was still to be seen at racecourses, and it was suggested that he still made large sums selling racing cards.[581] A resolution for bankruptcy was passed.

Threatened with a warrant for his arrest, Sabini appeared at the London Bankruptcy Court on 29 June. Described as a thick-set man, he was now living in apartments in Russell Street, Brighton, with his wife and three children and he stressed that a lot of harm had been done to him by the article in the *Topical Times*. He denied that he was king of the Sabini Gang and that he was engaged in threatening bookmakers who refused to pay for particular pitches or to buy the racing lists he sold. Sabini revealed that these were sold for five shillings each, out of which he and another man made fivepence while the printer at Portsea Press made one shilling. Of course, this was Emanuel's printing company. Sabini said that bookmakers bought these cards because they were members of the BPA. No threats were made to them if they did not want to buy them.

Refuting the suggestion that he had made from £20,000 to £30,000 a year as head of the Sabini Gang, he laughed and said, 'No.' Out of his earnings at £8 a week he had to pay £1, 5 shillings a day in travelling expenses, and a further five shillings a day for food and drink – and he went racing most days. Finally, he admitted that he did not carry on his action against the newspaper publishers as he could not find the £75 the solicitor wanted for costs, adding that he had no assets.[582]

By now, strong action had been taken against the racecourse gangs by the Flying Squad, the specialist crime and operations section within the Metropolitan Police Service. The Jockey Club had also set up a department to supervise the rings (enclosures) at racecourses. Tainted by their employment of members of the Sabini Gang, the BPA had disassociated themselves from the Sabinis and formed Pitch Committees to protect and safeguard racecourse bookmakers' rights. In 1929, this approach was supported by the Jockey Club and thenceforth pitches were allocated not by the gangs but by racecourse personnel liaising with the local BPA.

It is likely that by now the Sabini Gang was led by Darby's youngest brother, Harry 'Boy', who was providing 'minders' and other services for West End drinking and gambling clubs. As for Darby Sabini, he remained in Brighton and was named as a bookmaker in 1929 when he was fined £5 for assaulting another bookie at Hove greyhound racing stadium.[583] His erstwhile ally, Alfie Solomon, had resumed bookmaking following his release from prison and, according to police records, had once again pulled together a race gang. In February 1930, he went with his men to Clacton greyhound racing stadium and demanded money from bookmakers. Solomon and his men were ejected from the stadium. However, he later claimed that he was the one who was threatened that evening by men from the Bethnal Green Gang of Dodger Mullins.[584]

A notorious terror who hated the Sabinis and their associates, in early 1936 Mullins was very badly slashed across his face and back with cut throat razors by Solomon's men.[585] To gain revenge, Mullins teamed up with the Hoxton Mob and Wal McDonald of the Elephant Boys at Lewes Races in June. They arrived with hatchets, knuckle dusters and other dangerous weapons. Solomon was struck several blows and wounded on his head but managed to run away, although his clerk was not so fortunate and was viciously beaten.[586]

This 'Battle of Lewes' aroused sensationalist and inaccurate headlines about a new race track war and the involvement of American mobsters.[587] It was nothing of the kind, as the ageing racecourse gangsters had been in decline since the mid-1920s, but the attack did inspire Graham Greene's novel *Brighton Rock* (1938).[588] His criminal characters were well drawn and not hyped up examples of media fantasy, although it has become assumed widely that the wealthy gangster Colleone is based upon Sabini.[589] Greene wrote to me in 1988, explaining that:

> My novel *Brighton Rock* it is true deals a little with something similar to the Sabini Gang but I have forgotten now what I may have known when I wrote it. In those days I used to go frequently to Brighton and once spent an evening with a member of a gang who introduced me to a certain amount of slang in use and took me to one of the meeting places of his fellow gangsters.[590]

Two years after the book's publication, in April 1940, Sabini was arrested at Hove dog track and subsequently interned under Defence Regulation 18B. He was detained because the Metropolitan Police and the Security Service (MI5) believed him to be a 'dangerous gangster and racketeer of the worst type' with fascist sympathies who was 'liable to lead internal insurrections against this country' at the behest of an occupying power. This was a most strange belief and one that the local chief constable and others doubted.[591]

Sabini was eventually released, and in June 1943, he and another man were sentenced to two years' hard labour for receiving stolen goods valued at £383.[592] Later described as a dealer, he died in 1950.[593] A legend arose that he had lived in a penthouse flat in Brighton but that when he died he had little money.[594] He actually lived at 16 Old Shoreham Road.[595] His wife died there in 1978 and left £16,730.[596]

By the mid-1920s, Kimber was also involved in West End nightclubs and he continued to operate rackets on racecourses in the south west of England.[597] On 19 July 1926, he married Elizabeth Garnham, a sister of his friend and ally, John Garnham of the Chapel Street Market Gang.[598] Kimber stated that he was a widower. He was – just, as Maud had died very recently.[599] But he and the McDonalds were still rowing with the Sabinis and in about 1927, he and Bert McDonald shot through the windows of the Griffin, a public house in Clerkenwell favoured by the Sabini Gang.

The two men then fled to America, where Brian McDonald believes that Kimber may have killed a man who did not pay him the money owed for a favour. From Arizona, Kimber and

Bert McDonald went to Los Angeles, where Wag McDonald was living. He had fled there to avoid arrest after the Battle of Epsom in 1921 and was now a bodyguard to Jack Dragna, the city's Mafia boss. Kimber moved on to Chicago, where he was said to have been hidden by Murray Humphreys.[600] Born of Welsh parents, he was a leading figure in Al Capone's notorious gang.[601]

In his book *Elephant Boys*, Brian McDonald recounts the exciting tale of his uncle Wag in America, who was a great friend of the actor Victor McGlagen and who appeared in crowd scenes in films.[602] There is no evidence to suggest that Kimber did so or that he became actively involved in Capone's gang, and there is equally no evidence to support the suggestion that there was a strong connection between Kimber's Birmingham Gang and American mobsters other than in the maverick life of Jimmy Spenser.[603]

Spenser, or 'Birmingham's Gunman', as he was called in the *Birmingham Daily Gazette* in March 1933, moved to London and joined Kimber in the early 1920s.[604] According to Brian McDonald, his real name was Francis Harold Guest and he became friends with the Elephant Boys.[605] As recounted in his book *Limey*, in about 1925 Spenser jumped ship in America, where he became a gunman for Jack Brussi, a gangster and hijacker in Long Island City. Moving on to California, he joined the outfit of the racketeer Niley Payne, then teamed up with Wag and Bert McDonald and finally ended up in San Quentin Prison. After his release, he was deported to Britain in 1932.[606]

Kimber had returned to England three years before and

become a bookmaker. He advertised himself in the later 1930s as 'Bill Kimber a reliable man' and became president of the Devon and Cornwall Bookmakers' Protection Association.[607] There was an irony in that, as it was the founding of the BPA in 1921 by his arch rival Emanuel that had sounded the death knell for Kimber's protection rackets on England's racecourses.

Kimber died in 1945. His obituary in the local newspaper asserted, 'His great interest in life, both personal and professional, was racing and he was well known and respected on every racecourse in England.' He left his widow, Elizabeth, their house at 10 Park Hill Road in Torquay and £3,665.[608] They had two daughters, one of whom was married to an RAF squadron leader and holder of the Distinguished Flying Cross. Having been sent to finishing school in Switzerland, they led very different lives to the children Kimber had abandoned in Birmingham.[609]

Kimber's nemesis, Emanuel, made even more money. By 1930, his Portsea Printing Works was in Hackney and he and his wife, Elizabeth, were living in a large house at 965 Finchley Road, Golders Green – a district which was attracting middle-class Jewish families.[610] He died in 1943.[611] His wife died seven years later and left £22,656 in her will, which was administered by her two daughters.[612]

As for Alfie Solomon, he died in 1947. His last known address in 1924 was Gerrard Street in Soho, close to where he had grown up in Covent Garden.[613] A will has not yet been found. Although their lives are fictionalised in the series *Peaky Blinders*, Billy Kimber, Alfie Solomon and

Darby Sabini were real people. Luca Changretta, the mafioso of series four, was not.

AFTERWORD

In a brutal fight in episode two, series three of *Peaky Blinders*, John Shelby single-handedly assaults Angel Changretta and his minder. The son of the Birmingham Italian gangster, Vicente Changretta, he has been caught unawares after walking downstairs to a cellar-like area in a Chinese laundry. Directed to a hanger laden with cleaned suits, he pulls them apart to find the one marked with his name – but is startled to see John Shelby smirking dangerously through the gap. Swiftly the peaky blinder punches Changretta to the ground and then, with a heavy cosh, batters his minder into unconsciousness. His boss is struggling to get up but Shelby turns, kicks him back down and drags him around. Changretta slumps on to his back and Shelby takes off his peaky cap and slashes the right cheek of his enemy. In terrible pain, Changretta covers his face as blood seeps between his fingers.[614] In the ensuing wars between the two gangs, Angel Changretta is killed and his father is assassinated. Their deaths enrage another son Luca Changretta. A mafioso from New York, he vows revenge and becomes Tommy Shelby's main protagonist in series four.

The Changretta Gang did not exist, but from the late nineteenth century there was a real Changretta family in Birmingham. Its members were the antithesis of the fictional Italian gangsters of the series, and the use of their unusual name draws into sharp relief the tension between historical fiction and historical realities.

The real family arrived in Birmingham with Martino Ciangretta, which became spelled as 'Changretta' in England. Hard-working and peaceful, he was devoted to his family and made a positive and long-lasting impact upon Birmingham. He belonged to a small and law-abiding Italian community which had no connections with Sicily, the Mafia or gangsters. That community had developed from the late 1870s, when burgeoning numbers of southern Italians emigrated because of severe poverty.

The first links of a striking chain migration were formed by young people from the communes of Picinisco, Atina and Gallinaro and the village of Carnello in the Comino Valley. Now in the province of Frosinone, they are close to the town of Sora.[615] The emigrants settled in Bartholomew Street and Duddeston Row, close to the modern Millennium Point. They did so because of the availability of cheap back-to-back housing for rent; the proximity to the Bull Ring, which gave the opportunity to earn money by playing barrel organs to shoppers; and the closeness of St Michael's Roman Catholic church on Moor Street – which came to be regarded as the Italians' church.[616]

Baptismal and marriage certificates point to the importance of a Giuseppe Delicata in beginning the chain in the early 1880s. He and his family were the base for newcomers connected to them by communal and kinship loyalties.[617] But he was also a *padrone*, a man established in England who returned regularly to Italy to find youths whom he could bring back to Birmingham. He would pay for their passage and board and keep, but they had to reimburse him by labouring for him for a specified time. Their task was to walk the streets playing a barrel organ.[618] One of them was Martino Changretta.

Born in 1868, he stated that he was from Sora, as did all the Birmingham Italians from the Comino Valley.[619] He arrived in 1887 in his late teens.[620] Six years later, in February 1893, Ciangetto Martino, as he was named in a newspaper report, and another 'piano grinder' were assaulted. Speaking through an interpreter, he told the court that they had been playing on the Hagley Road when they were told to leave by two other Italians as their *padrone* had worked the road for thirteen years. If they did not do so, they would be killed. The threat was ignored, but soon after, one of the men struck Changretta on the lip and the head with a small knife and beat him with an iron bar. The assailant was fined merely two shillings.[621]

By this time, Martino Changretta was twenty-five and he had met his wife, Ann Kitchen. Their granddaughter, Victoria Hooper, wrote that although her grandmother had been born in Chipping Norton in the Cotswolds in 1873, the family had moved to Bartholomew Street by the mid-1880s. In the Italian Quarter: 'Gran met Martino Ciangretta, a strapping dark-eyed, curly-haired Italian. He was well over six foot while Gran was a tiny, little young woman of 4 foot 10 inches with long blonde hair that was waist length. The cart was put before the horse, so to speak, and they were married at St Michael's in October 1893 and my Aunt Chris was born a month later.'[622]

The Changrettas had fourteen children. Another grand-daughter, Pam Ovethrow, explained that the oldest was born in 1893 and the youngest in 1917. Four of them died in infancy. She was told that her grandfather had gone to America, 'to see if it would be a better life for his family. It didn't work out and he came back to Annie and the children.'[623]

Sometime after his marriage, Changretta left Delicata's service and became a bricklayer. By 1922, he was the foreman in charge of the work to clear the Broad Street site for Birmingham's Hall of Memory, which would honour the men from the city who had died in the First World War. Amongst some, that role aroused anger and letters were written to the local newspapers asking why foreigners had been taken on instead of those who had fought and helped pay for the memorial. The contractors replied that of the sixteen men employed, the only foreigner was an Italian, who was an expert in demolition work, whilst their foreman was a naturalised Englishman.

Changretta himself also responded to the critics in the name of T(homas) Martin, the English name he had adopted.

He emphasised that he had been in Birmingham for thirty-five years, that he was married to an Englishwoman and that he had served in the Boer War. Moreover, his oldest son had made the supreme sacrifice, having been killed in action during the First World War. The other 'foreigners' were his sons-in-law, 'born of an English mother in this city'. They had each served 'in the late war and went through the thick of it'. Expressing his personal hurt at the criticisms, Changretta stated that he was in 'in charge of a job that is to be a memorial to the fallen, among whom, if the names are inscribed, will be that of my son'.[624] So it was. Gunner K. G. Changretta of the Royal Garrison Artillery is remembered in Birmingham's Roll of Honour in the Hall of Memory.

Changretta went on to start his own demolition business in Lawley Street, doing some large jobs for Birmingham Council and also clearing out all the inside walls of Curzon Hall so that it could be converted into the West End Cinema.[625]

However, the ageing Martino and Annie Changretta were to suffer more sorrows in the Second World War. Their house in Belmont Row was bombed in 1942 and, as Hooper recollected, 'Gran and my cousins, Alfie and Ray, had to be dug out of the ruins with petrol pouring down the street from the garage next door. Thank God they were all OK, although Gran went stone deaf afterwards. More sadness was to follow with the death of Uncle Vic in Italy in September 1943. His name continues to live on in the family as he was so loved by all his nieces and nephews.'[626]

Victor Changretta was the youngest child, having been

born in 1917. He served as a private with the 1/6th Battalion, the Queen's Royal Regiment (West Surrey). A married man aged twenty-five, he was killed in action on 30 September 1943. Poignantly, he died in the Allied landings at Salerno, Italy – his father's country. A year later, his extended family remembered him with ten notices in the 'In Memoriam' column of the *Birmingham Mail*. His wife, Florrie, wrote that he had marched bravely away to fight for Britain.[627] Industrious, law-abiding, honourable and true, the real Changrettas gave to their country and to their city, unlike the real gangsters of England in the 1920s.

Yet it is not respectable and respected real families like the Changrettas that have an alluring appeal for drama, it is glamorised fictional gangsters. As with the mafiosi, they are held up as caring for their families and defenders of their communities. Men of honour, they inflict violence only upon opposing gangsters or on people who have violated a code of conduct that is regarded as 'moral'. Those who have no dealings with such mobsters have nothing to fear; wives and motherly women are respected, the elderly are honoured, and children are protected. Loyal, truthful, unafraid, trustworthy and principled, they are admired as anti-establishment figures who have created an 'alternative' society. Though outsiders and criminals, they are successful, moneyed, well-dressed and respected. Psychologically distant from onlookers, the gangster thus becomes a romanticised figure – like Tommy Shelby.[628]

In reality, there was nothing romantic or glamorous about the racecourse gangsters of 1920s England who have been brought to the fore in the series *Peaky Blinders*. Billy Kimber was a pickpocket and extortionist who became prosperous through brute force and the fear of violence. Disloyal to his first wife and their children, he abandoned them to a life of poverty. Though regarded by some as 'the gentleman of the gang', Darby Sabini was another thug who gained his wealth through open intimidation and ruthless attacks on those who crossed him. Although not as powerful as either Sabini or Kimber, like them Alfie Solomon was violent and after he killed a man in a row in the Eden Club, was fortunate to be found guilty of manslaughter and not murder, for which he would have been hanged.

None of them, nor others such as Edward Emanuel and Harry 'Boy' Sabini, were men to be admired as honourable, principled or moral. And nor were the real peaky blinders and sloggers of back-street Birmingham. Vicious youths and men who revelled in inflicting pain and bloody injuries upon their enemies, many were akin to John Sheldon, who shunned fair fighting and instead fought mob-handed and with weapons.

Others were the same as my great grandfather, Edward Derrick, a petty thief who physically abused his wife, assaulted a policeman and wounded another person. They were despicable men and those who should be admired are those who stood up to them. People like Edward Cook, who confronted sloggers; like Constable Lines, who was killed by a gang in saving another officer; and like the courageous Harriet Chaplin, who followed ruffians who had assaulted a number of men and identified them to the police.

And we should also admire the great majority of the poor, who did not turn to criminality and violence and who had to endure the reign of the peaky blinders until it was ended. Despite living in an unfair and mostly uncaring society, and despite the unending battle against the unrelenting enemy of poverty, they strove daily to stay clean, honest and decent. In the midst of what ill-informed onlookers denigrated as 'slums', mothers, aunts, grandmothers and big sisters, in particular, forged viable neighbourhoods through their kinship and neighbourly relationships. Unlike the peaky blinders and the racecourse gangsters, it was these women who were the ones who were loyal, honourable, truthful and principled and who adhered to a moral code of conduct. It is they whom we should respect.

SELECT FURTHER READING

The detailed Endnotes list many books and articles for further reading. This list highlights those that are most pertinent to reading on the peaky blinders and gangs of the 1920s.

Carl Chinn, *The Real Peaky Blinders, Billy Kimber, the Birmingham Gang and the Racecourse Wars of the 1920s* (Studley 2014).

Andrew Davies, 'Youth, Violence, and Courtship in Late-Victorian Birmingham: 'The Case of James Harper and Emily Pimm', *History of the Family*, volume 11, issue 2 (2006) pp. 107–20.

Andrew Davies, *The Gangs of Manchester. The Story of the Scuttlers Britain's First Youth* Cult (Preston 2008).

Philip Gooderson, *The Gangs of Birmingham. From the Sloggers to the Peaky Blinders* (Lancashire 2010).

Brian McDonald, *Elephant Boys Tales of London and Los Angeles Underworlds* (Edinburgh and London, 2000).

Brian McDonald, *Gangs of London. 100 Years of Mob Warfare* (Wrea Green, 2010).

Heather Shore 'Criminality and Englishness in the Aftermath: The racecourse wars of the 1920s', *Twentieth Century British History,* volume 22, issue 4 (1 December 2011) pp. 474–497.

Heather Shore 'Rogues of the Racecourse. Racing men and the press in interwar Britain', *Media History*, volume 20, issue 4: (Published online: 28 Aug 2014) pp. 352–367.

Heather Shore, *London's Criminal Underworlds, c.1720– c.1930. A Social and Cultural History* (Basingstoke 2015).

ENDNOTES

1 **Introduction**
Nick Cave and the Bad Seeds,
Songwriters: Mick Harvey, Nick
Cave and Thomas Wydler, from
Let Love In, produced by Tony
Cohen (Mute Records, 1994)

2 Series 1, Episode 1, *Peaky Blinders*
(BBC2, 2013).

3 Lanre Bakare & Gwilym
Mumford, 'Peaky Blinders:
Brummie Boardwalk or shop-
soiled Sopranos?', *Guardian*,
29 September 2014 (https://
www.theguardian.com/tv-and-
radio/2014/sep/29/peaky-blinders-
cillian-murphy); and Alex
Fletcher, 'Peaky Blinders' review:
'Did the British "Boardwalk
Empire" cut it?', *Digital Spy*, 12
September 2013 (http://www.
digitalspy.com/tv/news/a514949/
peaky-blinders-review-did-the-
british-boardwalk-empire-cut-it/)

4 Julian Ralph, 'The best-governed
city in the world', *Harper's
Magazine* (June 1890); and see,
for example, 'Street Ruffianism in
Birmingham', *Portsmouth Evening
News* (21 September 1883).

5 'Black Country Memories: Black
Country Irish', *Express and Star*
(14, 21 and 28 May 2009).

6 'The Perils of the Police',
Birmingham Mail (hereafter *BM*)
(12 June 1871).

7 'Balsall Heath Police Court', *BM*
(13 February 1891).

8 'Penn Street Industrial School,
Birmingham, Warwickshire',
http://www.childrenshomes.org.
uk/BirminghamPennStreetIS/

9 Edward Derrick, Calendar of
Prisoners, General Quarter
Sessions of the Peace,

QS/B/20/65 (29 Oct 1906).

10 William Chinn, Interview, BirminghamLives Archive hereafter *BLA* (1979).

11 'For the Sake of Beer', *BM* (30 July 1906).

12 Carl Chinn, *The Real Peaky Blinders* (Studley, 2015) p.16.

13 TNA, Divorce Court File: 4333. Appellant: Ada Derrick. Respondent: Edward Derrick. Type: Wife's petition for divorce [wd], J 77/1744/4333 (1921)

14 'Woman's Divorce', *Birmingham Daily Gazette* [hereafter *BDG*] (25 April 1923).

15 'Cleaned Up Black Spots', *BDG* (24 August 1935).

Chapter One: Before the Peaky Blinders: The Slogging Gangs

16 Michael Bradley, 'Birmingham's real Peaky Blinders', *BBC News, West Midlands* (12 September 2013, http://www.bbc.co.uk/news/uk-england-birmingham-24047750).

17 Charles Anthony Vince, *History of the Corporation, vol. III* (Birmingham, 1903) pp.226, 228-229 and 23; and Joseph Trevor Jones, *History of the Corporation of Birmingham, vol. V (1915–1935), part II* (Birmingham, 1940), pp.354 and 373. The noticeable jump in population is explained by the extension of Birmingham in 1911 to bring in the local authorities of Aston, Erdington, Handsworth, Kings Norton and Yardley and their various districts.

18 'Year's Crime in Birmingham', *BDG* (1 September 1920).

19 Jones, *History of the Corporation of Birmingham, vol. V, part II* (Birmingham, 1940) p.371; 'Glasgow Disorder', *The Scotsman* (1 February 1919); 'Riot Act read in Birkenhead', *Aberdeen Press and Journal* (4 August 1919); 'Mob Law', *Leicester Daily Post* (23 July 1919); and 'Serious Riots', *Leeds Mercury* (2 June 1919) p.9.

20 'Mons Man Killed in Cardiff Riots', *Globe* (13 June 1919); and 'The Racial Riots', *Hartlepool Northern Daily Mail* (12 June 1919).

21 'Hooliganism Redivivus', *BM* (5 November 1901).

22 'Sparring', *Morning Advertiser* (23 July 1824).

23 'Riot in Birmingham by the Slogging Gang', *Birmingham Daily Post* [hereafter *BDP*] (8 April 1872).

24 'The Slogging Gang', *BDP* (10 April 1872).

25 'The Slogging Gang', *BDP* (11 April 1872).

26 'A Caution to Juvenile Stone Throwers', *BDP* (3 June 1872).

27 See, for example, 'Burslem Stone Throwing Battle', *BDG* (27 April 1870).

28 'Infringement of the Bye-Laws', *BDG* (10 May 1872).

29 Jerry White, *The Worst Street in North London. Campbell Bunk, Islington, Between the Wars* (London, 1986), p.69.

30 Dyke Wilkinson, *Rough Roads. Reminiscences of a Wasted Life* (London, 1912), p.12.

31 Donald Philips, *From Biggles to Biggles: A Birmingham Childhood* (unpublished MS, no date; thanks to David Phillips), p.2.

32 George Wood, Interview, BLA (1985).

33 Fred Franklin, Interview, BLA (1982).

34 Buck Chinn, Interview, BLA (1989).

35 Jones, *History of the Corporation of Birmingham*, vol. V, part 2, p.373.

36 Sydney Hetherington, *From the Slums to Eastbourne's Belgravia* (unpublished MS, 1998), pp.16–17.

37 'Sunday Nuisances', *Birmingham Journal* [hereafter *BJ*] (16 November 1839).

38 Geoffrey Floy, *Policing Birmingham: a study of a borough police force, 1839–1914* (University of Birmingham, M.Phil., 1997), pp.5–56 and p.92.

39 See for example: 'Bathing in the Canal', *BDP* (26 August 1859); 'A Pigeon Flyer Caught' and 'Obstructions', *BDP* (12 April 1859); 'The Black Your Boots Nuisance', *BDP* (26 August 1859).

40 'Church Pastoral Society', *Aris's Birmingham Gazette* [hereafter *ABG*] (17 March 1856).

41 'Crusade against Street Gambling', *BJ* (27 September 1857).

42 'Caution to Street Gamblers', *BJ* (12 November 1853).

43 'Assault on the Police', *BJ* (2 May 1857).

44 'Gambling in the Streets and Assaulting the Police', *BDP* (28 April 1858).

45 'Police Crusade against Pitch and Toss in the Streets', *BJ* (1 September 1860); and, for example, 'New Vauxhall', *BDP* (5 April 1860).

46 'Sabbath Breaking and the Police', *BDP* (11 April 1861).

47 Floy, *Policing Birmingham*, p.128.

48 J. T. Bunce, *History of the Corporation of Birmingham, vol. II* (Birmingham, 1885), pp.294 and 300.

49 Barbara Weinberger, *Law Breakers and Law Enforcers in the*

Late Victorian City: Birmingham 1867–1877 (University of Warwick Ph.D. Thesis, 1981) p.231.

50 See for example, 'Street Ruffianism in the Ascendant', *The Era* (6 December 1863).

51 ''Street Ruffians', *ABG* (18 June 1864).

52 'Correspondence', *BDP* (7 July 1866).

53 'The Street Gambling Nuisance', *ABG* (23 May 1868).

54 Pitch and Toss', *BDG* (4 April 1871).

55 Gooderson, *The Gangs of Birmingham*, p.77.

56 'Barford Street', *BDG* (10 April 1871).

57 'Correspondence', *BDP* (16 March 1868); 'Capture of a Gang of Roughs', *BDP* (8 June 1870).

58 'Street Ruffians', *BDG* (28 September 1870); and 'News of the Day', *BDP* (8 November 1870).

59 'A Riot', *BDP* (4 May 1871).

60 Bunce, *History of the Corporation of Birmingham, vol. II*, pp.294 and 300.

61 'Eleven Weeks Ruffianism in Birmingham', *BDP* (11 April 1873).

62 'Rowdyism in Birmingham', *BDP* (12 August 1873).

63 'Street Ruffianism in Birmingham', *BDP* (1 April 1873).

64 'Eleven Weeks Ruffianism in Birmingham', BDP (11 April 1873).

65 'The Slogging Gang', *BDP* (29 March 1873).

66 'The Slogging Gang', *BDP* (22 September 1873); 'A Terror to the Neighbourhood' *BDP*, (30 October 1873).

67 Weinberger, *Law Breakers and Law Enforcers in the Late Victorian City*, pp.233–38.

68 'Ruffianism in Birmingham. Dastardly Assaults', *BDP* (24 June 1873).

69 'News of the Day', *BDP* (2 July 1873).

70 'News of the Day' (2 July 1873) and 'Warwickshire Assizes', *BDP* (9 July 1874).

71 'A Caution to Rioters', *BDP* (8 July 1874).

72 'The Barn Street 'Sloggers', *BDP* (12 September 1874).

73 'Incidents of the 'Slogging Gang'', BM (28 September 1874).

74 1871 Census, TNA, Class: RG10; Piece: 3086; Folio: 129; Page: 59; GSU roll: 838895.

75 1881 Census, TNA, Class: RG11; Piece: 2987; Folio: 23; Page: 39; GSU roll: 1341714.

76 'Incidents of the 'Slogging Gang', *BM* (28 September 1874).

ENDNOTES

77 Weinberger, *Law Breakers and Law Enforcers in the Late Victorian City*, p.174.

78 Gooderson, *The Gangs of Birmingham*, p.35.

79 The 'Murphy Riots'. Demolition of Park Street, Birmingham 17 and 18 June 1867 (Birmingham, 1867), p.9.

80 Patsy Davis, 'Birmingham's Irish Community and the Murphy Riots of 1867', *Midland History* 31 (2006), pp.50–51.

81 'Sunday Riots', *BDP* (30 April 1872).

82 Gooderson, *Gangs of Birmingham*, p 111

83 'Violent Assault upon "A Copper"', *BDP* (30 May 1872).

84 'Our Roughs' and 'A Warning to Street Rioters', *BM* (14 July 1874).

85 'The Stone-Throwing Nuisance at Ashted', *BDP* (23 March 1875).

86 'Navigation Street Riot. Death of Police-Constable Lines', *BDP* (25 March 1875).

87 'The Riot in Navigation Street. The Sentences', *BDP* (13 July 1875).

88 'Murder of PC Lines', *BWP* (27 May 1955).

89 'The Suppression of Rowdyism in Birmingham' and 'News of the Day' *BDP* (21 May 1875).

90 'More Persecution of Witnesses' *BDP* (19 July 1875).

91 'News of the Day' *BDP* (21 May 1875) and 'The Suppression of Rowdyism in Birmingham', *BDP* (21 May 1875).

92 'News of the Day', *BDP* (15 February 1876).

93 'Birmingham Watch Committee', *BDP* (28 February 1877).

94 'Street Crimes in Birmingham.-A warm dis-.' The *Times* [London, England] 28 Nov. 1877: 12. The Times Digital Archive. Web. 28 June 2018.

95 *Weinberger, Law Breakers and Law Enforcers in the Late Victorian City, pp.63–64.*

96 J. T. Bunce, *History of the Corporation of Birmingham, vol. II* (Birmingham, 1885), p.300.

97 See, for example, 'A Street Waif', *BM* (25 March 1881).

98 'Sunday Gambling at Aston', *BDP* (28 April 1885).

99 *'News of the Day', BDP* (8 May 1883).

100 Lil Perry, 'Old Days of Aston', BLA (1978) and for London see White, *The Worst Street in North London*, pp.118–119.

101 'Slogging Gangs' in Birmingham', *BM* (5 June 1882).

102 'Street Ruffianism', *BM* (13 September 1882); and 'Revival of the Slogging Gangs' *BM* (11 August 1882).

103 "Birmingham Watch Committee', *BM* (10 October 1882).

104 'A Warning to Stone Throwers', *BDP* (1 April 1884).

105 'A Warning to Street Ruffians', BDP (21 July 1886).

106 'The Aston Slogging Gang', *BDP* (18 August 1886).

107 'Street Rowdyism', *BDP* (11 August 1886; 'Stone-throwing', *BDP* (13 April 1886). More Attacks on Policemen', *BDP* (23 November 1886); and 'The Aston Slogging Gang' *BDP* (4 October 1888).

108 'Alleged Serious Wounding', *BDP* (22 December 1888).

109 'News of the Day', *BDP* (1 September 1888).

110 'Punishment for "Sloggers"', *BDP* (26 February 1889).

111 'A Violent Assault', *BDP* (20 February 1889).

112 'Ruffianism at Aston', *BDP* (31 July 1889).

113 Malcolm Archibald, *Liverpool Gangs, Vice and Packet Rats: 19 Century Crime and Punishment* (Edinburgh, 2015), pp.171–182; Heather Shore, *London's Criminal Underworlds, c.1720–c.1930: A Social and Cultural History* (Basingstoke, 2015), pp.141–166 and for London, see also Brian McDonald, *Gangs of London: 100 Years of Mob*

Warfare (Wrea Green, 2010), pp.59–73; and Andrew Davies, *The Gangs of Manchester: The Story of the Scuttlers Britain's First Youth Cult* (Preston, 2008) pp.38–141.

114 Davies, *Gangs of Manchester*, pp.17–18.

115 'Members of the 'Slogging Gang'', *BDP* (6 April 1886); and 'Street Rowdyism', *BDP* (11 August 1886).

116 'Deeds of Violence', *Liverpool Mercury* (4 August 1887); and 'Assaulted by a Slogging Gang', *BDP* (21 September 1888).

117 'A Slogging Gang', *BDP* (24 July 1889); 'The Outrage by Militia Men at Small Heath', *BDP* (2 July 1889); 'An Ornament to the Slogging Gang', *BDP* (1 July 1889); 'A Slogging Gang', *BDP* (13 June 1889); 'A 'Slogging Gang' Broken Up', *BDP* (1 June 1889); and 'Tackling 'Slogging Gangs'', *BDP* (27 February 1889).

118 'Notes and Comments', *Sheffield Daily Telegraph* (10 June 1882).

Chapter Two: The City of Peaky Blinders

119 Series 1, Episode 2, *Peaky Blinders* (BBC2, 2013). For a full discussion of tossing, see Chinn, *Better Betting*, pp.85–93.

ENDNOTES

120 Louise Mellor, 'Steven Knight on Peaky Blinders, Series 2', Den Of Geek (11 September 2013) https://www.denofgeek.com/tv/peaky-blinders/27113/steven-knight-on-peaky-blinders-birmingham-accents-working-class-drama-sam-neill-cillian-murphy-more

121 John Crace, 'Peaky Blinders; The Guilty – TV review', *Guardian* (13 September 2013) https://www.theguardian.com/tv-and-radio/2013/sep/13/peaky-blinders-tv-review

122 'Incidents of Full Career. Campaign Against the 'Peaky Blinders'', *Warwick and Warwickshire Advertiser* (2 November 1929).

123 R. E. Corder, 'The Seamy Side' *Daily Mail* [London, England] 3 April 1929: 8. *Daily Mail* Historical Archive.

124 'Belt and Buckle Days. Saga of Birmingham's Peaky Blinders', *BM* (15 April 1939).

125 'Death of Norman Tiptaft. Vigilante Extraordinary', *BDP* (14 October 1970).

126 'Mr Butler Urged to Punish or Resign', *BDP* (20 July 1961).

127 Norman Tiptaft, *The Individualist* (Birmingham, 1954).

128 John Douglas, *A Walk Down Summer Lane* (1st published 1977, London, 1983 ed.), p.126.

129 Pauline and Bernard Mannion, *The Summer Lane and Newtown of the Years between the Wars 1918–1938* (Birmingham, 1985), pp.1, 31 and 81.

130 'Gang Warfare and the 'Peaky Blinders', Letter from George Morris, *Birmingham Weekly Post* [hereafter *BWP*] (6 May 1955).

131 Arthur L. Matthison, *Less Paint, More Vanity* (London, 1937), pp.62–63.

132 'A Cowardly Rogue', *BDP* (29 October 1891); 'Table Talk', *BM* (11 October 1890), and 'Local News and Jottings', *BM* (25 June 1891).

133 'The 'Peaky Blinders' Barber', (*BM* 30 May 1914).

134 'Man Found Drowned', *BDP* (19 May 1891).

135 F. Atkins, Letter, (15 October 1936), cited in Gooderson, *The Gangs of Birmingham*, p.217.

136 'Letter from Norma K. Beattie', BLA, (19 July 1987).

137 Corinne Brazier, 'Potentially the oldest police custody photo... in the world?-*WM Peelers* (19 March 2018) [https://www.wmpeelers.com/single-post/2018/03/19/Potentially-the-oldest-police-custody-photo-in-the-world accessed 24 June 2018).

138 V. W. Garrett, *A Man in the Street* (London, 1939), pp.65–6.

139 Fred Sutton, Interview, BLA (1989).

140 'Table Talk', BM (30 May 1896); 'Table Talk', *BM* (14 May 1904); and 'The 'Peaky Blinders' Barber' (30 May 1914).

141 The 'Peaky Blinders' Barber', *BM* (30 May 1914).

142 'Local News and Jottings', *BM* (13 August 1906).

143 Geoffrey Pearson (2008) Disturbing continuities: 'peaky blinders' to 'hoodies', Criminal Justice Matters, 65:1, 6-7, DOI: 10.1080/09627250608553010.

144 Davies, *Gangs of Manchester*, p.22. See also Charles E. B. Russell, *Manchester Boys: Sketches of Manchester Boys at Work and Play* (Manchester 1905), p.16, where it is stated that a scuttler wore 'a peaked cap rather over one eye'.

145 J. R. C. 'Peaky Blinders', *Central Literary Magazine* vol. XIV, no. 2, (April 1879) p.71.

146 Andrew Davies, 'Youth, violence, and courtship in late-Victorian Birmingham: The case of James Harper and Emily Pimm', *History of the Family*, 11 (2006), p.111.

147 Shore, *London's Criminal Underworlds*, p.165.

148 See, for example, 'Sidelights on Low Life. Birmingham "Peaky" sent to Prison', *BM* (26 May 1900); Davies, 'Youth, Violence, and Courtship in Late-Victorian Birmingham'.

149 See Alan Mayne, *The Imagined Slum: Newspaper representation in three cities, 1870–1914* (Leicester, 1993) and Alan Mayne, 'Representing the slum', *Urban History*, Volume (17 May 1990), pp.66–84.

150 Davies, 'Youth, Violence, and Courtship in Late-Victorian Birmingham', pp.108–09 and 118.

151 'The Peaky's Courtship', *BDM* (19 November 1898).

152 'Table Talk', *BM* (14 May 1904).

153 Benny Green, 'Introduction', to Clarence Rook, *The Hooligan Nights* (first published 1899, new edition Oxford 1979), p.viii.

154 2–7 'My Bloke's a Peaky' (Roud 24185) *Cecilia Costello, Old Fashioned Songs*.

155 Davies, *Gangs of Manchester*, pp.277–295.

156 J. R. C. 'Peaky Blinders', p.71.

157 'Slogging Gang', *Lakes Herald* (7 May 1897).

158 'Brummagem Beauties', *Sheffield Evening Telegraph* (29 July 1897).

159 *The Wellington Journal & Shrewsbury News* (26 August 1899)

160 'A Man's Skull Fractured', *BM* (24 March 1890).

161 'The Birmingham "Slogging Gangs"', *St James's Gazette* (9 April 1890).

162 "Slogging Gangs" of Birmingham', *Aberdeen Evening Express* (10 April 1890); 'Slogging Gangs', *Chichester Observer* (16 April 1890).

163 Gooderson, *The Gangs of Birmingham*, pp.219–219.

164 'Serious Charges of Assault', *BM* (28 May 1890).

165 'A Brutal Assault', *BM* (25 June 1890).

166 1891 Census, TNA, Class: RG12; Piece: 2407; Folio: 10; Page: 16.

167 'The Crusade Against Ruffianism', *BD* (16 April 1890).

168 'The Highgate Street Slogging Gang', *BM* (11 April 1890); 'Ruffianism in Birmingham', *BM* (12 April 1890).

169 'A Slogging Gang at Perry Barr', *BM* (11 April 1890); 'The Sparkbrook Slogging Gang', *BDP* (10 April 1890).

170 'The Chief Constable and the Sloggers', *BM* (23 April 1890).

171 'News of the Day', *BDP* (10 April 1890).

172 'Ruffianism at Sparkbrook', *BDP* (24 March 1890).

173 'Heavy Sentences on Sloggers', *BDP* (16 April 1890).

174 'Notes and News', *BM* (15 April 1890).

175 'The Band of Friendship', *BDP* (21 June 1890).

176 William Chinn, Interview, BL (1979).

177 'One of a Gang' BDP (24 March 1891)

178 'Assault by a 'Ganger', *BDP* (14 April 1891) and 'Assaulted by Roughs', BM, (28 April 1891).

179 'A Cowardly Ruffian', BM (28 October 1891).

180 'The Stone-Throwing Nuisance', *BM* 8 July 1891 and 'Street Ruffianism in Birmingham', *BDP* (24 June 1892).

181 'Cliveland Street v Weaman Street', *BDP* (2 August 1893) and 'A Nechells Slogging Gang', *BDP* (18 October 1893).

182 'A Heavy List', *BDP* (26 June 1894).

183 'Birmingham Slogging Gangs', *Manchester Evening News* (27 June 1895).

184 'Assault on the Police', *BDP* (29 October 1895) and 'The Bromsgrove Street Disturbance', *BDP* (30 October 1895).

185 'Slogging in Kenyon Street', *BDP* (5 November 1895); 'Unlawful Wounding at Aston', BDP (10 December 1895).

186 Archibald, *Liverpool Gangs*, pp.189–191.

187 'Heavy Sentence on Slogging Gang' *BDP* (11 December 1895)

188 'A Violent Ruffian' *BDP* (3 December 1895).

189 'Balsall Heath Police Court', *BDP* (13 January 1877).

190 'Ruffianism at Balsall Heath', *BDP* (20 November 1879).

191 'Riotous Proceedings in Balsall Heath Road', *BM* (9 March 1883).

192 'Hardened Young Criminals', *BDP* (2 November 1888).

193 Henry Lightfoot, Calendar of Prisoners 1870–1935 [hereafter Calendar of Prisoners], Birmingham Quarter Sessions, 1839–1971 (QS/B/20/69). Library of Birmingham, (29 April 1907).

194 Henry Lightfoot 3200, New Soldiers Records. Short Service Attestation, [hereafter Short Service Attestation], TNA, War Office: Soldiers' Documents from Pension Claims, First World War, WO364; Piece: 2097 (1914).

195 Henry Lightfoot 201128, Territorial Force Attestation, TNA, War Office: Soldiers' Documents from Pension Claims, First World War, WO364; Piece: 2097 (1925).

196 "Tommy Giblin' and the Roughs generally', *BM* (8 January 1896).

197 C. H. Lea, 'The Fair – But Not the Onions', *BDG* (26 September 1935).

198 'Seventy years a Showman', *BDP* (4 November 1939).

199 Terry Proctor Letter, BLA (8 March 1996).

200 'Peaky Blinders', *Coventry Evening Telegraph* (30 December 1896).

201 'Topics of the Day' *Coventry Evening Telegraph* (11 October 1895).

202 'Tommy Giblin and Roughs Generally', *BM* (10 January 1896).

203 See for example, 'The Reign of the Rough in Birmingham', *Dundee Courier* (22 July 1897) and 'Birmingham Roughs on the Rampage', *Leeds Times* (24 July 1897).

204 'Policeman Killed in Birmingham', *Manchester Evening News* (19 July 1897).

205 'Assault on a Policeman' *BDP* (29 September 1891); 'Cowardly Assaults on the Police', *BDP* (23 February 1892); 'Assaults on the Police', *BDP* (26 April 1892); 'Assaulting Neighbours and Policeman', *BDP* (23 August 1892); 'Assaulting Policemen' *BDP* (13 March 1894); 'Assaults on Constables', *BDP* (9 April 1895); and 'Violent Assaults on Policemen', *BDP* (12 November 1895).

206 'Funeral of Snipe', *Sports Argus* (24 July 1897); 'The Reign of Violence in Birmingham', *Lloyd's Weekly Newspaper* (25 July 1897).

207 'VIOLENCE IN BIRMINGHAM', *The Times* [London, England] (14 October 1897) The Times Digital Archive. (accessed 28 June 2018).

Chapter Three: The Reign of the Peaky Blinders Ended

208 Series 1, Episode 2, *Peaky Blinders* (BBC2, 2013).

209 'Chief Constable Rafter. A Character Sketch, *Weekly Irish Times* (28 October 1899); and 'An Epidemic of Brutality', *Globe* (30 July 1897).

210 See Gooderson, *The Gangs of Birmingham*, pp.263–64.

211 'The Epidemic of Ruffianism in Birmingham', *Edinburgh Evening News*, (12 August 1897).

212 Vince, *History of the Corporation, vol. III*, p.218.

213 Geoffrey Pearson, 'Victorian Boys, We are Here!' in Yvonne Jewkes and Gail Letherby (eds), *Criminology. A Reader* (London, 2002), p.8.

214 Vince, *History of the Corporation, vol. III*, pp.218, 226–229 and 232, and Bunce,

History of the Corporation, vol II (Birmingham, 1885), p.300.

215 'Cheltenham Man Injured', Cheltenham Chronicle (30 April 1898).

216 *The Moseley and Kings Heath Journal*, vol. 8 (August 1899). pp.1–14.

217 'Street Ruffianism', Globe – Saturday, 21 January 1899

218 'Exit Mr Farndale', *The Birmingham Owl* (20 June 1899), p.9; see also, Death of Mr Joseph Farndale', *BDG* (9 August 1901).

219 See, for example, 'Playing Space Problem', *Sports Argus* (29 June 1901).

220 'Cleaned Up Black Spots', *Birmingham Gazette* [hereafter *BG*] (24 August 1935).

221 'Thousands See the Passing of Sir Charles Rafter in Birmingham', *BG* (28 August 1935).

222 'Death of Sir C. Rafter', *Police Review* (30 August 1935).

223 'Cleaned Up' Black Spots', *BG* (24 August 1935).

224 'The New Chief', *The Birmingham Owl* (21 July 1899) p.9.

225 'Chief Constable Rafter. A Character Sketch', *Weekly Irish Times* (28 October 1899).

226 Percy Langridge, MEPO 6 Metropolitan Police: Habitual

Criminals Register 1904, piece 15.

227 'Ruffianism in Birmingham', BM (29 June 1900).

228 Vince, *History of the Corporation of Birmingham, vol. IV*, pp.226 and 246.

229 Sentence on a "Peaky Blinder"', *Cheltenham Chronicle* (12 January 1901). Constable Bennett rose to become a chief superintendent and was credited with playing a leading role in the suppression of the Garrison Lane Vendetta by bringing the ring leaders to justice; 'B'ham Former Police Chief Dies', newspaper cutting thanks Ruby Massa, Bennett's granddaughter.

230 'A Ruffian Silenced for a Time', *Ross Gazette* (10 January 1901); 'Penal Servitude for a Hooligan', *Sheffield Daily Telegraph* (10 January 1901).

231 'Rowdysim in Garrison Lane' *BM* (10 July 1901).

232 Walter G. Chinn, *From Victoria's Image (A Reminiscence in Reflection)* (unpublished MS, Birmingham c. 1978), p.18.

233 'Ruffianism in Birmingham the Stipendiary's Resolution', BM (5 November 1901).

234 J. Cuming Walters, *Scenes in Slumland: Pen Pictures of the Black Spots in Birmingham* (Birmingham, 1901), p.5.

235 'The Gunter Case', *BM* (14 December 1901).

236 'Verdict of Wilful Murder', *BM* (30 October 1901).

237 'Funeral of the Victim', *BM* (31 October 1901).

238 'The Gunter Murder Trial. Verdict and Sentences', *BM* (14 December 1901).

239 T. J. Bass, *Hope in Shadowland* (Birmingham, 1903), p.31; 'The Birmingham Peaky Blinders', *BDG* (14 December 1901).

240 For intimidation see 'The Gunter case. Alleged intimidation of Witnesses', *BM* (7 November 1901).

241 'Terrible Assault in Birmingham', *Coventry Herald* (31 January 1902).

242 'The Murderous Attack on PC Blinko', *BDG* (15 March 1902).

243 'Murderous Attack on a Police Constable', *London Daily News* (29 January 1902).

244 'The Murderous Attack on PC Blinko', *BDG* (15 March 1902).

245 *BDG* (25 March 1903).

246 Vince, *History of the Corporation of Birmingham. Vol. IV*, pp.346.

247 *BDG* (13 September 1905).

248 'Two Murder Trials', *BDG* (16 December 1905).

249 Vince, *History of the*

Corporation of Birmingham,
vol. IV, pp.346.

250 'Hooligan outrages', BDG (11
January 1907).

251 'Night Adventure', BDG
(19 November 1912).

252 Davies, Gangs of Manchester,
pp.334–343.

253 Gooderson, Gangs of
Birmingham, p.255; also
see 'Birmingham's Sporting
Parson', BDG (11 December
1934).

254 'The Rev. Arnold Pinchard', Pall
Mall Gazette (4 October 1907);
and for Father Jay see Raphael
Samuel, East End Underworld.
Chapters in the life of Arthur
Harding (London, 1981), pp.2,
19 and 286–288 and for the Old
Nicholl, Sarah Wise The Blackest
Streets: The life and death of a
Victorian slum (London,
2009 edn).

255 Sarah Wise, 'Inside the Skin of
a Slum', Church Times (2 July
2008).

256 J. R. C. 'Peaky Blinders', p.72.

257 'Table Talk', BM (16 April
1881).

258 'Sparkbrook Boxing Club', BDG
(12 August 1908).

259 'Changed a Bad Parish', BDG
(11 December 1934).

260 'Women's Election
Preparations', BDG (23 January
1929).

261 'Birmingham Kyrle Society in the
Seven Dials', BDP (8 July 1889);
'The Birmingham Kyrle Society.
A Proposed "Kyrle Hall"', BDP
(27 November 1891).

262 'The Birmingham Kyrle
Society', BDP (27 September
1893).

263 'Birmingham Street Boys Union',
BM (27 September 1906).

264 Arnold Freeman, Boy Life and
Labour: The Manufacture of
Inefficiency (London 1914)
p.130.

265 Davies, Gangs of Manchester,
pp.343–44 and 353.

266 See, for example, 'Aston Board
School Football Association',
BDP (12 May 1886); 'Junior
League', Sports Argus
(21 October 1905).

267 Freeman, Boy Labour, pp.110–
115.

268 Davies, Gangs of Manchester,
pp.353–54.

269 Freeman, Boy Labour, p.133 and
pp.88–89.

270 'Ruffianism in Birmingham the
Stipendiary's Resolution', BM
(5 November 1901).

271 'Hooliganism Redivivus', BM
(5 November 1901).

272 'The Navigation Street Riot',
BDP (25 March 1875).

273 T. J. Bass, Everyday Life in
Blackest Birmingham: Facts Not
Fiction (Birmingham 1898), p9.

274 'Hooliganism in Birmingham', *BM* (13 May 1901).

275 'Police Attacked at Key Hill. Civilians to the Rescue', *BM* (27 March 1905).

276 Vince, *History of the Corporation of Birmingham vol. IV*, pp.326–7.

277 'Local News and Jottings', *BM* (14 December 1901).

278 'Birmingham Watch Committee', BM (13 November 1901).

279 'Wanted', *Cheltenham Chronicle* (30 July 1910).

280 'Cowardly Constable', *Worcestershire Chronicle* (19 September 1903).

281 'Memories of Peaky Blinder Gangs', *Evening Despatch* (29 January 1930).

282 'Murder of PC Lines', *BWP* (27 May 1955).

283 'News of the Day', *BDP* (2 July 1900).

284 'Police Orders 17 Dec. 1901 To 8 Oct. 1903'.

285 'Testing the Police Staves', *BDP* (22 November 1890).

286 'Notes and News', *BM* (9 December 1890).

287 Walter Chinn, Interview, BLA (number 2 1979).

288 See 'The History of Police Uniform in Manchester Up Until WW2', http://www. gmpmuseum.co.uk/collection- item/the-history-of-police- uniform-in-manchester-up- until-ww2/ [accessed 15 July 2018).

289 'Connaught Man', *Weekly Irish Times* (19 October 1907).

290 'Reservists and the Birmingham City Police', *BM* (11 February 1901).

291 'Table Talk', *BM* (24 August 1901).

292 'The Birmingham Police Force. Where The Recruits Come From', *BM* (26 October 1901).

293 'Chief Superintendent C. W. Lloyd, Letter, BLA (18 June 1987).

294 'Ex-Police Chief', *BDG* (13 February 1928).

295 'Half-Century of Police Service', *BDG* (6 March 1918).

296 'Juvenile Slogging Gangs', *BM* (21 September 1918).

297 'The Resignation of Superintendent Walker', *BM* (6 February 1900).

298 'The Disappearance of Tramps' *BM* (4 December 1915).

299 'Murder of PC Lines', *BWP* (27 May 1955).

300 'The Ten Arches Gang', *BM* (10 January 1883); 'Aston Police Cricket Club', *BDP* (18 January 1895).

301 'Rowdyism at Ten Arches', *BDP* (22 May 1900).

302 George Hickling 145403, Short Service Attestation, TNA,

Soldiers' Documents, First World War 'Burnt Documents' (1915).

303 C. R. S., 'Forward. How Birmingham is Changing', *BDG* (30 December 1925).

304 'Less Crimes. Birmingham Returns', *BDG* (9 May 1929).

305 'Bricks and Bottles Thrown by a Hostile Crowd', *BDG* (21 June 1910).

306 'Street Terrorists. Six Months' Hard Labour for Young Hooligans', *BDG* (15 June 1920).

307 *Dundee Evening Telegraph* (21 March 1927).

308 'Terrorising Gang Sent to Prison. Expert Crooks' Crimes', *BDG* (8 May 1930).

309 There is also no mention of peaky blinders in the 1920s in Deritend and Bordesley, where they had been rife until a few years before the First World War. See, for example, Mary Elizabeth Shott, *Brum and Candlelight: A Walk Down Memory Lane*s (1995), and also Tom Golding, *96 Years a Brummie, 1889–1896* (1986).

310 Beattie Hamill, née Carson, Interview, BLA (1987).

311 Victor J. Andrews, *Patched Parts* [originally serialised in the *Sunday Mercury* as 'I Remember Garrison Lane'] (Birmingham, 1999), p.37–40.

Chapter Four: Illegal Bookmakers and a Vendetta

312 Series 1, Episode 1, *Peaky Blinders* (BBC2, 2013).

313 'Behind the scenes on the set of BBC drama Peaky Blinders', http://www.bbc.co.uk/news/av/ entertainment-arts-23795850/ behind-the-scenes-on-the-set-of-bbc-drama-peaky-blinders.

314 Chinn, *Better Betting*, p.102; and Geoffrey Floy, *Policing Birmingham*, p.226 and p.203.

315 See David Dixon, '"Class Law": The Street Betting Act of 1906', *International Journal of the Sociology of Law*, vol. 8 (1980), p.109.

316 Charles Vince, *History of the Corporation of Birmingham, vol. IV (1900–1915)* (Birmingham, 1923) pp.348–49.

317 Floy, *Policing in Birmingham*, p.228.

318 Chinn, *Better Betting*, pp.136–40.

319 'Year's Crime in Birmingham', BDG (1 September 1920).

320 Chinn, *Better Betting*, pp.136–40.

321 Harry Vokes, Letter, BLA (1988).

322 Hetty Bradbury, Letter, Carl Chinn Bookmaking Archive [hereafter BA], Cadbury Research Library, University of Birmingham.

323 See 'Law on Betting', *BDG* (9 May 1913).

324 Chinn, *Better Betting*, pp.109 and pp.142–4.

325 Clements, 'Historia Interviews: Steven Knight'.

326 Albert Judd, Interview, BA (1988).

327 Mr A. T. Richardson, Letter, BLA (23.3.88).

328 George W. Langham, Letter, BLA (1988).

329 Vokes, Letter, BLA (1988).

330 Chinn, *Better Betting*, p.125.

331 Richardson, Letter, BLA (1988).

332 Carl Chinn, *The Anatomy of a Working-Class Neighbourhood: West Sparkbrook 1871 to 1914* (University of Birmingham Ph.D. thesis, 1986), p.151.

333 'Successful Novel Police Ruse', *BDG* (17 November 1928).

334 Chinn, *Better Betting*, p.208.

335 William Chinn, Interview, BLA (1987).

336 Mrs V. G. Pullin (née Foster), Letter, BLA (2007).

337 Olga Packer, nee Pickering, Interview (1988); and for women betting see Chinn, *Better Betting*, pp.144–47.

338 Richard Pickering, Interview, BA (1993).

339 Chinn, *Better Betting*, pp.130–31.

340 Katherine Clements, 'Historia Interviews: Steven Knight', Historia (2 May 2016), http://www.historiamag.com/historia-interviews-steven-knight/

341 Jonathan Wright, 'Peaky Blinders: behind the scenes with creator Steven Knight', *HistoryExtra*, (2018), https://www.historyextra.com/period/20th-century/peaky-blinders-behind-the-scenes-with-creator-steven-knight/

342 For the Burger Boys and Johnson Crew see Caroline Gall, 'Birmingham gangs: How two rivals poisoned a city's streets', (23 August 2017 https://www.bbc.co.uk/news/uk-england-birmingham-41024825).

343 1871 Census, TNA, Class: RG10; Piece: 3015; Folio: 17; Page: 27; GSU roll: 838861.

344 1881 Census, TNA, Class: RG11; Piece: 3013; Folio: 108; Page: 51; GSU roll: 1341720.

345 See G. C. Allen, *The Industrial Development of Birmingham and the Black Country 1860–1927* (firstpublished 1929, New York edn 1866), pp.233–43).

346 1891 Census, TNA, Class: RG12; Piece: 2413; Folio: 76; Page: 4.

347 1911 Census, TNA, Class: RG14; Piece: 18165.

348 1901 Census, TNA, Class: RG13; Piece: 2855; Folio: 44; Page: 38; and *Census* 1911, Class: RG14; Piece: 18357.

349 'Birmingham Police Court', *BM* (23 April 1881).

350 'Riding without a Ticket', *BM* (10 January 1884).

351 'Unprovoked Attack', *BDP* (6 November 1895).

352 'Alleged Counterfeiters at Warwick', *Leamington Spa Courier* (4 July 1896); 'Counterfeiters get their Deserts', *Leamington Spa Courier* (11 July 1896).

353 'Samuel Sheldon, 147', *Convicts on License 9* (Birmingham City Police, 1911–1912), West Midlands Police Museum; 'Samuel Sheldon 2546, Prisoners' Photographs (29 October 1907), West Midlands Police Museum.

354 'An Intolerable Nuisance', *BDP* (29 June 1886).

355 'Assaulting the Police', *BM* (14 May 1887).

356 'Another Rough Severely Punished', *BDP* (15 November 1888).

357 'The Assault in Allison Street', *BDP* (3 August 1889).

358 'Disgraceful Assault on a Girl', *BDP* (5 November 1889).

359 'Street Ruffianism', *BDP* (9 July 1890).

360 'Committed for Trial', *BDP* (20 March 1895) and Samuel Sheldon, Calendar of Prisoners (28 Oct 1907), QS/B/20/72.

361 Banns, St Laurence, Samuel Sheldon (22 September 1890), Reference Number: EP 69/2/3/1; Archive Roll: 12.

362 1891 Census, TNA, Class: RG12; Piece: 2403; Folio: 55; Page: 12.

363 'The Most Lawless Part of Birmingham', *BDP* (28 February 1900).

364 1901 Census, TNA, Class: RG13; Piece: 2855; Folio: 37; Page: 23.

365 1911 Census, TNA, Class: RG14; Piece: 18264.

366 Banns, St James the Less Ashted, Ella Maria Small (6 August 1917) Reference Number: DRO 10; Archive Roll: 643.

367 'Daring Robbery in Leicester', *Leicester Chronicle* (28 July 1900).

368 Samuel Sheldon, Calendar of Prisoners (28 Oct 1907), QS/B/20/72.

369 See https://www.legislation.gov.uk/ukpga/Geo4/5/83/section/4.

370 'The Stratford Road Riot', *BM* (5 June 1905).

371 'Quarter Sessions', *BDG* (31 October 1907).

372 Samuel Sheldon, 147, *Convicts on License 9*.

373 Joseph Sheldon, Calendar of Prisoners (19 November), QS/B/20/94.

374 John Sheldon, MEPO 6, The Metropolitan Police Criminal Record Office containing the

Habitual Criminals Registers and Miscellaneous Papers (1914).

375 'Charge of Uttering Base Coin', *Worcestershire Chronicle* (27 June 1903).

376 'House Ransacked', *BDG* (20 May 1905).

377 1901 Census, TNA, Class: RG13; Piece: 2855; Folio: 32; Page: 13; and 'John Sheldon', Calendar of Prisoners (17 March 1906), QS/B/20/112.

378 'Racecourse Pests', *Nottingham Evening Post* (3 September 1919).

379 'John Sheldon', MEPO 6, The Metropolitan Police Criminal Record Office containing the Habitual Criminals Registers and Miscellaneous Papers (1903).

380 'Policeman and a Commission Agent' (21 March 1906).

381 1901 Census, TNA, Class: RG12; Piece: 2403; Folio: 62; Page: 25

382 Janice Jackson Email (21 November 2014); 'William Beach', Militia Attestation (22 September 1898); 'William Beach 24109,' Canada, WWI CEF Personnel Files, 1914–1918, Bea – Bel Box 0530 (Beach, Oliver – Beech, William James).

383 Margaret Beale, Email (1 October 2014).

384 Mr Beasley, Interview, BA (1989).

385 Ray Lewis, Interview, BA (1989); Terry Lines, Email (24 February 2014).

386 'Garrison Lane Vendetta', *Birmingham Gazette and Express* [hereafter *BGE*] (14 October 1912).

387 'Shooting Affray', *BDG* (9 January 1909).

388 'Shots in a City Street', *BDG* (22 June 1908).

389 'Charles Jones', Calendar of Prisoners (19 November 1910), QS/B/20/112.

390 Acting Superintendent, 'Re Unlawful Assemblies in Watery Lane and district' (Handwritten MS 1909) [West Midlands Police Museum], p.1.

391 Beasley, Interview, BA (1989).

392 'Shooting Affray', *BDG* (9 January 1909).

393 'Birmingham Vendetta', *BM* (30 January 1909).

394 'Theft of Cheese', *BDP* (1 May 1900); 'A Question of Time' *BDP* (29 September 1900); 'Peace and Goodwill', *BDG* (29 December 1903).

395 'The Dartmouth Street Vendetta', *BDG* (3 May 1909); 'Garrison Street Vendetta' *BGE* (20 September 1920).

396 Acting Superintendent, 'Re Unlawful Assemblies in Watery Lane and District', pp.1–2.

397 'Arthur Morris', Calendar of Prisoners (26 February 1913), QS/B/20/110.

398 'Dartmouth Street Vendetta', BED (5 May 1909).

399 'William Beach', Calendar of Prisoners, (26 March, 1909), QS/B/20/83.

400 'Lewis, Interview, BA (1989)

401 'Garrison Street Vendetta', BDG (20 September 1910).

402 'Garrison Street Vendetta Case', BDG (29 November 1910).

403 'Garrison Street Vendetta. Heavy Sentences', BDG (1 December 1910).

404 'Birmingham Stabbing Case', BM (25 January 1911).

405 'Women Stabbed', BDG (22 March 1911).

406 'Garrison Lane Vendetta', BM (27 March 1912).

407 Beasley, Interview, BA (1989).

408 Anonymous, 1912, Oct 15. A BIRMINGHAM VENDETTA: MAN SHOT IN THE HEAD IN A PUBLIC HOUSE. The Manchester Guardian (1901-1959), 11.

409 Garrison Lane Vendetta', BGE (30 October 1912).

410 'A Vendetta in Garrison Lane', BDP (7 December 1912).

411 'Rival Gangs', BDP (5 November 2912).

412 'Garrison Lane Vendetta', BGE (30 October 1912).

413 'Birmingham Vendetta', News of the World (8 December 1912).

414 'Garrison Lane Feud', BDP (14 October 1912).

415 'Garrison Lane Vendetta', BGE (30 October 1912).

416 'Reign of Terror', newspaper cutting (West Midlands Police Museum).

417 'Garrison Lane Vendetta', BM (7 December 1912) and 'Sentence Reduced', BDG (21 January 1913).

418 'Watery Lane Shooting Affray', BM (20 March 1906).

419 'The End of the Peaky Blinders', Sheffield Independent (28 June 1923).

420 'Racecourse Pests', Nottingham Evening Post (3 September 1919).

421 Janice Jackson, Email, (21 November 2014).

422 'William Beach 24109,' Canada, WWI CEF Personnel Files, 1914–1918, Bea – Bel Box 0530 (Beach, Oliver – Beech, William James). I thank Janice Jackson for alerting me to this material. For the battle in which Beach was wounded, see R.C. Fetherstonhaugh (edited and compiled) 13th Battalion Royal Highlanders of Canada 1914–1919 (Canada, 1925).

423 'William Beach', Midlands, England, Electoral Registers,

1832–1955, 33 Homes Buildings, Palmer Street, Deritend (1920).

424 Midlands, England, Electoral Registers, 1832–1955, Deritend, 1925, Charles Henry Street; and TNA, 1939 Register; Reference: RG 101/5538I.

425 England & Wales, Civil Registration Death Index, 1916–2007, Samuel Sheldon, December 1943, Birmingham, Volume 6d, Page 638.

426 TNA, 1939 Register; Reference: RG 101/5541B.

427 England & Wales, Civil Registration Death Index, 1916–2000, John Sheldon, December 1941, Birmingham, Volume 6d, p.208.

Chapter Five: The Real Gangsters of the 1920s

428 Series 1, Episode 2, *Peaky Blinders* (BBC2, 2013).

429 William Kimber, W168959, Certified Copy of an Entry of Birth, General Register Office (3 February 2005).

430 1891 Census, TNA, Class: RG12; Piece: 2387; Folio: 125; Page: 37. For a full discussion of Kimber's background see Chinn, *The Real Peaky Blinders*, pp.44–6.

431 William Kimber, TNA, HO140, Calendar of Prisoners, piece 239 (27 October 1904).

432 'Chase among the Chimney Pots', *Leominster News and North West Herefordshire & Radnorshire Advertiser* (5 October 1900); Census 1901, Class: RG13; Piece: 2853; Folio: 155; Page: 7.

433 William Kimber, TNA, MEPO 6, The Metropolitan Police Criminal Record Office containing the Habitual Criminals Registers and Miscellaneous Papers, (1913).

434 William Kimber, Calendar of Prisoners, (27 October 1904).

435 William Kimber, Banns, Reference Number: DRO 9; Archive Roll: 608 (1 November 1902).

436 Juliet Banyard, Email (7 September 2013).

437 William Kimber, Calendar of Prisoners (27 October 1904); 'A Question of Identity', *BM* (29 October 1904).

438 'Trip Tickets', *BM* (29 January 1906).

439 'After the Races. Sequel to the Birmingham Derby. Loiterers Sentenced', *BDG* (24 May 1907).

440 1911 Census, TNA, Class: RG14; Piece: 24018.

441 Justin Jones, Email (27 August 2013).

442 Maude Kimber, Midlands, England, Electoral Registers, 1832–1955, West Birmingham, 5 Charlotte Street (1920 and 1925).

443 Banyard email (7 September 2013).

444 1911 Census, TNA, Class: RG14; Piece: 17989.

445 'Roughs of the Turf', *The Daily Telegraph* (13 August 1898). For a discussion of the Brummagem Boys see Chinn, *The Real Peaky Blinders*, pp.20–30.

446 'Cup Tie Prosecution', *Derby Daily Telegraph* (16 January 1913).

447 Joseph Kimber, Calendar of Prisoner, QS/B/20/64 (27 July 1906); 'Doncaster Police Court. After the St Leger', *Yorkshire Post and Leeds Intelligencer* (13 September 1912); and 'Scene at the Maze Races', *Northern Whig* (4 August 1913).

448 'Crowd Looks on While Constable is Attacked', *BDG* (17 February 1922).

449 Thomas McDonagh, 154 and 83, Convicts on License 9 (Birmingham City Police, 1911–1912; West Midlands Police Museum); 'Slashed with a Razor', *BDG* (17 June 1925).

450 McDonald, *Gangs of London*, p.218 and p.123.

451 Brian McDonald, *Elephant Boys Tales of London and Los Angeles Underworlds* (Edinburgh and London, 2000), p.62

452 Brian McDonald, Email (28 August 2013).

453 McDonald, *Gangs of London*, pp.125–28.

454 'A Charge of Stabbing', *Illustrated Police News* (20 February 1913).

455 'Alleged Wounding', *East London Observer* (15 March 1913).

456 *Illustrated Police News* (20 February 1913). Tamplin was named as Templar in this account.

457 'After the Races', *Bedfordshire Advertiser and Luton Times* (17 April 1914).

458 See Wray Vamplew, *A Social and Economic History of Horse Racing* (London, 1976) pp.62–75.

459 Denny Green, Interview, BA (2005).

460 Chinn, *The Real Peaky Blinders*, pp.92–3.

461 'Englishmen Charged in Dublin', *Dublin Daily Express* (11 May 1917). For Cope, see Chinn, *The Real Peaky Blinders*, pp.92–3.

462 W. Kimber, ADM 194: Courts Martial Registers, WO 86: Judge Advocate General's Office: District Courts Martial

Registers, Home and Abroad, Piece 078: Register of Charges: Home and Abroad (1917), Page 203 (11 October 1917).

463 'How Fortunes Have Been Lost and Won', *Hull Daily Mail* (14 November 1931); Thomas Henry Dey, *Leaves from a Bookmaker's Book* (London, 1931).

464 Mike Huggins, *Horseracing and the British 1919–1939* (Manchester, 2003), p.21.

465 Tom Divall, *Scoundrels and Scallywags (And Some Honest Men)* (London, 1929) p.199.

466 *Centenary Supplement of the 'Sporting Chronicle'* (29 May, 1971).

467 'Charge of Molesting Bookmakers', *The Times* (24 June 1919).

468 Sam Dell, Interview, BA (1987)

469 Dave Langham, Interview, BA (1988).

470 Dell, Interview and Simmy Lewis (Simeon Solomon), Interview (1988).

471 Dell, Interview.

472 Chinn, *Better Betting*, pp.177–8.

473 Divall, *Scoundrels and Scallywags*, pp.207–8.

474 McDonald, *Gangs of London*, pp.140–1.

475 'Desperate Thieves.' *Daily Mail* (18 October 1919) : 5. Daily Mail Historical Archive. Web. 2 Sept. 2018.

476 'Rogues of the Racecourse', *The Times* (17 July 1920): 13. The Times Digital Archive. Web. 2 Sept. 2018.

477 McDonald, *Gangs of London*, p.140 and pp.103–128.

478 W. Bebbington, *Rogues Go Racing* (London, c. 1947) p.95.

479 Ali Harris, *Interview*, BA (1987) and Dell 1987).

480 Tommy Garnham, *Interview*, BA (2013).

481 Divall, *Scoundrels and Scallywags*, p.199 and McDonald, *Gangs of London*, pp.153–4.

482 1901 Census 1, Class: RG13; Piece: 240; Folio: 103; Page: 42 and Census 1911, Class: RG14; Piece: 1191.

483 'Alfred Solomon 83939, Short Service Attestation'.

484 'Betting in City Road', *Hackney and Kingsland Gazette* (30 August 1907).

485 'Alfred Solomon, 83939, Short Service Attestation'.

486 Simmy Lewis (Simeon Solomon), Interview, BA (1989

487 Edward Greeno, *War on the Underworld* (London, c. 1960), p.17.

488 Moss Deyong, *Everybody Boo* (London, 1951), p.55.

489 For a full account of the attack by Armstrong, see Chinn, *The Real Peaky Blinders*, pp.68–9.

ENDNOTES

490 McDonald, *Gangs of London*, p.160 and pp.146 and 155–59.

491 Garnham, Interview, BA (2013).

492 ALFRED SOLOMON charged with the wilful murder of BARNET BLITZ, TNA, MEPO 3/374, Image 3.

493 For Emanuel's family see 1871 Census, TNA, Class: RG10; Piece: 413; Folio: 38; Page: 1; GSU roll: 824629; 1841 Census, TNA, Class: HO107; Piece: 725; Book: 5; Civil Parish: St Botolph Aldersgate; County: Middlesex; Enumeration District: 16; Folio: 33; Page: 2; Line: 8; GSU roll: 438830; and England & Wales, Civil Registration Death Index, 1837–1915 for Barnet Emanuel, (1873) Q3 Jul-Aug-Sep E.

494 1871 Census, TNA, Class: RG10; Piece: 413; Folio: 38; Page: 1; GSU roll: 824629; 1881 Census, TNA, Class: RG11; Piece: 567; Folio: 75; Page: 25; GSU roll: 1341129; and 1891 Census, TNA, Class: RG12; Piece: 376; Folio: 82; Page: 17. For Emanuel's family see 1871 Census, TNA, Class: RG10; Piece: 413; Folio: 38; Page: 1; GSU roll: 824629; 1841 Census, TNA, Class: HO107; Piece: 725; Book: 5; Civil Parish: St Botolph Aldersgate; County: Middlesex; Enumeration District: 16; Folio: 33; Page: 2; Line: 8; GSU roll: 438830; and England & Wales, Civil Registration Death Index, 1837–1915 for Barnet Emanuel, (1873) Q3-Jul-Aug-Sep E.

495 1891 Census, TNA, Class: RG13; Piece: 262; Folio: 56; Page: 22.

496 Edward Emanuel, Calendar of Prisoners (25 April 1902).

497 'North London', *London Evening Standard* (24 December 1904).

498 Old Bailey Proceedings Online (www.oldbaileyonline.org, version 8.0, 24 August 2018), September 1908, trial of JOHN McCARTHY, (27, contractor) (t19080908-48).

499 1911 Census, TNA, Class: RG14; Piece: 1410

500 Prince, Interview, BA (1987); Samuel, *East* Underworld, p.131.

501 'A Whitechapel Case', *Sheffield Daily Telegraph* (22 January 1912) and 'The East End Gambling Raid', *East London Observer* (10 February 1912).

502 'Recruiting Scandal', *Lincolnshire Echo* (17 September 1917', 'London Gambling Den. Patronised Mostly by Jews'; *Nottingham Evening Post* (17 September 1917); *BDP* (18 September 1917); 'Aliens Crowd Police Court', *The People* (23 September 1917).

503 'Aliens Crowd Police Court', *The People* (23 September 1917); £300 fine for Gaming, *Daily Mirror* (18 September 1917).

504 Prince, Interview, BA (1987) and see also McDonald, pp.145–6.

505 Raphael Samuel, *East Underworld: Chapters in the Life of Arthur Harding* (London, 1981), p.131.

506 Prince, Interview, BA (1987).

507 £300 Fine for Gaming, *Daily Mirror* (18 September 1917).

508 1891 Census, TNA, Class: RG12; Piece: 201; Folio: 96; Page: 104.

509 1901 Census, TNA, Class: RG13; Piece: 1616; Folio: 7; Page: 5.

510 'The Savoy Club Raid', *Globe* (12 May 1922); 'The Raid on a Strand Club'; and 'The Police Raid on a Club', *Sunderland Daily Echo* (22 May 1902). Always First to Start Betting', *Daily Herald* (7 September 1931).

511 'Always First to Start Betting', *Daily Herald* (7 September 1931).

512 Netley Lucas, *London and Its Criminals* (London, 1926) p.76.

513 http://www.bbc. co.uk/programmes/ profiles/3rgnlRdfWMFs MMwDXN14yW5/darby-sabini

514 Norman Lucas, *Britain's Gangland* (London 1969), p.23;

and 'Ugly violent criminals of the past' (22 April 2005) https:// www.telegraph.co.uk/news/ uknews/1488384/Ugly-violent-criminals-of-the-past.html

515 Catharine Arnold, *Underworld London: Crime and Punishment in the Capital City* (London, 2012) pp.284–6.

516 Edward T. Hart, *Britain's Godfather* (London, 1993) pp.3, 6–7, 13, 15, and 56–71. This discussion on the representation of Sabini as Italian benefitted from discussions with Sam Bernard, an undergraduate student at the University of Birmingham who graduated in 2017 and whose final-year dissertation on the Sabini gang I supervised.

517 1911 Census, TNA, Class: RG14; Piece: 902.

518 Ottavio Sabini, London Metropolitan Archives; Reference Number: p76/phi/016 (21 December 1913); Doris Annie Amelia Sabini, London Metropolitan Archives, Church of England Parish Registers, 1754–1906; Reference Number: p90/jud/005 (25 January 1916).

519 TNA: HO45/23691, 'Octavius Sabini, alias Darby Sabini Internment'.

520 Lucio Sponza, *Italian immigrants in Nineteenth*

Century Britain Realities and Images (Leicester 1988) pp.32–6; and https://www.genesreunited.co.uk/boards/board/ancestors/thread/1163482 (16 July 2009).

521 David R. Green, 'Little Italy in Victorian London. Holborn's Italian Community', *Camden History Review*, vol. 15 (1988) pp.5–6.

522 'Serious Assault Cases', *Morning Post* (28 December 1883).

523 London Metropolitan Archives, School Admission and Discharge Registers; Reference: LCC/EO/DIV03/LAS/AD/002; England & Wales, Civil Registration Birth Index, 1837–1915, London, Holborn, Volume: 1b, Page: 683 (Jul-Aug-Sep 1888). In this latter he is registered as Q?tavia hHndley.

524 General Register Office, England & Wales, Civil Registration Birth Index, 1837–1915, London, Holborn, Volume: 1b, Page: 76881 (Jan-Feb-Mar 1881); General Register Office, England & Wales, Civil Registration Birth Index, 1837–1915, London, Holborn, Volume: 1b, Page: 775 (Jan-Feb-Mar 1883); and Census 1871, TNA, Class: RG11; Piece: 351; Folio: 12; Page: 17; GSU roll: 1341076.

525 'Denies He Is King of Sabini Gang', *Sunday Post* (4 July 1926); TNA: CRIM1/209; Charles Sabini statement, (5 December 1922); TNA: HO45/23691, 'Octavius Sabini, alias Darby Sabini Internment'.

526 1891 Census, TNA, Class: RG13; Piece: 253; Folio: 170; Page: 1

527 London Metropolitan Archives, School Admission and Discharge Registers; Reference: LCC/EO/DIV03/LAS/AD/002.

528 http://www.childrenshomes.org.uk/DruryLancID/.

529 Shore, *Organised Crime*, p.183.

530 Ottavio Sabini, London Metropolitan Archives; Reference Number: p76/phi/016 (21 December 1913); and Doris Annie Amelia Sabini, London Metropolitan Archives, Church of England Parish Registers, 1754–1906; Reference Number: p90/jud/005 (25 January 1916).

531 'Denied he was the King of the Sabini Gang', *Sunday Post* (4 July 1926).

532 Shore, *Organised Crime*, pp.186–7

533 *Globe* (20 May 1898).

534 'Serious Assault Cases', *Morning Post* (28 December 1883); 'Stabbing in Clerkenwell', *Islington Gazette* (30 August 1888).

535 'Italians in Trouble', *Islington Gazette* (27 June 1895) and

'Italian Stabbing case', *Henley Advertiser* (10 March 1894).

536 'Not Willing to be Killed for 5s 6d', *Islington Gazette* (24 June 1909). Darby is often confused with Charles. However the latter was born in 1883, as indicated by his age in this court case and censuses.

537 Old Bailey Proceedings Online (www.oldbaileyonline.org, version 8.0, 27 August 2018), January 1910, trial of CORTESI, George (20, wireworker) SABINI, Vincent (24, carman) (t19100111-46).

538 'Italian Affray', *Daily Telegraph & Courier* (28 December 1909).

539 1891 Census, Class: RG12; Piece: 223; Folio: 58; Page: 8.

540 Calendar of Prisoners, HO140, Piece 226 (3 May 1903); and TNA, Central Criminal Court: After Trial Calendars Of Prisoners, CRIM9, Piece 59, Folio 5 (22 April 1913).

541 See Chinn, *The Real Peaky Blinders*, p.70.

542 Shore, *Organised Crime*, p.178.

543 Prince, Interview, BA (1987).

544 Dival, *Scoundrels and Scallywags*, p.199.

545 For Alf White see McDonald, *Gangs of London*, pp.101–2, 139–40 and James Morton, *Gang*land (London, 1993) pp.29–31, 33–4 and 42–4.

546 'Crowd Shot at on Trotting Ground', *Nottingham Evening Post* (31 March 1921).

547 Greeno, *War on the Underworld*, p.21.

548 Ugly Scene at Race Meeting', *The Courier* (Dundee) (25 March 1921).

549 'Crowd Shot at on Trotting Ground', *Nottingham Evening Post* (31 March 1921).

550 McDonald, *Gangs of London*, p.156; Samuel, *East End Underworld*, pp.204–5.

551 'Shot after Orgy', *BDG* (6 April 1921).

552 'King's Cross Mystery', *Nottingham Journal* (29 March 1921).

553 'Hit First Then Shot', *BDG* (20 April 1921).

554 'A Gang of Terrors', *Nottingham Journal* (28 April 1921).

555 'Epsom Road Battle', *The Times* (4 June 1921).

556 For a full discussion of these events, see Chinn, *The Real Peaky Blinders*, pp.72–6.

557 'Racing Gang's Vendetta', *The Gloucester Citizen* (18 August 1921).

558 'Rival Bookies' Vendetta', *The Sunday Post* (21 August 1921).

559 'Racecourse Feud. Is it a Settlement?', *Western Daily Press* (5 October 1921).

560 *The Bookmakers and Backers*

Racecourse Protection Association. *What It Has Done and What It Can Do, with YOUR Help*, National Association of Bookmakers File, 'History' (1921)

561 'General Committee Minutes, Bookmakers and Backers Racecourse Protection Association' (12 September 1921).

562 'The B.P.A.', *The Sportsman* (10 December 1921).

563 For a full discussion of these events see Chinn, *The Real Peaky Blinders*, pp.82–91.

564 McDonald, *Gangs of London*, pp.167–185.

565 General Committee Minutes, Bookmakers and Backers Racecourse Protection Association (15 May, 12 June and 4 September)

566 'Sentence in Sabini Case', *Derby Daily Telegraph* (18 January 1923).

567 'Wild West in London Club', *Nottingham Journal* (16 January 1923).

568 Langham, Interview, BA (1988).

569 'Racing Feud Sentences', *Pall Mall Gazette* (3 November 1922).

570 'Attempt to Bribe Warders', *The Scotsman* (2 July 1923).

571 'Club Tragedy Trial', *Hull Daily Mail* (18 November 1924).

572 McDonald, *Gangs of London*, p.182.

573 'A Terrific Hit', *Nottingham Journal* (18 November 1924).

574 'A Silent Quarrel', *Sheffield Daily Telegraph* (10 October 1924).

575 'Club Tragedy Trial', *Hull Daily Mail* (18 November 1924).

576 'Street Stabbing Affray', *Dundee Evening Telegraph* (24 September 1924).

577 Alfred Solomon, MEPO6, Habitual Criminals Register 1927, piece 39 (21 February 1927).

578 For attacks on bookmakers see 'Assault on bookmakers', *Western Daily Press* (14 October 1924); for the knuckle duster case see 'It was a Fight among the Jews', *Evening Telegraph* (Dundee) (8 June 1923) and 'Alleged use of a Knuckleduster', *The Scotsman* (19 June 1923).

579 'How We Outwitted a Rival Gang', *Topical Times* (19 March 1924).

580 'A Libel Action Discontinued', Hull Daily Mail (15 December 1925).

581 'Sabini Bankruptcy', *Daily Herald* (11 June 1926).

582 'Sabini's Admissions in Bankruptcy Court', *Dundee Evening Telegraph* (29 June 1926).

583 For the Sabini Gang and nightclubs see Morton, *Gangland*, pp.27–8.; 'Dispute Over a Bet', *The Citizen* (Gloucester) (30 October 1929).

584 TNA, MEPO 3/374 – ALFRED SOLOMON charged with the wilful murder of BARNET BLITZ (Image 2)

585 Bebbington, *Rogues Go Racing*, pp.102–3.

586 'Racecourse Scene Sequel', *Coventry Evening Telegraph* (27 July 1936).

587 For a full discussion see Chinn, *Better Betting*, p.182.

588 Norman Sherry, *The Life of Graham Greene, vol. 1, 1904–1939* (London, 1989), pp.634–5.

589 See, for example, Morton, *Gangland*, p.32.

590 Graham Greene, Letter, BA (9 May 1988).

591 TNA HO 45/23691, WAR: Octavius Sabini, alias Darby Sabini, alias Frederick Handley, notorious race-course gangster and racketeer: internment (1940–1941).

592 'Heavy Sentence on Receivers', *Kent & Sussex Courier* (25 June 1943).

593 £50 Produced from Sock, *Mid Sussex Times* (16 May 1945); Civil Registration Death Index, 1916–2007, Volume: 5h, p.351, Hove, Sussex, Ollavio Sabini (December 1950).

594 Morton, *Gangland*, pp.31–2.

595 1939 Register; TNA, Reference: RG 101/2511A.

596 Annie Emma Sabini, National Probate Calendar (Index of Wills and Administrations), 1858–1966, 1973–1995 (30 October 1978).

597 McDonald, *Gangs of London*, p.188; 'Nottingham Bookmaker Fined', *Nottingham Evening Post* (23 March 1925).

598 General Register Office. England and Wales Civil Registration Indexes, Holborn, (August–September 1926) vol. 1b, p.1341 (19 July 1926).

599 General Register Office. Civil Registration Death Index, 1916–2007 for Maud B Kimber, Volume: 6d, Page:11 (1926 Q3-Jul-Aug-Sep K).

600 McDonald, *Gangs of London*, pp.344–5.

601 Federal Bureau of Investigation, 'Subject: Murray Humphreys', https://archive.org/details/ MurrayHumphreys

602 McDonald, *Elephant Boys*, pp.102–31.

603 Stuart McGurk, 'Peaky Blinders creator Steven Knight on last night's cliffhanger and the all-out war to come', *GQ* (16 November 2017), (https://

ENDNOTES

www.gq-magazine.co.uk/
article/peaky-blinders-creator-
steven-knight-on-last-nights-
cliffhanger-and-the-all-out-war-
to-come).

604 'Birmingham's Gunman', *BDG*
(4 March 1933).

605 McDonald, *Gangs of London*,
pp.262–4.

606 *Ibid.*, and James Spenser, *Limey.
An Englishman Joins the Gangs*
(London 1934).

607 *The Western Morning News*
(18 April 1938); and 'Late Mr
Bradshaw Smith', *Devon and
Exeter Gazette* (25 October
1940).

608 William Kimber, England
& Wales, National Probate
Calendar (Index of Wills and
Administrations), 1858–1966,
1973–1995 (20 Oct 1945).

609 See Chinn, The *Real Peaky
Blinders*, pp.100–1.

610 London, England, Electoral
Registers, 1832–1965, Hackney,
Portsea Works; and see Pam
Fox, *The Jewish Community of
Golders Green: A Social History*
(Stroud, 2016).

611 General Register Office,
England & Wales, Civil
Registration Death Index,
1916–2007, Volume: 3a; Page:
948, Edmonton, Essex, Edward
Emanuel (March 1943).

612 Elizabeth Mary Emanuel,

National Probate Calendar
(Index of Wills and
Administrations), 1858–1966,
19731995 (3 February 1951).

613 *Yorkshire Post and Leeds
Intelligencer* (10 October 1924).

Afterword

614 Episode 2, Series 3, *Peaky
Blinders* (BBC2, 2016).

615 Carl Chinn, 'We All Come
from Round Sora: Italians in
Birmingham', in Owen Ashton,
Robert Fyson and Stephen
Roberts (eds), *The Duty of
Discontent. Essays in Honour of
Dorothy Thompson* (London,
1995), pp.255–7.

616 Doreen Hopwood and Margaret
Dilloway, *Bella Brum: A
History of Birmingham's Italian
Community* (Birmingham,
1996), p.2.

617 Chinn, 'We All Come from
Round Sora', pp.258–9; 'Serious
Affray in Bartholomew Street',
BDP (24 April 1886).

618 'Importing Organ grinders',
BDP (3 February 1891).

619 1901 Census, Class: RG13;
Piece: 2868; Folio: 95; Page:
32; and 1939 Register; TNA,
Reference: Class: RG 78 Piece:
18142, Chinn, 'We All Come
from Round Sora', p.260.

620 'Unemployed and the War Memorial', *BDM* (17 July 1922).

621 'Angry Italians', BDP (4 February 1893).

622 Victoria Hooper (née Jennings), 'Gran and Granddad Ciangretta's Family', *Carl Chinn's Brummagem Magazine*, Issue 194 (May 2017), p.6.

623 Pam Overthrow, Letter (14 May 2018).

624 'Unemployed and the War Memorial', *BDM* (17 July 1922).

625 Charles Alberici, unpublished MS, BLA, (ND), pp.14–15.

626 Hooper nee Jennings, 'Gran and Granddad Ciangretta's Family',

627 'Deaths on Active Service', *BM* (30 September 1944).

628 For an informed and thoughtful discussion of these issues see Maria Konnikova, 'Why Do We Admire Mobsters?' *The New Yorker* (16 September 2015), https://www.newyorker.com/science/maria-konnikova/why-do-we-admire-mobsters